IMPORTANT NOTICE

The Forest Service is in the process of renumbering all of the forest roads in western Washington. They expect to make the change in 1982, at which time the forest maps and road signs will show the new numbers.

The present numbering system was derived thirty years ago before road planners had any indication of the maze of roads that would eventually be developed. The new numbering system should make road directions easier to follow.

101 hikes

IN THE
NORTH CASCADES

Text: Ira Spring and Harvey Manning
Photos: Bob and Ira Spring
Maps: Helen Sherman

THE MOUNTAINEERS • SEATTLE

Second edition

Glacier Peak from ridge above Cub Lake – Hike 36

The Mountaineers: Organized 1906 ". . . to explore, study, preserve and enjoy the natural beauty of the Northwest."

Copyright © 1970, 1972, 1979 by The Mountaineers
All rights reserved

Published by The Mountaineers, 719 Pike Street
Seattle, Washington 98101

Published simultaneously in Canada by
Douglas & McIntyre Ltd., 1615 Venables Street
Vancouver, British Columbia V5L 2H1

Manufactured in the United States of America
First edition, July 1970
Second edition, January 1979; second printing, May 1980;
third printing, May 1981

Book design by Marge Mueller

*Photographs for trips 4 and 63 By John Spring; trip 79 By Dick Brooks;
    trip 95 By Harvey Manning.*

*Cover: Frozen pond on Park Butte below Easton Glacier
    on Mt. Baker – Hike 13.*
Title: Glacier Peak from ridge above Cub Lake – Hike 36

Library of Congress Cataloging in Publication Data:

Spring, Ira.
    101 hikes in the North Cascades.

    1. Hiking—Washington (State)—Cascade Range—Guide-books. 2. Cascade
Range—Description and travel—Guide-books. I. Manning, Harvey, joint author.
II. Title.
GV199.42.W22C376 1979   917.97'5   79-10865
ISBN 0-916890-82-1

PRESERVATION AGENDA FOR THE 1980s

When the drive for protection of North Cascades wildlands gathered new force in the 1950s, the initial goal was to carry out the plan drawn up in the 1930s by a pioneer of the wilderness movement, Bob Marshall of the U.S. Forest Service. Fruits of that effort were, in 1960, the Glacier Peak Wilderness.

The area set aside was magnificent but too small, a mere fragment of the old vision. Thus seeing how far the Forest Service had swung from the Marshall-era balance between "esthetics" and "utility," preservationists turned to the National Park Service and Congress, and the triumph of this second decade was the 1968 North Cascades Act creating the North Cascades National Park, Ross Lake and the Lake Chelan National Recreation Areas, and the Pasayten Wilderness.

In the third decade the preservation coalition shifted attention south and won, in 1976, the Alpine Lakes Wilderness. This fine achievement seemed only the beginning — the sense of the middle 1970s was of victory possible throughout the Cascades. Those officials of the Forest Service who favored a balanced position could warn their less preservationist-minded associates, "We don't have the only game in town anymore. Remember 1968. . ." And indeed the comprehensive management plans the Forest Service was developing in the middle 1970s for the North Cascades included a number of proposals for wilderness and related classifications.

However, the regional planning was cut off in midcourse, preempted by the nation-wide Roadless Area Review and Evaluation (RARE) intended to settle in one fell swoop the fate of every roadless area in all the national forests. The enterprise appeared laudable, if crushingly gigantic. But public input crashed head-on into local economy, and while the attention of preservationists was diffused by myriad battlegrounds, the input evaluation system was changed in mid-stream; trail country was to be processed by computer and come out ticketed for roading and logging. Fairness of the process challenged in court, the Forest Service withdrew RARE.

And came forth with RARE II. Preservationists expected a different game, as promised. But as they unraveled the computer categories, even more confusing than before, they found an even more egregious tilt. The centrist, even-handed officials who continued to warn, "Remember 1968 . . ." were not being heard. Although additional letters to the Forest Service have little effect, letters to your Congressmen have a great impact. Meanwhile, another threat raises an ugly specter.

The Crunch is Coming

For the present, private tree farms have given up the sustained yield practice and are cutting their slow-growing, old-growth timber as fast as they can find a market, and then replacing their virgin forest with a "super tree" that matures in 50 to 60 years instead of the usual 80 to 100 years. This is no secret. The logging industry has been boasting (and rightfully so) about their super tree in national ads, and from any Puget Sound city, one has only to look at the miles of scalped hills to tell where the boundary of Forest Service and private land is.

The "super tree" may be the answer to future timber demands, but what will happen 10 to 15 years from now when the private lands have been stripped of their last old growth trees and the first super trees are still 20 to 30 years from being ready to cut? And this in an area when even a year's interruption could be an economic catastrophe. If this impending collision course of events is allowed to continue, either sawmills will have to go out of business or the Forest Service will have to abandon its sustained yield program to fill the gap, scalping their high ridges where even super trees will take 100 to 300 years to regrow. Dedicated wilderness areas and national parks would be spared at first, but when they contain the only old growth trees, when jobs and houses are at stake, tremendous pressure could be brought on Congress to undo what it has done, and boundaries adjusted to unlock valuable forest.

Already hikers have lost hundreds of miles of trails in the Cascades to logging roads, but they will feel the pinch even more when the highest hillsides and ridge tops are crisscrossed with logging roads. Easier access to fragile wilderness areas brings even more use. Young hikers now commencing exploration with parents or youth groups would find by middle age that the only nonroaded pristine wilderness would be the subalpine forest, parkland, meadows, rock, and ice.

This need not happen. There is an alternative: **Balanced Forest Management.** The Forest Service presently has no say in the management of private land, but it can and must adjust its harvest to allow for the depletion of private forest. At the same time a Balanced Forest Management Plan must come from Congress, but this can only come about through your letters to your Congressmen. When testifying at hearings, hikers need not be pro esthetics and anti utility; a balanced management can supply both logs and wilderness.

Stamping Out Brushfires

Forests are not alone on the agenda. There are other burning issues.

Seattle City Light still is striving to raise Ross Dam, drowning the Big Beaver and more of the Skagit. It now is also considering plans to drown Thunder Creek and a long stretch of the Skagit between Copper Creek and Newhalem.

Kennecott Copper Company resolutely intends to dig an open-pit copper mine on Miners Ridge in the heart of the Glacier Peak Wilderness.

And there are other dam notions, other mine proposals, other brushfires constantly blazing up to keep preservationist boots busy.

Roadless Area Review

Whatever the fate of RARE II, or RARE III, or XVI, there will be no magic end to controversy, there will be a contest over every portion of the North Cascades that preservationists feel has a low value for production of cellulose, a high value for those many tangible and intangible commodities produced by wilderness.

The message to hikers: Do your fieldwork — walk the trails, learn the wildlands. Then do your homework — testify at hearings, write letters to the Forest Service, to Congressmen and Senators. And join a conservation organization that supports an active lobbying corps in Washington, D. C.

The Second North Cascades Act

The lesson of 1968 having been forgotten, legislation is being prepared for Congress to mandate a Second North Cascades Study looking toward a Second North Cascades Act. The entire periphery of the North Cascades National Park must be examined to determine a suitable adjustment of boundaries outward.

The message to hikers of the 1980s is: The debt you owe Gifford Pinchot and Theodore Roosevelt for halting the giveaway of public lands in the Cascades, for preserving a residue in national forests, and to Bob Marshall and his associates and followers for achieving wildernesses and a park in the North Cascades, you can now repay by working for the Second North Cascades Act. Shall we tentatively pencil in as its date, 1985?

February 1979   Norman L. Winn
Conservation Division Chairman
Immediate Past President
The Mountaineers

Cedar trees and Big Beaver trail

UNITED STATES DEPARTMENT OF AGRICULTURE
FOREST SERVICE

Dear Trail Users:

Welcome to the trails of the Mt. Baker-Snoqualmie National Forest. I hope they lead you to many pleasant adventures in the western Cascade Range of Washington.

The Forest trail system, about 1,200 miles in total length, has a mixed heritage. Some are as old as human history, used by Native Americans, explorers, and early-day trappers. Others were built by the boots of early-day miners or the trailing of cattle and sheep to high mountain ranges. Later, trails were built for fire and administrative access. Only a small part of the trail mileage was built in recent years with recreation as a primary purpose.

We recently prepared, with public participation, a Forest Trail Plan that charts the future management of the trail system. The plan states what level of maintenance each trail will receive, what trails will be reconstructed to what standard, and where new trails will be built in the future. Some guiding principles that were broadly endorsed by the public were basic to the plan. The main ones are:

1. The trail country of the Forest should provide for a variety of recreation opportunities, including some opportunities for access by horse and trailbikes.
2. Trails should vary from easy to difficult and primitive and some areas should be left without trails.

The Forest has also prepared an Off-Road Vehicle Management Plan that, in accordance with Executive Order 11644, states where use of motorized vehicles will be permitted, restricted, or prohibited.

These plans will be revised from time to time. An interdisciplinary team of Forest personnel will recommend changes needed to the District Ranger concerned. If he approves, the recommendation goes on to the Forest Supervisor. Some of the recommended changes will result from public comment during the time the earlier edition of the plan has been in effect. Before a revised plan is approved by the Forest Supervisor, the public is again given an opportunity to comment on it.

In addition, you are welcome to write to me or the District Ranger whose District is involved at any time to tell us what you think about the condition, maintenance, or use of any trail.

I also invite your active participation in the care of the trail system. Join one of the volunteer work parties* that is scheduled from time to time. As you hike a trail, do some minor maintenance, such as removing limbs and rocks or diverting running water from the trail tread. Report major maintenance problems, such as large windfalls and washed-out bridges, to the nearest Ranger Station. Report illegal or damaging trail use that you observe, too, such as motorbikes on a trail closed to such use, along with enough identifying information to help us to follow up.

Most of all, I hope you enjoy your use of the trail system. Treat it and the country it serves gently. Respect the right of others to enjoy it also. For variety, and a feeling of exploration, try some of the trails that **are not** featured in the guidebooks.

Sincerely,

DON R. CAMPBELL
Forest Supervisor

P.S. Although this letter is primarily about the Mt. Baker-Snoqualmie National Forest, most of the thoughts expressed apply to other National Forests, too.

*Editor's Note

It is too time consuming for a ranger to show one volunteer at a time what work is needed and how to do it, so join a work party sponsored by outdoor clubs such as the Explorer Scouts, Signpost Magazine, phone: 743-6944, Recreational Equipment, Inc., phone: 323-8333, and our own Mountaineers, phone: 623-2314.

Mt. Baker from Winchester Mountain trail

HELP! HELP! HELP!

Hikers! Don't just walk there — **do** something!

The Forest Service has considerable money to spend on motorcycle trails, but instead of building new trails where they will not conflict with other users, they are reconstructing hiking trails to motorcycle standards. Among the early shocks was in the mid-1960s, when Wenatchee National Forest cut a swath through the trees to smooth the Entiat River trail into a roadlet for wheels. In the past 5 years it has similarly rebuilt the trails of Mad River, Foggy Dew Creek, Horsehead Pass, Chelan

Summit, and South Fork Twisp River — and these are only those discovered while researching this new edition — there's no telling how many other trails have been so "improved" by Okanogan and Wenatchee National Forest. And Gifford Pinchot National Forest has also stepped up the pace.

And, folks, this is only the beginning. In 1979 alone federal funds were allocated to regrade for motorcycles these trails: Devil's Backbone, Prince Creek, Quartz Creek, Taneum Ridge, Fishhook Flat, Manastash Ridge and Divide, Blowout Mountain, North Ridge, Jolly Mountain, Mission Creek, and Devil's Gulch. That's a single year!

The Forest Service is opening these trails to wheels in response to pressures from motorcyclists. Hikers must exert more pressure or the wheels will roll, the engines roar, farther each year.

Some Forest Service rangers are bitterly opposed to motorcycles on hiking trails and urgently need your letters to support their position. Others, indifferent to the conflict, typically say: "This is multiple-use country. You'll just have to learn to live with motorcycles." But even these rangers will react if enough letters are written.

The Forest Service asks for and respects your comments. Letters about a specific trail can be addressed either to the district ranger or the forest supervisor. In either case the letter will be read by the person who makes the decision concerning opening or closing the trail to motorcycles. The most useful comments are those that give a reason for eliminating motors based on your own experience. Was your child endangered by a speeding cyclist? Was your wilderness mood diluted by motors? Is it to escape the tensions of a wheel-freaky civilization, to preserve your mental health, that you take to the trails?

Do not dispiritedly suppose that Forest Service minds are made up and cannot be changed. Forest Service officers have told me, off the record, and cited specific examples, where objections to motorcycles made in the previous edition of this guidebook have directly resulted in banning wheels.

It's the squeaking wheel that gets the grease. The squawking boot that gets the peace.

Walk softly, but squawk loudly and often.

Ira Spring

Canadian dogwood or bunchberry

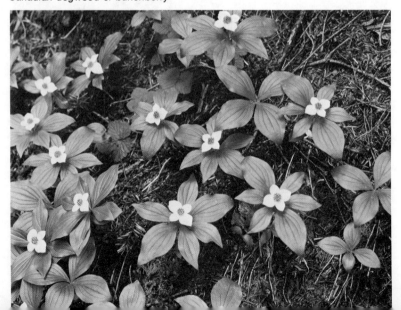

INTRODUCTION

Broad, smooth, well-marked, heavily-traveled, ranger-patroled paths safe and simple for little kids and elderly folks with no mountain training or equipment, or even for monomaniacs dashing from Canada to Mexico. Mean and cruel and mysterious routes through evil brush, over fierce rivers, up shifty screes and moraines to treacherous glaciers and appalling cliffs where none but the skilled and doughty should dare, or perhaps the deranged. Flower strolls for an afternoon, heroic adventures for a week.

A storm side (the west) where precipitation is heavy, winter long, snows deep, glaciers large, peaks sharply sculptured, vegetation lush, and high-country hiking doesn't get comfortably underway until late July. A lee side, a rainshadow side (the east) where clouds are mostly empties, summer is long, vegetation sparse, ridges round and gentle, and meadows melt free of the white by late June.

Places as thronged as a city park on Labor Day, places as lonesome as the South Pole that Scott knew. Scenes that remind of the High Sierra, scenes that remind of Alaska.

In summary, to generalize about the North Cascades: To generalize about the North Cascades is foolish.

Rules, Regulations, and Permits

Except for blocks of state (Department of Natural Resources) land around Chopaka Mountain and Mount Pilchuck-Sultan River, scattered enclaves of private lands mostly dating from mining and homestead days, and such miscellaneous bits as the Seattle City Light holdings on the Skagit River, the entirety of the North Cascades is federally administered. The U.S. Forest Service is the principal trustee, responsibility shared by Mt. Baker-Snoqualmie, Wenatchee, and Okanogan National Forests. Since 1968 the National Park Service has been on the scene in the North Cascades National Park and the accompanying Ross Lake and Lake Chelan National Recreation Areas, essentially parts of the park but permitting some activities, such as hunting, banned within the park proper.

Most of the national forest lands are under "multiple-use" administration, with roads, with logging, mining, and other economic exploitation, and with motorcycles allowed on many trails. Some areas, however, are proposed for statutory protection as wilderness. Already existing are the Glacier Peak (established 1960) and Pasayten (1968) Wildernesses; here the Wilderness Act of 1964 applies and these are areas where "the earth and its community of life are untrammeled by man, where man himself is a visitor who does not remain."

The North Cascades National Park (1968) was set aside, to use the words of the National Park Act of 1916, "to conserve the scenery and the natural and historic objects and the wildlife. . ." Each visitor therefore must enjoy the park "in such manner and by such means as will leave it unimpaired for the enjoyment of future generations." Most of the park is further covered by the Wilderness Act, giving the highest degree of protection in the North Cascades.

While most of the North Cascades continue in the First Stage of Preservation, where the goal is to save the land from racketing exploiters on bulldozers and loud recreationists on wheels, the dedicated areas of park and wilderness have entered the Second Stage, where the concern is to save the land from quiet boots. Even tenny-runners.

In dedicated lands each party on the trails overnight or longer must obtain and carry

Magic Mountain from Doubtful Lake

a "wilderness permit" (Forest Service) or "backcountry permit" (Park Service) that must be shown on request to a wilderness ranger (FS) or backcountry ranger (PS). Permits may be obtained by mail from the national forest headquarters (see below) or in person from forest or park ranger stations on the major entry roads. Where a planned itinerary lies on both Forest Service and Park Service lands, either agency can issue a single permit covering the entire trip.

Regulations differ from place to place (because not all places are the same), from agency to agency (because land managers disagree on the necessary and sufficient regulation), and from year to year (because population pressures on the backcountry vary, more is learned about the "carrying capacity" of ecosystems, and land managers change their minds). In the North Cascades as throughout America, the Second Stage of Preservation will be a period of experiment, discussion, argument, and — sometimes — confusion, over- or under-regulation, and unhappiness. Hikers can share in the great debate by expressing opinions to land managers. But to avoid unhappiness (and/or tickets for illegal camping) they must learn in advance the regulations applying to any given place in any given year, and then obey. Do not come flinging blithely in from New Jersey expecting the situation to be the same as it was a decade ago, or a year ago — you may end in frustration and despair by fleeing home to finish your vacation in the Great Pine Barrens.

Maps

Each hike description in this book lists the appropriate topographic maps published by the U.S. Geological Survey. These can be purchased at map stores or mountaineering equipment shops or by writing the U.S. Geological Survey, Federal Center, Denver, Colorado 80225.

The national forests and the park publish recreation maps that are quite accurate and up-to-date and are either free or inexpensive. Forest Service maps may be obtained at ranger stations or by writing:

Mt. Baker-Snoqualmie National Forest
919 2nd Avenue
Seattle, WA 98104

Wenatchee National Forest
P.O. Box 811
Wenatchee, WA 98801

Okanogan National Forest
P.O. Box 432
Okanogan, WA 98840

Park Service maps may be obtained, along with backcountry permits, at the ranger stations at Sedro Woolley, Marblemount, Chelan, and Stehekin.

Clothing and Equipment

No one should set out on a North Cascades trail, unless for a brief stroll, lacking warm long pants, wool shirt or sweater, and a windproof and rain-resistant parka, coat, or poncho. Many "freeway" trails can be negotiated in any footgear and gentle travelers treat meadows tenderly by wearing sneakers or the like. However, on the typical rude paths and in cross-country travel the feet need the protection of sturdy shoes or boots, with a 5-9-inch top to support ankles and keep out mud and dirt; the boots should be of such size as to permit wearing of two pair of wool socks, a third pair carried in the rucksack. For traction — and thus security — on snow and steep scree, moraines, and grass, the rubber-lug sole has been standard for several decades. Some authorities now consider the lug unnecessarily destructive of plants and soil and favor a smooth composition sole. Obviously there is a trade-off: saving plants versus saving feet and perhaps bodies. Experienced North Cascades travelers agree that 9 out of 10 hikers wear bigger, heavier, more wearying, more destructive boots than they need.

The rucksack should contain the Ten Essentials, found to be so by generations of North Cascades travelers, often from sad experience:

1. Extra clothing — more than needed in good weather.
2. Extra food — enough so something is left over at the end of the trip.
3. Sunglasses — necessary for most alpine travel and indispensable on snow.
4. Knife — for first aid and emergency firebuilding (making kindling).
5. Firestarter — a candle or chemical fuel for starting a fire with wet wood.
6. First-aid kit.
7. Matches — in a waterproof container.
8. Flashlight — with extra bulb and batteries.
9. Map — be sure it's the right one for the trip.
10. Compass — be sure to know the declination, east or west.

Camping and Fires

The laissez-faire camping of the past is pretty well gone from the North Cascades. The pioneer did as he pleased, when and where he pleased, and indeed took satisfaction in leaving his mark (meadows and lakeshores trampled bare, fire rings erected in profusion, ditches dug, wires strung between trees, nails pounded, initials carved.) The modern ideal is "without a trace" camping (kill only curiosity, take only photographs and memories, leave not even a footprint, emulate Nattie Bumpo, The Deerslayer). In the early days of the North Cascades the concern was how a small band of travelers could survive in an enormous wilderness. Now the concern is how a small wilderness can survive an enormous number of people. Whether or not rangers are on hand to enforce rules, the ethical hiker adheres to a code of walking light, camping light.

Backcountry regulations of the Park Service are strict. To protect fragile sites, and also the quality of the experience, the number of travelers in any zone of the park at any time is restricted, trail camping is limited to specified sites, cross-country camping is not allowed near trails, and wood fires cannot be built at any off-trail sites nor at many of the trail camps.

The Forest Service is similarly strict at such high-use areas as Image Lake but elsewhere is introducing regulations more slowly. Camping has been banned at many long-used spots within 100 feet of lakes or streams, at some beaten-to-death meadows, and the wood fire eliminated at the bulk of timberline sites.

In forested valleys, in remote areas with relatively few visitors, wood fires may still be built at many places with a clear conscience and no violation of the law. Even here a party should minimize impact by using only established fire pits and using only dead and down wood and, when finished, should drown the coals and stir them with a stick and then drown the ashes until the fingers can probe every corner of the pit and find no warmth.

At higher elevations, both because it is immoral to burn ingredients of the scenery and usually illegal, the wood fire is gone. But the loss is small because most of the easy wood anyway was gone years before the ban. Few long trips in the North Cascades do not require a backpacker stove — arrive at the trailhead without one and that may be as far as you get. Smokey Bear is watching.

Litter, Garbage, and Sanitation

The pioneer's technique was to toss garbage in the brush or drop it on the trail and walk away. Manners were improved to the level of "Burn Bash and Bury," the prevailing rule for decades. Today's rule is: PACK IT OUT.

On a day hike, take back to the road (and your garbage can at home) every last orange peel and band-aid.

On an overnight or longer hike, where a wood fire is built, burn all paper but carry back all unburnables. With no fire, carry back everything.

Don't bury garbage. If fresh, animals will dig it up and strew the remnants. Messy. Also, by providing this food supply you help build a resident population of hiker-menacing bears, mice, rats, skunks, and squirrels. No sleep. Burning before burying is no solution. Tin cans take as long as 40 years to disintegrate completely; aluminum and glass last for centuries. Further, digging pits to bury junk disturbs the ground cover, and iron often leaches from buried cans and "rusts" springs and creeks.

Don't leave leftover food for the next travelers; they will have their own food and won't be tempted by contributions spoiled by time and animals.

Especially don't cache plastic tarps. Weathering quickly ruins the fabric, little creatures nibble, and the result is a useless, miserable mess.

Keep the water pure. Even if you camp close to the source — as can be conscientiously done (where allowed) on gravel bars and lakeshore morainal or delta barrens and the like — do not wash dishes or bodies in creeks or lakes — haul water away from the shore to do the job. Do not swim in small lakes used for drinking water.

Finally, avoid RE (random elimination). Where privies are lacking, take care of toilet needs (1) far from watercourses, and (2) far from potential campsites. Choose a spot where the soil can be disturbed without damaging plant communities, scratch a shallow hole, just as cats do, and afterward cover the evidence. In this near-surface layer of high bacterial action nature will take care of things quickly.

Use This Land, Your Land, But Protect It

One generalization about the North Cascades that is not foolish: Hikers must use the land or lose it. What is not walked will be motorcycled and/or logged.

But even as they participate in the First Stage of Preservation, hikers must join, too, in the Second Stage, or be lumped with the eco-criminals.

A tangible reward for hiking may be cited. According to Professor Valerius Geist, Associate Dean of the University of Calgary, "exploring is life-giving." Your life's occupation, your life's recreation, help determine the state of your health. Persons who work in healthful surroundings and whose recreation centers on the strenuous physical activities characteristic of wilderness travel live on the average 7 to 14 years longer than they otherwise might.

That's so many more years to walk the trails, lightly, and to write letters and testify at hearings, so that your children, and grandchildren, also may have wilderness in which to live longer.

Pets

It is time to leave pets at home. Dogs have become so numerous on trails they sometimes outnumber hikers and, like humans, are having an impact on the fragile environment. Pets have always been forbidden on national park trails, and park rangers issue hundreds of citations every year to hikers who choose to violate the regulation. Outside of the parks, dogs have had free rein, but their impact on meadows and wildlife has been so great the Forest Service has been forced to prohibit dogs in some areas, and as the problem is better documented, there will be more closures in the future.

Where pets are permitted, even a well-behaved dog can ruin someone else's trip. Some dogs noisily defend an ill-defined territory for their master, snitch someone else's food, and are quite likely to defecate on the flat bit of ground the next hiker will want to use for a campsite.

Dogs belong to the same family as coyotes, and even if no wildlife is visible, the presence of dogs is sensed by the small wild things into whose home they are intruding.

Theft

Twenty years ago theft from a car left at the trailhead was rare. Not now. Equipment has become so fancy and expensive, so much worth stealing, and hikers so numerous, their throngs creating large assemblages of valuables, that theft is a growing problem. Not even wilderness camps are entirely safe; a single raider hitting an unguarded camp may easily carry off several sleeping bags, a couple tents, and assorted stoves, down booties, and freeze-dried strawberries — maybe $1000 worth of gear in one load! However, the professionals who do most of the stealing mainly concentrate on cars. Authorities are concerned but can't post guards at every trailhead.

Rangers in Olympic National Park have the following recommendations.

First and foremost, don't make crime profitable for the pros. If they break into a hundred cars and get nothing but moldy boots and tattered T shirts they'll give up. The best bet is to arrive in a beat-up 1960 car with doors and windows that don't close and leave in it nothing of value. If you insist on driving a nice new car, at least don't have mag wheels, tape deck, and radio, and keep it empty of gear. Don't think locks help — pros can open your car door and trunk as fast with a picklock as you can with your key. Don't imagine you can hide anything from them — they know all the hiding spots. If the hike is part of an extended car trip, arrange to store your extra equipment at a nearby motel.

Be suspicious of anyone waiting at a trailhead. One of the tricks of the trade is to sit there with a pack as if waiting for a ride, watching new arrivals unpack — and hide their valuables — and maybe even striking up a conversation to determine how long the marks will be away.

The ultimate solution, of course, is for hikers to become as poor as they were in the olden days. No criminal would consider trailheads profitable if the loot consisted solely of shabby khaki military surplus.

Water

Hikers traditionally have drunk the water in wilderness in confidence, doing their utmost to avoid contaminating it so the next person also can safely drink. But there is no assurance your predecessor has been so careful.

No open water ever, nowadays, can be considered safe for human consumption. Any reference in this book to "drinking water" is not a guarantee. It is entirely up to the individual whether he wants to take a chance — or to treat the water with chemicals or boil it for 20 minutes.

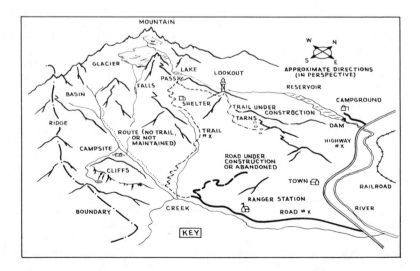

TABLE OF CONTENTS

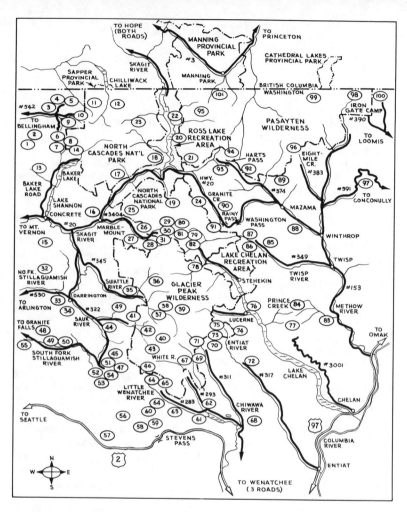

Round trip to Heliotrope Ridge 6 miles
Hiking time 5 hours
High point 6000 feet
Elevation gain 2300 feet
Best August to October
One day or backpack
USGS Mt. Baker

1 Heliotrope Ridge

A splendid forest walk leading to a ramble-and-scramble on flowery moraines below (and above) the ice-chaos of the rampaging Coleman Glacier. See the mountain climbers — by the hundreds on many summer weekends, because this is the most popular route to the summit of Mt. Baker. They're a harmless and unobtrusive lot, boisterous in camp but sacking out early, rising somber-and-quiet in the middle of the night and spending all day on the glaciers, out of sight and sound. Along the trail, hikers can enjoy the colorful displays of tents and axes and ropes and helmets and ironware.

Drive State Highway 542 to the town of Glacier and about 1 mile beyond to Glacier Creek road. Turn right some 8 miles to a parking lot at a sign, "Mt. Baker Trail," elevation 3700 feet. Hike 2 miles, traversing and switchbacking through tree shadows, over cold little creeks, to Kulshan Cabin, built by the Mt. Baker Club and now maintained by the Western Washington Outdoor Club. (Respect the historic and deteriorating old cabin and the efforts of those who keep it going; don't use it unless necessary, and then only with care.)

The cabin is at 4700 feet, near but still below timberline, and camping inside and out is of the sort only a climber (his thoughts on high) can enjoy, so hike along and past. No reason to loiter.

The fun country is above. From the cabin the trail (such as it is, built by boots) crosses the creek and switchbacks first in forest, then in meadows. Diverge left from the main-line climbers' path and continue on a lesser track to the moraine overlook on Heliotrope Ridge, at about 1¼ miles and 1300 feet above Kulshan Cabin. At 6000 feet the moraine touches ice-polished buttresses with a panorama of glaciers, Black Buttes, Baker, and the Nooksack valley. Hikers please note: be wary of the snow, which here merges indistinguishably into a crevassed glacier, strictly climbers' terrain. Hikers also have badly banged themselves up glissading on snowfields below here.

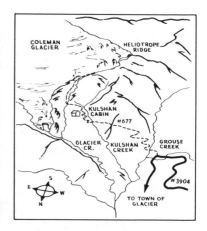

Mountain daisy

Coleman Glacier from trail's end

For one among numerous other possible wanders: above timberline, drift left (east) on meager man-and-animal tracks over a moraine and a rocky draw whistling with marmots to an alpine-forested ridge (another moraine). Burst suddenly through old, old trees to the surprising brink of a gravel precipice falling down and down to the blue-white jumble of the Coleman Glacier. Good camps here. Then climb the ancient moraine—stopping well short of the living glacier above.

Because of the enormous snowfall on Mt. Baker, and because this is the north side of the mountain, hikers who come earlier than August are liable to be surrounded by snow—and potential danger — above Kulshan Cabin. The crevasses, of course, are always there, visible or invisible.

NOOKSACK RIVER

2 Skyline Divide

Round trip to knoll 6 miles
Hiking time 4 hours
High point 6215 feet
Elevation gain 2200 feet
Best August to October
One day or backpack
USGS Mt. Baker

A large green meadow. An enormous white volcano — pound for pound, the iciest in all the Cascades. Views of forests and glaciers, rivers and mountains. Miles of ridges and basins to explore.

Drive State Highway 542 to 1 mile beyond the town of Glacier. Turn right on the Glacier Creek road and within 100 yards turn sharply left onto Dead Horse road No. 3907. Follow the south side of the Nooksack River a pleasant 4 miles. The road then climbs abruptly. At 7½ miles pause to view a lovely waterfall splashing down a rock cleft. At 12 miles is a parking lot and trailhead, elevation 4000 feet.

The trail, moderate to steep, climbs 2 miles in silver firs and subalpine glades to an immense meadow, the beginning of wide views. South are the vast glaciers of the north wall of Mt. Baker. North, beyond forests of the Nooksack valley, are the greenery of Church Mountain and the rock towers of the spectacular Border Peaks, and, across the boundary, the Lucky Four Range. On a clear day saltwater can be seen, and the Vancouver Island mountains, and the British Columbia Coast Range. Eastward is Mt. Shuksan, and for a gentle contrast, little Table Mountain, above Heather Meadows.

The meadow is superb but the supreme viewpoint is the 6200-foot knoll to the south. (From the meadow, it partly blocks out Baker.) Follow the trail ¾ mile along the ridge and around the knoll to the far side. Once the ridge crest is regained, walk back up the easy slope of the knoll to the summit. Sprawl in flowers and enjoy. (Note to photographers: generally the best pictures of Baker from here are taken before 10 a.m. or after 4 p.m.)

The trail continues along the meadow ridge another mile and then peters out. No matter; in these open highlands the roaming is easy, so walk where you will. There is enough country here to keep a party happy for several days of exploration. The trail, the big meadow, and Skyline Divide are waterless except in early summer. However, well-watered basecamps for wandering can be found in the flower gardens of Smith and Chowder Basins. Experienced alpine hikers can travel cross-country from here to Bastile Ridge.

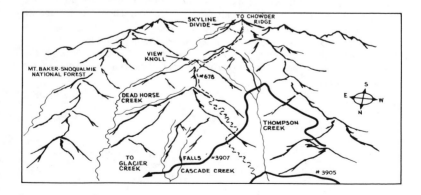

Mt. Baker from Skyline Ridge trail. Black Buttes on right skyline

Hikers who don't mind plugging steps in snow can enjoy a brilliant trip here in late spring-early summer. Since road No. 3907 may not be open then, start instead on road No. 3905, from which a 2-mile trail climbs virgin forest to join road 3907 near the Skyline Divide trailhead.

Mt. Baker from Excelsior Mountain

NOOKSACK RIVER

3 Excelsior Mountain

Round trip from Canyon Creek road 7 miles
Hiking time 4 hours
High point 5699 feet
Elevation gain 1500 feet
Best mid-July to October
One day or backpack
USGS Mt. Baker

Views from this meadow summit include Nooksack valley forests and Puget Sound lowlands, Mt. Baker and the Border Peaks, the southernmost portion of the British Columbia Coast Range, and more. Flowers in July, berries and colors in September. Three trails lead to the site of a long-gone lookout cabin; the easiest is recommended here, but take your pick.

Drive State Highway 542 to the town of Glacier and 2 miles beyond to Canyon Creek road No. 400. Turn left 15 miles to the parking lot in a clearcut at the start of trail No. 625; elevation, 4200 feet.

Climb gently through forest ½ mile to the junction with Canyon Ridge trail No. 689 and a bit more to 4500-foot Damfino Lakes, two small ponds surrounded by acres of super-delicious blueberries (in season). Campsites and running water near the smaller lake.

Climb another timbered mile, then go up a narrow draw and shortly enter meadows. Cross a notch, sidehill forest, then broad meadows, rising in ½ mile to 5300-foot Excelsior Pass, some 2½ miles from the road. (Pleasant camps at and near the pass when there is snowfield water — perhaps until early August.) Leave the main trail at the pass and climb a way trail ¼ mile east to the 5699-foot peak.

Sit and look. See the glaciers of Mt. Baker across forests of the Nooksack. See more ice on Mt. Shuksan and other peaks east. See the steep-walled Border Peaks and snowy ranges extending far north into Canada. And see green meadows everywhere.

The summit is a magnificent place to stop overnight in good weather, watching a sunset and a dawn; no water, though, except possible snowmelt.

Two alternate trails can be used to vary the descent. (They can also be used to ascend the peak, but for reasons that will be obvious are not the best choices.)

Alternate No. 1. From Excelsior Pass, descend trail No. 670 4 miles and 3500 feet to the highway, reached 8 miles east of Glacier at a small parking area (with trail sign on opposite side of road) between Wells Creek road No. 403 and the highway overlook. The trail switchbacks steeply on south-facing slopes that melt free of snow relatively early in the season; an excellent hike from the highway in May or June, turning back when snowfields halt progress. In summer this route to high country is long and hot and dry.

Alternate No. 2. From the lookout, traverse High Divide trail No. 630 east 5 miles to Welcome Pass. At 4960-foot Welcome Pass, find a steep trail dropping south 2 miles to an unmaintained logging road; descend the road 2 more miles to the highway, reached at a point some 13 miles east of Glacier.

Experienced off-trail roamers can extend their flower wanders west from Excelsior Pass toward Church Mountain and east from Welcome Pass to Yellow Aster Butte.

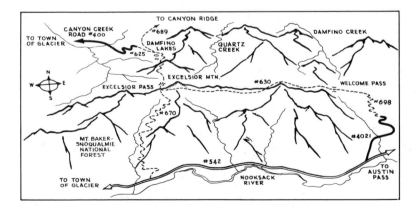

4 Gold Run Pass

Round trip to Gold Run Pass 4 miles
Hiking time 4 hours
High point 5400 feet
Elevation gain 1800 feet
Best July through October
One day or backpack
USGS Mt. Shuksan

Views across the Nooksack valley to Mt. Baker and Mt. Shuksan. Views over the headwaters of Tomyhoi Creek to Tomyhoi Peak and the tall, colorful walls of Mt. Larrabee and American Border and Canadian Border Peaks. Views down to a mile-long lake and north into Canada. Mountain meadows along a pretty trail — but a hot and dry trail on sunny days, so start early and carry water.

Drive State Highway 542 to Glacier and 13½ miles beyond to highway maintenance sheds. Just past is a sign, "Tomyhoi Trail 5, Twin Lakes 7." Turn left up narrow, steep, rough road No. 401. At 2½ miles pass the Keep Kool Trail (see below). At 3 miles is an intersection; go left. At 4½ miles is the Tomyhoi Lake trail sign, elevation 3600 feet; park here.

The trail switchbacks steadily up meadows, then trees, then meadows again. In 1½ miles the way leaves forest the last time and enters an open basin, snowcovered until July. South are Baker and a shoulder of Shuksan. Above is Yellow Aster Butte. The display of wildflowers begins here with avalanche lily and lanceleaf spring beauty in mid-June and continues with other species through the summer. At 2 miles is Gold Run Pass, 5400 feet.

Two further explorations are inviting. Tomyhoi Lake, 3800 feet, is 2 miles and 1600 feet below the pass. The lake is less than 2 miles from the border; Canadian logging roads can be seen. Avalanche snow floats in the waters until early summer. Good campsite. The trail from Gold Run Pass down to Tomyhoi Lake crosses a steep, hard-packed, north-facing snow patch that is often treacherous most of the summer.

The other choice is 6200-foot Yellow Aster Butte, 800 feet higher than the pass. The route to the summit is not difficult but requires care on the steep greenery. Avoid little cliffs and settle for the comfortable first summit, with views just as big as from the slightly-higher rock crag. Meadows lead easily down to Yellow Aster Lakes.

Starting at 2900 feet, the Keep Kool Trail climbs forest, then meadows, 2½ miles to an end at 5500 feet in a cold basin not too long ago filled with ice, and more recently picked at by miners. A dozen little lakes and tarns are scattered through the basin and in ridge-top scoops. The higher views of Yellow Aster Butte are a short and easy stroll away. A boot-beaten path climbs the broad ridge to mind-boggling panoramas beside and above the Tomyhoi Glacier, and to just below the climbers-only 7451-foot summit of Tomyhoi. Camping should be confined to bare dirt and sterile gravel — stay off the flowers.

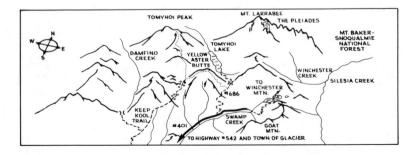

Mt. Shuksan from Yellow Aster Butte

5 Winchester Mountain

Round trip from Twin Lakes 4 miles
Hiking time 3 hours
High point 6521 feet
Elevation gain 1300 feet
Best late July to October
One day
USGS Mt. Shuksan

An easy and popular trail through alpine meadows to a summit view of Baker, Shuksan, Icy, Border Peaks, and Tomyhoi, with looks far down to Tomyhoi Lake and forests of Silesia Creek. Especially beautiful in fall colors.

Drive to Twin Lakes road (Hike 4). This road is not the work of the Forest Service, or built to its specifications. A "mine-to-market" road, it was constructed by the county and is maintained in the upper reaches solely by the miners, and then only when they are engaged in their sporadic activity, and then only minimally. The first 4½ miles to the Tomyhoi Lake trail usually are in decent condition but the final 2 miles to Twin Lakes are something else, culminating in five wickedly-sharp switchbacks. Many people prefer to protect cars and nerves from damage by driving 1 mile past the Tomyhoi Lake trail, parking near an old mine road, and walking the final mile (gaining 1000 feet) to the lakes. Road maintenance is so difficult this last stretch is not open to automobiles until the middle of August, some years not at all; when the miners finally give up, the road will be abandoned, returning Twin Lakes to the realm of trail country where they belong.

The two lakes, lovely alpine waters at an elevation of 5200 feet, often are frozen until early August, though surrounding parklands melt free earlier. Between the lakes is an undeveloped campsite with a classic view of Mt. Baker.

Find the Winchester Mountain trail at the road-end between the lakes. Within ¼ mile is a junction with the High Pass (Gargett Mine) trail. Take the left fork and climb a series of switchbacks westerly through heather, alpine trees, and flowers. Near the top there may be a treacherous snow patch, steep with no runout, often lasting until late August. It may be possible to squirm between the upper edge of the snow and the rocks. Otherwise, drop below the snow and climb to the trail on the far side. Don't try the snow without an ice ax and experience in using it.

In 1½ miles the trail rounds a shoulder and levels off somewhat for the final ½ mile to the summit, site of an abandoned fire lookout cabin and a fine place to while away hours surveying horizons from Puget Sound lowlands to the Pickets and far north into Canada.

Twin Lakes make a superb basecamp for days of roaming high gardens, prowling old mines, and grazing September blueberries. Even if the upper road must be walked, access is easy for backpacking families with short-legged members.

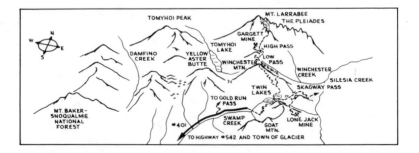

Winchester Mountain trail. Goat Mountain across valley

For one of the longer explorations of the many available, take the High Pass trail (see above). A steep snowfield near the beginning may stop all but trained climbers; if not, there is no further barrier to Low Pass (about 1½ miles) and 5900-foot High Pass (2½ miles). Follow an old miner's trail high on Mt. Larrabee to a close view of the rugged Pleiades. Investigate the junkyard of the Gargett Mine. Wander meadow basins and admire scenery close and distant.

6 Chain Lakes Loop

Round trip 6 miles
Hiking time 4 hours
High point 5400 feet
Elevation gain 1500 feet
Best late July through October
One day
USGS Mt. Shuksan

Alpine meadows loaded with blueberries (in season), a half-dozen small lakes, and at every turn of the trail a changing view, dominated by "the magnificent pair," the white volcano of Mt. Baker and the massive architecture of Mt. Shuksan. The area is a wildlife sanctuary, so deer are frequently seen. All this on an easy hike circling the base of a high plateau guarded on every side by impressive lava cliffs.

Drive State Highway 542 to closed-in-summer Mt. Baker Lodge (Heather Meadows Recreation Area). Continue on gravel road 3 miles upward to the 5200-foot road-end on Kulshan Ridge. The winter snowpack here is often 25 feet deep on the level, with much greater depths in drifts, so the road commonly is snowbound until late August. Drive as far as possible and walk the rest of the way.

Find the Chain Lakes trail on the west side of the road-end parking lot. In a few hundred feet keep left. (The right fork, the Table Mountain trail, climbs 500 feet through lava cliffs to grand views atop the plateau; to here, the walk is easy and rewarding. The trail then continues over Table Mountain and descends cliffs to meet the Chain Lakes trail. However, on the way it crosses a steep and dangerous snowfield which has killed enough hikers that the summit traverse is not recommended.) The Chain Lakes trail makes an almost level traverse a short mile around the south side of Table Mountain to a saddle between Table Mountain and Ptarmigan Ridge. At the junction here take the right fork, dropping 300 feet to the first of the four Chain Lakes, tiny Mazama Lake. A bit beyond is aptly-named Iceberg Lake, which many years never melts out completely. (Halfway around the shore, one can take the left trail for a short sidetrip on a narrow ridge between Hayes Lake and Arbuthnot Lake.)

Climb 600 feet to 5400-foot Herman Saddle, a narrow slot whose cliffs frame Baker west, Shuksan east. Spend some time sitting and looking from one to the other. Then descend amid boulders, heather, and waterfalls, dropping 1100 feet to meadow-sur-

Mt. Baker from Kulshan Ridge

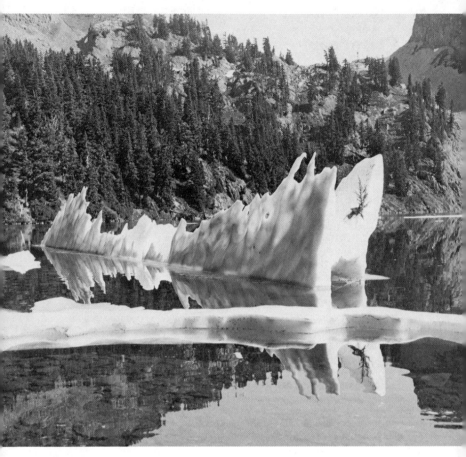

Iceberg Lake

rounded Bagley Lakes. Pause to wander flower fields of the inlet stream. Look for skiers on the north side of Table Mountain; diehards ski the permanent snowfields all summer and fall, until winter sends them to other slopes.

Between the Bagley Lakes find an unmaintained path (easy going even if the tread is lost) climbing to the Cascade Field Station of the University of Washington and the Kulshan Ridge parking area, gaining 900 feet in 2 miles. If transportation can be arranged (by use of two cars, or by means of a helpful friend), this final ascent can be eliminated.

NOOKSACK RIVER

7 Ptarmigan Ridge

Round trip to Camp Kiser about 12 miles
Hiking time 8 hours
High point 6000 feet
Elevation gain about 1200 feet
Best August through September
One day or backpack
USGS Mt. Baker and Mt. Shuksan

Begin in meadows, climb a bit to the snowy and rocky crest of a ridge open to the sky, and wander for miles on the high line toward the lofty white mass of Mt. Baker. This hike has no single destination; a party may go a short way until stopped by snow, or continue a long way to close views of the splendid Rainbow Glacier, or accept the invitation of sidetrips. Everything is purely delightful.

Keep in mind, though, that Ptarmigan Ridge is basically "climbers' country." In late summer of light-snowfall years, in good weather, hikers can venture into the wild and lonesome highland, but even then they must be well-equipped and experienced. Indeed, climbers' gear and training are usually essential to get very far in safety.

Drive to Kulshan Ridge road-end at 5200 feet and hike 1 mile to the saddle between Table Mountain and Ptarmigan Ridge (Hike 6). At the junction take the left fork, Camp Kiser trail No. 683. The trail drops a bit and then climbs around the side of the 5628-foot hump marking the north end of Ptarmigan Ridge. Snowfields often linger here through the summer and may force casual walkers to turn back.

Beyond the hump the trail climbs (usually on snow) to a ridge crest and traverses some 2½ miles to Camp Kiser. The tread is sketchy, snow crossings are frequent, and the route becomes increasingly difficult to follow and increasingly easy to lose, despite rock cairns. In fog, even skilled alpine navigators get confused; spur ridges may be mistaken for the main ridge and lead a party far astray.

The Baker-Shuksan scenery is steadily dazzling and off-trail tours of high rocks and waterfall-loud basins are constantly tempting. Listen to marmots and conies whistling and squeaking. Watch for goats. And ptarmigan.

The trail swings around the south side of 6414-foot Coleman Pinnacle to Camp Kiser, which is not a specific place but rather a ½-mile stretch of ridgeslope benches sprinkled with alpine fir and mountain hemlock. Here is where the occasional climbers camp.

Camp Kiser offers many fine spots to stop overnight or longer. Water is plentiful but not wood; carry a stove. The place cries out for a basecamp to enjoy the explorations. Walk to near the top of Coleman Pinnacle — and scramble to the summit if competent to do so. Wander the climbers' track another mile or two closer to the glaciers. Or drop 500 feet down meadows to the cold little basin southeast of Coleman Pinnacle, only recently evacuated by a glacier, remnants of which linger; roam the shores of a new-born, ice-fed lakelet.

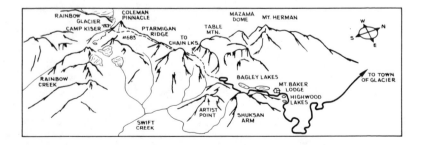

Mt. Baker from Camp Kiser

NOOKSACK RIVER

8 Lake Ann

Round trip to Lake Ann 8 miles
Hiking time 6-8 hours
High point (at saddle) 4800 feet
Elevation gain about 1000 feet in
    and about 1000 feet out
Best August to October
One day or backpack
USGS Mt. Shuksan
Park Service backcountry permit
    required for camping at Lake Ann

When North Cascades climbers and hikers compare memories of favorite sitting-and-looking places, Lake Ann always gets fond mention. The Mt. Shuksan seen from here is quite different from the world-famous roadside view, yet the 4500-foot rise of glaciers and cliffs is at least as grand. And there is much to do.

Drive State Highway 542 to Mt. Baker Lodge, closed in summer. Continue on gravel road about 1½ miles upward to the parking lot at Austin Pass, 4700 feet. Until August, snow blocks the road somewhere above the Lodge, adding ½ mile or so of walking.

The trail begins by dropping 600 feet to a delightful headwater basin of Swift Creek. Brooks meander in grass and flowers. Marmots whistle from boulder-top perches. Pleasant picnicking.

From the basin the trail descends a bit more and traverses forest, swinging around the upper drainage of Swift Creek. At 2¼ miles is the lowest elevation (3900 feet) of the trip, an attractive camp in meadows by a rushing stream, and a junction with the Swift Creek trail.

Now starts a 900-foot ascent in 1½ miles, first in heather and clumps of Christmas trees, then over a granite rockslide into forest under a cliff, to a cold and open little valley. If the way is snow-covered, as it may be until mid-August, plod onward and upward to the obvious 4800-foot saddle, beyond which is Lake Ann. When whiteness melts away, the waterfalls and moraines and flowers and ice-plucked buttresses of the little valley demand a slow pace.

What to do next? First off, sit and watch the living wall of Shuksan. Then, perhaps, circumnavigate the lake, noting the contact between granitic rocks and complex metamorphics. In September, blueberry upward on the ridge of Mt. Ann. If time allows, go on longer wanders.

Recommended Wander No. 1.   Follow the trail from Lake Ann as it dips into the headwater basin of Shuksan Creek, then switchbacks up and up toward Shuksan. At a rocky gully a climbers' track branches steeply to the left. Just here the main trail may

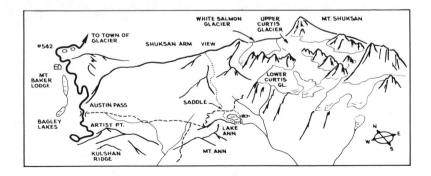

Curtis Glacier and Mt. Shuksan from near Lake Ann

be nonexistent for a few yards; if so, scramble across gravel to regain the tread. Continue to a promontory a stone's throw from the snout of the Lower Curtis Glacier. Look up to the mountain. Look down forests to Baker Lake. Look beyond Swift Creek to the stupendous whiteness of Mt. Baker.

Recommended Wander No. 2.   From the Lake Ann saddle climb the heathery spur to Shuksan Arm. No trail, but logic leads the feet. Views down to the Nooksack River and north to the splinter-summits of the Border Peaks.

Nooksack Cirque

NOOKSACK RIVER

9 Nooksack Cirque

Round trip 11 miles
Hiking time 6-10 hours
High point 3500 feet
Elevation gain 1100 feet
Best late May through October
One day or backpack
USGS Mt. Shuksan
Park Service backcountry permit required

A wild, lonesome cirque, a wasteland of glacial violence, one of the most dramatic spots in the North Cascades. Icefalls, waterfalls, moraines, a raging river, the stark pinnacle of Nooksack Tower, and the 5000-foot northeast wall of Mt. Shuksan. But not much trail, mostly miles of bushwacking and/or ankle-twisting boulders. The trip is best taken either in late spring when snow covers the brush or in fall when the river is low enough to fully expose gravel bars.

Drive State Highway 542 east from Glacier 13 miles to the Nooksack River bridge. Just before the bridge turn left on Nooksack River road No. 402. In about 1½ miles take the right fork, road No. 404. Go 4 miles to another fork; take the lower and most-used road and follow it 1 rough mile to end, elevation about 2400 feet. Road and trail should be marked "Nooksack Trail."

The trail goes 1 mile to an abrupt end at the river bank. From here on, lots of luck. No problems getting lost, just problems getting there.

When the river is low, as during extended periods of cool weather and in fall, gravel bars can be walked all the way from trail-end into the cirque. The bouldery travel is slow and occasional side-channels must be crossed by hopping or wading but the going is easy.

Not so when the river is high, covering some or all the gravel bars, flooding the side-channels. A route must then be picked through the woods, which offers some open travel but a lot of brush, including patches of 6-foot-high huckleberry bushes. (More than one party has hiked into the cirque on gravel bars and been forced by a downpour and rising waters to beat brush to get out.)

In 2 miles, views of Icy Peak. In 3 miles, the hanging ice cliffs of the East Nooksack Glacier, falling from Cloudcap (Seahpo) Peak and Jagged Ridge. Now, rounding a bend in the valley, the way enters the cirque and at 4 miles reaches "the deepest, darkest hole in the North Cascades."

For the most impressive views climb a few hundred feet up slopes to the north. See the East Nooksack Glacier tumbling 5000 feet from the Summit Pyramid of Shuksan. See the startling thrust of 8268-foot Nooksack Tower. For higher views scramble to the 6000-foot saddle between Icy Peak and Cloudcap Peak.

Many campsites on gravel bars and moraines; no fires allowed, not even on the gravel. Within the cirque, several hundred feet above the river, is the famous Great Trog, well worth finding in bad weather; this overhang of a giant boulder offers comfortable camping, dry and protected, for as many as a dozen people (and dozens of varmints!).

The National Park Service may build a trail into the cirque. The trip will then be much easier but much less wild. Go now, before the crowds.

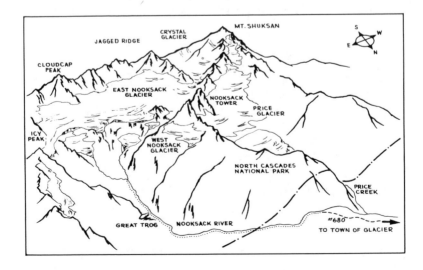

NOOKSACK RIVER

10 Hannegan Pass and Peak

Round trip to Hannegan Pass 8 miles
Hiking time 6 hours
High point 5066 feet
Elevation gain 2000 feet
Best mid-July to October
One day or backpack
USGS Mt. Shuksan

Round trip to Hannegan Peak 10 miles
Hiking time 8 hours
High point 6186 feet
Elevation gain 3100 feet
Best mid-July to October
One day or backpack

A prime entry to the Chilliwack and Picket section of the North Cascades National Park. The walk begins in a delightful valley dominated by the white serenity of Ruth Mountain and concludes with a relaxed wander to a meadow summit offering a panorama of the north wall of Shuksan, the Pickets, and wildness high and low.

Drive State Highway 542 east from Glacier 13 miles to the Nooksack River bridge. Just before the bridge turn left on Nooksack River road No. 402. In about 1½ miles take the left fork, Ruth Creek road No. 402, and continue 4½ miles to road-end at Hannegan Campground, 3000 feet.

The first trail mile ascends gently through trees and avalanche-path greenery near Ruth Creek, with looks upward to the waterfall-streaked cliffs and pocket icefields of Mt. Sefrit and Nooksack Ridge. At a bit more than 1 mile the snow dome of Ruth Mountain comes in sight — a startling expanse of whiteness for so small a peak. Now the path steepens, climbing above the valley floor.

Rest stops grow long, there is so much to see and so much good water to drink. At 3½ miles, 4600 feet, the trail swings to the forest edge beside a meadow-babbling creek; across the creek is a parkland of heather benches and alpine trees. Splendid campsites, the best on the route; those least harmful to the terrain are designated by the Forest Service, which wishes campers would not build fires here. The final ½ mile switchbacks in forest to Hannegan Pass, 5066 feet.

Views from the pass are restricted by trees; the camping is so poor (scarce wood, undependable water) and so damaging to the tiny meadow it is strongly discouraged

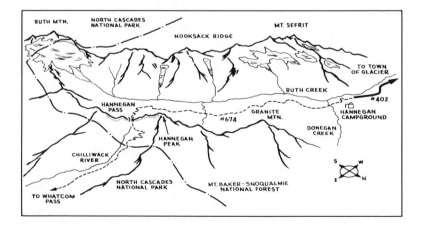

Looking north from side of Hannegan Peak

and ought to be forbidden. Hikers who come only to the pass will feel richly rewarded by scenes along the way but may be disappointed by the lack of a climactic vista. A sidetrip is therefore recommended.

Visitors usually are drawn southward and upward on the climbers' track toward Ruth Mountain. This path leads to lovely meadows and broader views but dwindles to nothing before long, tempting the unwary onto steep and dangerous snow slopes. Leave Ruth to the climbers. There's a better and safer sidetrip.

From the pass, saunter westerly up open forest, following game traces when available. Emerge into a steep, lush meadow (slippery when wet), at the top break through a screen of trees to heather and flowers, and wander wide-eyed up the crest of a rounded ridge to the summit plateau of Hannegan Peak, 6186 feet. Roam the meadow flats, looking down into valley forests of Ruth and Silesia Creeks and Chilliwack River, looking out to glaciers and cliffs of Baker, Shuksan, Ruth, Triumph, Challenger, Redoubt, Slesse, and dozens of other grand peaks. Many of these peaks and valleys — including the entire route of this hike — have been omitted from the North Cascades National Park. This grievous error must be rectified.

In good weather a party can camp comfortably on the summit; carry a stove for cooking, collect water from snowfield trickles, and enjoy the panorama in sunset and dawn. Experienced highland travelers can run the open ridge north to connect with the Copper Mountain trail (Hike 11). The ridge-running west to Granite Mountain is also inviting.

11 Copper Mountain

Round trip to Copper Mountain
  Lookout 20 miles
Allow 2-3 days
High point 6260 feet
Elevation gain about 4800 feet in,
  1500 feet out
Best August to October
USGS Mt. Shuksan and Mt. Challenger
Park Service backcountry permit required
  (obtain at Glacier Ranger Station)

A remote meadow ridge on the west edge of the North Cascades National Park, offering a rare combination of easy-walking terrain and panoramas of rough-and-cold wilderness. Views across far-below forests of the Chilliwack River to the Picket Range — and views west to other superb peaks and valleys proposed for addition to the Park. However, hikers planning a visit should be aware of severe restrictions on use of the area. The Park Service currently permits only three parties to camp at any given time on the entire 6-mile length of the ridge.

Mt. Shuksan from Copper Ridge

Drive to Hannegan Campground and hike 4 miles, gaining 2000 feet, to Hannegan Pass (Hike 10). Descend forest switchbacks into avalanche-swept headwaters of the Chilliwack River, then sidehill along talus and stream outwash patched with grass and flowers. Note chunks of volcanic breccia in the debris and look up to their source in colorful cliffs — remnants of ancient volcanoes.

At 1 mile and 650 feet below Hannegan Pass is a 4400-foot junction. (Beside the nearby river is a nice campsite.) The Chilliwack River trail goes right, descending. The Copper Mountain trail goes left and up, entering forest and climbing steadily, switch-backing some, crossing the upper portion of Hells Gorge (sliced into volcanic rocks), and emerging into parkland.

At 7 miles the trail attains the 5500-foot ridge crest between Silesia Creek and the Chilliwack River. A memorable look back to Hannegan Pass, Ruth Mountain, and Shuksan — and the beginning of miles of constant views.

(From this point, experienced hikers can make an off-trail ridge-running return to Hannegan Peak and Pass; also, a short sidetrip leads to a tiny cirque lake.)

The trail continues along the open crest, up a bit and down a bit, then climbs around a knob to a wide, grassy swale at 8 miles. Some 300 feet and a few minutes below the swale is little Egg Lake, 5200 feet, set in rocks and flowers. One permitted campsite is at the lake, another in the swale.

The way goes up and down another knob to a broad meadow at 9 miles. Now comes the final mile, gaining 1100 feet to 6260-foot Copper Mountain Lookout, the climax. Beyond the green deeps of Silesia Creek are the Border Peaks and the incredible fang of Slesse — and far-off in haze, ice giants of the British Columbia Coast Range. Look down and down to the white thread of the Chilliwack River and beyond its forest valley to Redoubt and Bear and Indian and the magnificent Pickets. Also see Shuksan and Baker. And more peaks and streams, an infinity of wildland.

Beyond the lookout the trail descends about 1½ miles to the third permitted campsite at 5200-foot Copper Lake (blue waters under steep cliffs), then traverses and descends about 7 more miles (views much of the way) to the Chilliwack River trail at 2300 feet; this junction is 14.4 miles from Hannegan Pass. A 34-mile loop trip using this return route adds low-valley forests to the high-ridge wander.

For another exploration leave the trail before the steep descent to Copper Lake and investigate ridges and basins toward the 7142-foot summit of Copper Mountain. It'll be a few years before crowds are a problem here.

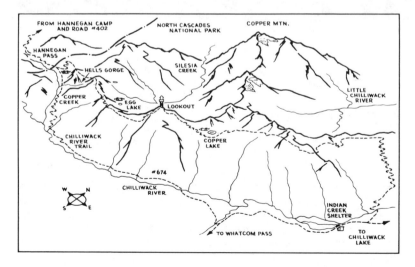

Mt. Challenger from Whatcom Pass

NOOKSACK RIVER

12 Whatcom Pass

Round trip to Whatcom Pass 34 miles
Allow 3-5 days
High point 5200 feet
Elevation gain 4600 feet in,
   2600 feet out
Best late July to October
USGS Mt. Shuksan and Mt. Challenger
Park Service backcountry permit required

A long hike on an old miners' route to the Caribou goldfields in Canada, entering the heart of the most spectacular wilderness remaining in the contiguous 48 states. Virgin forests in a U-shaped valley carved by ancient glaciers; rushing rivers; mountain meadows; and a sidetrip to lovely Tapto Lakes, the ultimate blend of gentle beauty and rough grandeur. Whatcom Pass is the high point on the increasingly-popular walk across the North Cascades National Park from the Mt. Baker region to Ross Lake. However, hikers planning a trip should be aware the Park Service has banned camping between Graybeal Shelter and Twin Rocks Camp; they thus must be prepared to cover in one day 9 miles, gaining 1200 feet and losing 2200. This chore discourages extensive sidetrip explorations along the way.

Drive to Hannegan Campground and hike 4 miles, gaining 2000 feet, to Hannegan Pass (Hike 10). Descend the Chilliwack River trail, which drops rapidly at first and then gentles out in delightful forest, reaching the U.S. Cabin shelter (camping) at 10 miles.

At about 11 miles, elevation 2468 feet (2600 feet down from Hannegan Pass), the trail crosses the Chilliwack River. The footbridge has been gone for several years and despite two drownings there are no immediate plans for replacement. Do not try to ford the river in high water; look downstream ½ mile for a footlog. The way now climbs moderately to the crossing of Brush Creek at about 12 miles. Here is a junction.

The Chilliwack trail goes north 9 miles to the Canadian border and about 1 mile more to Chilliwack Lake. The forest walk to the border is worth taking in its own right; parties visiting the region during early summer when the high country is full of snow may prefer pleasures of the low, green world.

From the 2600-foot junction the Brush Creek trail climbs steadily, gaining 2600 feet in the 5 miles to Whatcom Pass. At 14 miles is Graybeal Shelter, and at 17 miles 5200-foot Whatcom Pass.

Views from the meadowy pass are superb, but there is vastly more to see. Plan to spend at least a full day touring the area; Graybeal makes the best base. The first thing to do is ramble the easy ridge south of the pass to a knoll overlooking the mind-boggling gleam of the Challenger Glacier.

Tapto Lakes are next. (However, don't bother if snow is still deep around the pass; the lakes will then be frozen and their basins solid white.) Climb steep slopes north from the pass, following a boot-built path in alpine forest. When the hillside levels off continue left in meadows to rocky ground above the lakes. Enjoy the waters and flowers, the stupendous view of Challenger.

The classic "across the National Park" hike from Hannegan Campground to Big Beaver Landing on Ross Lake covers 38½ up-and-down miles on easy trail beside wild rivers, through gorgeous forests, over three passes. Total elevation gain on the way, 5400 feet. To have time for sidetrips a party should allow 7-9 days. From Whatcom Pass drop abruptly (56 switchbacks!) into headwaters of Little Beaver Creek, an enchanting place where waterfalls tumble from cliffs all around. Camping here at Twin Rocks Camp, 3000 feet. At 6 miles from Whatcom Pass is Stillwell Camp and the 2400-foot junction with the Beaver Pass trail. To conclude the cross-Park journey, see Hike 23.

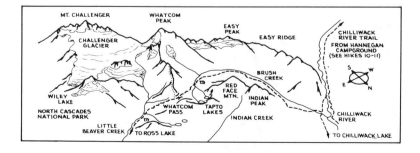

BAKER RIVER

13 Park Butte— Railroad Grade

Round trip to Park Butte 7 miles
Hiking time 6-8 hours
High point 5450 feet
Elevation gain 2250 feet
Best mid-July through October
One day or backpack
USGS Hamilton and Mt. Baker

Recommending any one hike in the parklands of Mt Baker's southwest flank is like praising a single painting in a museum of masterpieces. There are days of wandering here, exploring meadows and moraines, waterfalls and lakes, listening to marmots and watching for mountain goats. The trail to Morovitz Meadow gives a good sampling of the country, with impressive near views of the glaciers of Baker, the towering Black Buttes (core of an ancient volcano), the Twin Sisters, and far horizons.

Drive State Highway 20 east from Sedro Woolley 14½ miles and turn left on the Baker Lake-Grandy Lake road. In 12½ miles, just past Rocky Creek bridge, turn left on Loomis-Nooksack road No. 3725, go 3 miles to Sulphur Creek road No. 372, and follow it 6 miles to the end in a logging patch (inside the Mt. Baker Recreation Area!) at about 3200 feet. Find the trail west of the road, near Sulphur Creek.

The trail immediately crosses Sulphur Creek into the heather and blueberries (in season) of Schreibers Meadow, passes frog ponds and a dilapidated shelter cabin, then enters forest. In 1 mile is an interesting area where meltwater from the Easton Glacier has torn wide avenues through the trees. The drainage pattern changes from time to time; generally three torrents must be crossed by footlog or boulder-hopping.

Beyond the boulder-and-gravel area the trail enters cool forest and switchbacks steeply a long mile to lower Morovitz Meadow. The grade gentles in heather fields leading to upper Morovitz Meadow, 4500 feet. Pleasant campsites here, some in alpine trees, some in open gardens beside snowmelt streams.

At the trail junction in the upper meadow, go left to Park Butte, climbing to a ridge and in a mile reaching the 5450-foot summit. Views of Mt. Baker glaciers (and much more) are magnificent. Parties with spare time and energy may well be tempted to descend to the delightful basin of Pocket Lake, or roam the ridge to 6100-foot Survey Point.

There is another direction to go from Morovitz Meadow. Leave the trail near the junction and ramble upward to the intriguing crest of Railroad Grade, a moraine built by the Easton Glacier in more ambitious days. Look down the unstable wall of gravel and

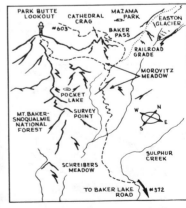

Snout of the Easton Glacier

Mt. Baker from Park Butte

boulders to the naked wasteland below the ice. Walk the narrow crest higher and yet higher, closer and closer to the gleaming volcano. In late summer hikers can scramble moraine rubble and polished slabs to about 7000 feet before being forced to halt at the edge of the glacier.

From either Railroad Grade or Baker Pass, inventive walkers can pick private ways through waterfall-and-flower country to the edge of a startling chasm. Look down to the chaotic front of the Deming Glacier, across to stark walls of the Black Buttes. All through the wide sprawl of Mazama Park are secluded campsites, beauty spots to explore. Don't forget little Mazama Lake or nearby Meadow Point.

14 Baker River

Round trip to Sulphide Creek 6 miles
Hiking time 3-4 hours
High point 900 feet
Elevation gain 200 feet
Best March through November
One day or backpack
USGS Lake Shannon, Mt. Shuksan,
and Mt. Challenger
Park Service backcountry permit required

Luxurious rain forest, a lovely green-milky river, and tantalizing glimpses of glacier-covered peaks. Because of the very low elevation (and such low-altitude virgin valleys are now rare indeed in the Cascades) the trail is open except in

Baker River

midwinter and offers a delightful wildland walk when higher elevations are buried in snow. Even bad weather is no barrier to enjoyment, not with all the big trees, understory plants, and streams. For a feeling of true lonesomeness, try the trip on a rainy day in early spring. It's also a good place to escape guns during hunting season, since the no-shooting North Cascades National Park is entered partway along.

Drive State Highway 20 east from Sedro Woolley 14½ miles. Turn left on the Baker Lake-Grandy Lake road 14 miles to Komo Kulshan Guard Station on Baker Lake and follow the Forest Service road 11½ miles to the lake head. Turn left ½ mile on a spur and on the first side-road turn right ½ mile to the start of Upper Baker trail No. 606, elevation 760 feet.

In ¼ mile is the first view — up and up the far side of the river to glaciers of 7660-foot Mt. Blum. At 1 mile the trail climbs a few feet above the river, a beautiful sight, and drops down again to go by large beaver ponds. In 1½ miles, about where the National Park is entered, see Easy Ridge at the valley head, and a little farther on, the sharp outline of 7574-foot Whatcom Peak, northern outpost of the Pickets. In a short 3 miles the way reaches raging Sulphide Creek, dominated by Jagged Ridge and its small glaciers. Partly hidden by trees is the huge expanse of the Sulphide Glacier on the south side of Mt. Shuksan.

If Sulphide Creek is high this is far enough for most hikers; there isn't any bridge. Five designated campsites are here, elevation 900 feet.

Unmaintained trail continues another 2 miles to Crystal Creek and once went 3 more miles to Bald Eagle Creek, 1100 feet. Currently the upper section is lost in brush and the best route beyond Crystal Creek is on gravel bars of the river.

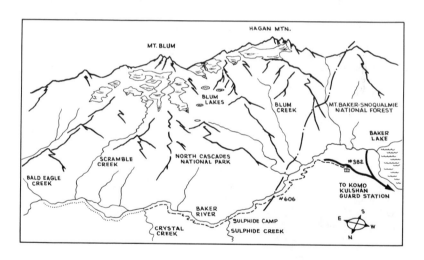

15 Finney Peak

Round trip 3½ miles
Hiking time 2 hours
High point 5079 feet
Elevation gain 900 feet
Best June to November
One day
USGS Oso and Finney Peak

Site of an old lookout cabin — nothing left now except a few rusty nails. But the view remains. The peak stands near Puget Sound lowlands, in wooded ridges completely surrounded by wide valleys; its position on the west edge of the range provides an unusual perspective on the North Cascades. An exceptional opportunity, too, for close observation of logging past, logging in progress, and logging yet to come; the entire "island" is due to be clearcut in the next few years.

Drive State Highway 20 to about 1 mile west of Concrete and turn south, crossing the Skagit River bridge to the South Skagit road. Turn left and continue east 9 miles to Finney-Cumberland road No. 353. Turn right on it 13 miles to road No. 3407. Turn left on it about 6½ miles to a spur road angling-off up right. Park here, elevation about 4200 feet.

Walk the spur to the end and pick a way up the old clearcut to the ridge crest, there intersecting the Finney Peak trail.

Note: In 1979-80 the spur will be extended about 1 more mile (more clearcutting); a new trailhead will then be built.

Tantalizing glimpses through trees of distant peaks, but the best is saved for the top. North across the broad Skagit River valley are Mt. Baker, Mt. Shuksan, and Baker Lake — plus a near view of the green slopes of Sauk Mountain and a far view of the jagged Pickets. More to the east are the Eldorado massif, Dome Peak, and Glacier Peak. Close to the south is a neighbor peak of the "island," Round Mountain and beyond the Stillaguamish River, the great north wall of Whitehorse. Carry a loaded canteen; there is no water on the route.

Under the concept of multiple use, Forest Service personnel had promised that the trail to Finney Peak would be kept open even though logging was taking place. However, a year after the first edition of this book the trail was shortened 1½ miles. Five years later another 1¼ miles were cut. Now, if hikers' protests are ignored, the

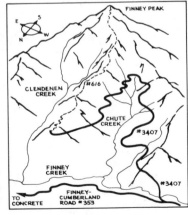

Pink pyrola

Mt. Baker from Finney Peak trail

walk will be reduced to a mere ¾ mile in 1979. New hikers may not have to huff and puff as much, but there will be less solitude. The view from the top will be just as great but there will be a lot less satisfaction getting there. The logging could be done from a temporary cat road and when finished give the trail back to the hiker. Time will tell whether the Forest Service officials are yet oriented to that kind of thinking.

49

Skagit valley from Cow Heaven. Whitehorse Mountain and Three Fingers in distance

SKAGIT RIVER—ROSS LAKE

16 Cow Heaven

Round trip 11 miles
High point 4400 feet
Elevation gain 4000 feet
Hiking time 8 hours
Best July to November
One day
USGS Marblemount and Lake Shannon

Years ago, Skagit ranchers herded cattle way up here to chew the alpine salads. Now only the occasional horse gobbles the flowers, so it's a heaven for hikers, with views from the Skagit Valley, to the Pickets, Eldorado, Whitehorse, and countless peaks between. But the route to heaven lies through purgatory — gaining 4000 feet in 5½ miles. Moreover, from August on a water shortage just about forces the trip to be done in a single grueling day, though in early summer snowmelt permits camping.

Drive State Highway 20 to Marblemount. At the town edge turn left .7 mile to the North Cascades National Park ranger station. Directly opposite the station take an unmarked road passing the information office. Go by a barn and small house and at 1.2 miles from the highway, where the road deadends at Olson Creek, spot the well-signed trailhead, elevation a meager, low-down 400 feet. The final ¼ mile of road often is washed out and must be walked.

The route is signed "Cow Heaven Trail 763, 4 miles." Don't believe it — the best views are at least 5½ miles. Eager to get the job done, the path wastes no time flirting, but starts steep and stays steep. The initial 2 miles are in fine shape, the tread wide and edged by soft moss, cooled by deep shadows of virgin forest. A creek is crossed at 1 mile and recrossed at 1½ miles — the last for-sure water. At about 2¼ miles the tread dips into a shallow ravine and for the next ½ mile often is gullied to naught. Just beyond 3 miles the way passes above an all-summer (usually) stream, absolutely the last chance to fill canteens and hot mouths. Tall trees yield to short ones and at 4 miles to a dense tangle of mountain ash, white rhododendron, and huckleberry. At 4½ miles, about 3600 feet, a brief flat with bits of heather invites camping — but provides no lake, pond, river, creek, dribble, or spring for the purpose, only (through July?) a snowfield.

Maintained trail ends here but a sketchy path, beaten out mainly by hunters, heads over the knoll on the skyline, climbing to the 4400-foot viewpoint. If aggrieved leg muscles and swollen tongue permit, continue up the alpine ridge to steadily broader views.

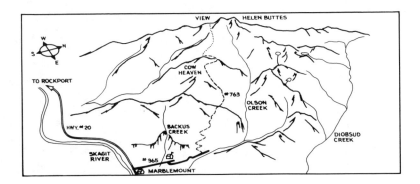

The Pickets from Trappers Peak

17 Thornton Lakes— Trappers Peak

Round trip to lower Thornton Lake 9½ miles
High point 4900 feet
Hiking time 6-8 hours
Elevation gain 2100 feet in, 400 feet out
Best mid-July through October
One day or backpack
USGS Marblemount
Park Service backcountry permit required

Three deep lakes in rock basins gouged by a long-gone glacier. Close by are living glaciers, still gouging. All around are icy peaks on the west edge of the North Cascades National Park. From a summit above the lakes, a splendid view of Triumph and Despair and the Picket Range. Not realizing they are in a National Park, many hikers come here with dogs and guns and without a permit, and sometimes go away with tickets.

Drive State Highway 20 to Marblemount and 11 miles beyond to Thornton Creek road. Turn left 5 steep miles to a parking area, elevation about 2800 feet.

The first 2 miles are on an abandoned logging road. Then begins the trail, which was never really "built" in a formal sense, but just grew; it's very steep in places and mucky in others. Except for the abandoned road across clearcuts, most of the way lies in forest. At a bit more than 1 mile from the abandoned road is an opening and a small creek to jump. The trail then switchbacks up a forested slope to the ridge crest.

Recuperate atop the 4900-foot ridge crest. Look down to the lake basin and out to Mt. Triumph. Then drop 400 feet to the lowest and largest Thornton Lake. Across the outlet stream are campsites designated by posts; no fires allowed.

To reach the middle and upper lakes, traverse slopes west of the lower lake. The middle lake usually has some ice until the end of July; the upper lake, at 5000 feet in a steepwalled cirque, ordinarily is frozen until mid-August.

If views are the goal, don't drop to the lakes. Leave the trail at the 4900-foot crest and follow a faint climbers' track up the ridge to the 5964-foot summit of Trappers Peak. See the fantastic Pickets. And see, too, the little village of Newhalem, far below in the Skagit valley. The route is steep in places and requires use of the hands, but is not really tough. Early in the season there may be dangerous snow patches; go above or below them. Turn around content when the way gets too scary for plain-and-simple hikers.

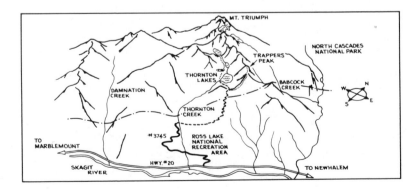

53

18 Sourdough Mountain

Round trip to TV tower 7 miles
Hiking time 7 hours
High point 4800 feet
Elevation gain 3900 feet
Best May through October
One day or backpack
USGS Diablo Dam and Ross Dam

Loop trip 14 miles
Allow 2 days
High point 5985 feet
Elevation gain 4500 feet
Best July through October
Park Service backcountry permit required

No other hike from the Skagit River can match these views of the North Cascades National Park. Look down to Diablo Lake and Ross Lake and out to forests of Thunder Creek. Look south to the ice of Colonial and Snowfield, and southeast to Buckner, and the sprawling Boston Glacier. Look east to the king of the Skagit, Jack Mountain, and north to Canada, and northwest and west to the Pickets.

There are two routes to Sourdough Mountain. One is an extremely steep trail — a strenuous day trip and even with an overnight camp not an easy weekend. The other is a loop which can be done in an arduous 2 days.

Drive State Highway 20 to the Seattle City Light town of Diablo, at the base of Diablo Dam. Park in the main lot; elevation 900 feet.

Direct Trail: Walk back from the parking lot past the powerhouse and tennis court and find the signed trail behind the covered swimming pool. The trail starts steep and stays steep; countless short switchbacks gain 3000 feet in the first 2½ miles before the way "levels off" to an ascent of 2000 feet in the final 4 miles to the summit.

After 1½ miles of zigzags from the road up a forested hillside, an opening gives a sample of panoramas to come. At 3 miles is an unmarked junction. The left fork climbs a steep ½ mile to a TV antenna serving Diablo. For most day hikers this 4800-foot viewpoint is far enough, adding northern vistas to the southern. The way to this turnaround point often is free of snow in May, offering a spectacular springtime hike.

The main trail climbs from the junction, on a gentler grade than before, reaching a designated campsite at Sourdough Creek, 4 miles, elevation 5000 feet. (Water can be

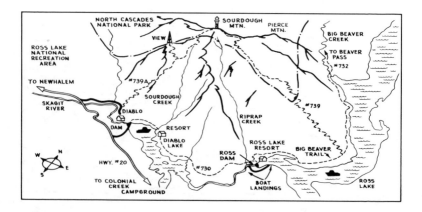

Diablo Lake from Sourdough Mountain

found at several places before this point, but it's thirsty travel at best.) In another 1½ miles the summit and fire lookout cabin are attained, with all the previous views plus additional ones north up Ross Lake and west to the Pickets.

Loop Trail: From the parking lot, hike the unmarked ½-mile trail to the top of Diablo Dam and take the Diablo Lake passenger boat to the base of Ross Dam. Climb the road 400 feet in 1 mile to the top of Ross Dam, cross the dam, and find the Big Beaver Trail. In 3 miles is a junction. Turn left on the Sourdough Mountain trail and climb 3000 feet in 4 miles to a designated campsite in Pierce Mountain saddle, and 1000 feet more in 1 mile to the 5985-foot lookout. Tread is indistinct or absent in the final rocky mile to the summit; watch for cairns. Descend to the parking lot via the "direct trail."

19 Thunder Creek

**Round trip to McAllister Creek
11 miles**
Hiking time 5-7 hours
High point 1800 feet
Elevation gain 600 feet
Best April through November
One day or backpack
**USGS Ross Dam and
Forbidden Peak**

Round trip to Park Creek Pass 36 miles
Allow 3-5 days
High point 6040 feet
Elevation gain 6000 feet
Best late July through October
**USGS Ross Dam, Forbidden
Peak, Mt. Logan, Goode Mtn.**
Park Service backcountry permit required

One of the master streams of the North Cascades, draining meltwater from an empire of glaciers. The first portion of the trail, easy walking, is nearly flat for miles, passing through groves of big firs, cedars, and hemlocks, with views of giant peaks. The route continues to a high pass amid these peaks; for experienced wilderness travelers, the trip from Thunder Creek over Park Creek Pass to the Stehekin River is a classic crossing of the range.

Drive State Highway 20 to Diablo Dam and 4 miles beyond to Colonial Creek Campground, where the trail begins, elevation 1200 feet.

The trail follows Thunder Arm of Diablo Lake about 1 mile, then crosses Thunder Creek on a bridge and in another ½ mile comes to a junction with a trail climbing to Fourth of July Pass and Panther Creek. The Thunder Creek trail continues straight ahead on the sidehill, going up and down a little. To increase its hydroelectric capacity (a minute amount in terms of Seattle's total consumption) Seattle City Light is considering flooding this part of the valley, turning one of the few remaining examples of low-altitude virgin forest into another desolate mud flat and ruining one of the five remaining wilderness valleys in the North Cascades.

At 5½ miles, after bright flowers and charred logs of a late-1960s forest fire, and neck-stretching looks to the summits of Snowfield and Colonial, the way reaches the site of now-gone Middle Cabin and passes a short sidetrail to a designated camp at

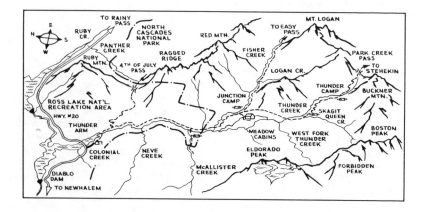

Thunder Creek trail

McAllister Creek, a good turnaround for a day or weekend trip. The trail to here offers one of the best forest hikes in the North Cascades and is open to travel early in the season and late.

At 7 miles the trail crosses Fisher Creek and follows it, climbing 1000 feet above the valley floor, which here is a vast marshland. At 9 miles are Junction Camp, 3000 feet, and a junction with Fisher Creek trail (Hike 24). Off the trail a bit are grand views down to the valley and across to glaciers of Tricouni and Primus Peaks. Shortly thereafter an obscure spur trail descends 1000 feet in 1 mile to the two Meadow Cabins, at the edge of the marsh. The main trail passes stunning viewpoints of the enormous Boston Glacier, Buckner and Boston and Forbidden thrusting above, drops steeply to the valley bottom at 2200 feet, and climbs to Skagit Queen Camp, 13 miles, 3000 feet, near where Skagit Queen Creek joins Thunder Creek. The way climbs steeply, gentles out somewhat in a hanging valley; at 15½ miles, 4300 feet, is the last designated campsite, Thunder Basin Camp. From here the trail ascends steadily up and around the meadow flanks of Mt. Logan to 6040-foot Park Creek Pass, 18 miles, a narrow rock cleft usually full of snow. To continue down to the Stehekin River, see Hike 80.

Lightning Creek bridge and Ross Lake

SKAGIT RIVER—ROSS LAKE

20 East Bank Trail

One-way trip from Panther Creek
to Hozomeen 31 miles
Allow 3-5 days
High point about 3500 feet
Elevation gain about 5000 feet
Best mid-June to November

Round trip from Panther Creek
to Rainbow Camp 15 miles
Elevation gain 900 feet in, 1250 out
Best May to November
USGS Ross Dam, Pumpkin Mtn.,
Skagit Peak, and Hozomeen Mtn.
Park Service backcountry permit required

When full, the reservoir known as Ross Lake simulates nature and is, indeed, a beautiful inland fjord. Unfortunately, draw-downs for power production expose dreary wastelands of mud and stumps. Because of the low elevation, the hike along the lake is especially attractive in spring, when most mountain trails are deep in snow — sorry to say, that's when the lake is at its visual worst. Generally the reservoir is full from late June to October and at a lower level other months, the maximum draw-down of as much as 150 feet usually coming in March or April.

However, even when stumps are showing there still are grand views across the waters to high peaks. To learn the valley in all its moods, to enjoy the panoramas from end to end, hike the East Bank Trail, mostly through forest, a little along the shore, and finally detouring inland to reach Hozomeen Campground. The complete trip can be done in several days or any portion selected for a shorter walk.

If only a portion of the trail is to be hiked, travel to Ross Dam (Hike 22) and arrange with Ross Lake Resort for water-taxi service to the chosen beginning point and a pick-up at trip's end.

To do the entire route, drive State Highway 20 the 8 miles from Colonial Creek Campground to Panther Creek Bridge and find the trailhead in the large parking area, elevation 2000 feet.

The trail drops 200 feet to the crossing of Ruby Creek and a junction beyond. Go left to Ruby Creek Barn, a scant 3 miles from the highway. The way leaves the water's edge to climb 900 feet over Hidden Hand Pass, returning to the lake near Roland Point Camp, 7½ miles.

The next 7½ miles to Lightning Creek are always near and in sight of the lake. Some stretches are blasted in cliffs; when the reservoir is full the tread is only a few feet above the waves, but when the level is down the walking is very airy. There are frequent boat-oriented camps, including the one at Lightning Creek, 15 miles from the highway.

Here the trail forks. The left continues 3 more miles up the lake, ending at the Desolation Peak trailhead (Hike 22).

For Hozomeen, take the right fork, switchback up 1000 feet to a glorious view of the lake, then lose all that elevation descending to a camp at Deer Lick Cabin (locked), 4 miles from the lake. The trail fords Lightning Creek to a junction with the Three Fools Trail (Hike 95). Go left 7 miles to the junction with the abandoned Freezeout trail; go left, fording Lightning Creek to Nightmare Camp in a spooky cedar grove. The way leaves Lightning Creek and climbs to Willow Lake at 2853 feet, 10 miles. Another 5 miles of some ups but mostly downs lead by a sidetrail to Hozomeen Lake and at last to the road-end at Ross Lake, 31 miles from the trailhead at Panther Creek.

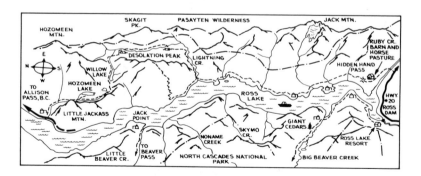

SKAGIT RIVER—ROSS LAKE

21 Crater-Devils Loop

One-way trip 27 miles to Devils Dome
  Landing, complete loop 43 miles
Allow 5-9 days
Elevation gain 7500 feet or so
High point 7000 feet
Best mid-July through October
USGS Crater Mtn., Azurite Peak,
  Shull Mtn., Jack Mtn., Pumpkin Mtn.
Forest Service wilderness
  permit required

Hoist packs and wander meadow ridges east of Ross Lake, encircling the far-below forests of Devils Creek and the cliffs and glaciers of 8928-foot Jack Mountain, "King of the Skagit," looking to peaks and valleys from Canada to Cascade Pass, the Pickets to the Pasayten. The trip is recommended as a loop but for shorter hikes the climaxes can be reached from either end.

Drive State Highway 20 eastward from Colonial Creek Campground, in 8 miles passing the Panther Creek trailhead; at 11 miles is the unmarked parking area along the riverbank at the junction of Canyon and Granite Creeks, which here unite to become Ruby Creek. Elevation, 1900 feet.

The trailhead is directly across both creeks and is not always easy or safe to reach. The Canyon Creek bridge rotted out years ago and though the Forest Service once announced plans to span both creeks, for whatever reason it hasn't. At present (1978) there is a huge log over Granite Creek about ¼ mile upstream, tilted, slippery when wet, often a hairy bit of business. Some years Canyon Creek has a handy log jam but ordinarily must be forded, a dangerous enterprise in high water.

The alternative to this double threat is to return westward on the highway 3 miles to Panther Creek and walk the trail up the north side of Ruby Creek to the Crater Mountain trailhead. Indeed, if the complete loop is contemplated, this is the logical beginning anyhow.

Once the trailhead is reached the work begins — the trail gains 3400 feet in 4 miles. Fortunately the labor is mostly shaded by big trees and there is water at several

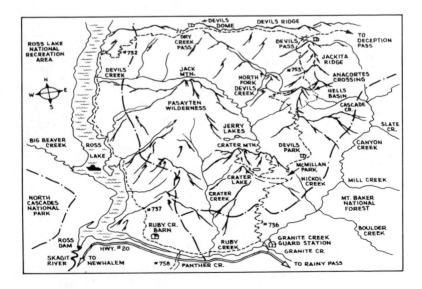

Crater Mountain

well-spaced points and ultimately glimpses of peaks. At 4 miles, 5280 feet, is a junction.

For a compulsory sidetrip, go left ¾ mile to the impressive cirque and shallow waters of 5800-foot Crater Lake. Just before the meadow-and-cliff-surrounded lake, a 2-mile trail climbs eastward to a lookout site on the broad 7054-foot east summit of Crater Mountain. From the lake a 2½-mile trail climbs westward to another lookout site on the 8128-foot main summit of Crater; the final ½ mile is for trained climbers

Crater Lake

only, but the panoramas are glorious long before difficulties begin. When this higher lookout was manned, the final cliff was scaled with the help of wooden ladders and fixed ropes. Maintenance proved too difficult and summit clouds too persistent, causing installation of the lower lookout. Now both cabins are long gone.

From the 4-mile junction the trail descends the gently-sloping table of McMillan Park to Nickol Creek, 4900 feet, then climbs an old burn, loaded with blueberries in season, to Devils Park Shelter, 7 miles, 5600 feet. One can roam for hours in this plateau of meadows, clumps of alpine trees, and bleached snags.

The way now climbs northward along Jackita Ridge into a larch-dotted basin. At 8¾ miles, some 6200 feet, is a junction of sorts. The well-maintained Jackita Ridge trail No. 753, the main route, continues up across the basin. The long-abandoned alternate Hells Basin trail, unsigned and with no tread at first, climbs to the 6700-foot ridge crest, drops more than 1000 feet into stark Hells Basin, regains the elevation to climb over Anacortes Crossing, and loses it again to rejoin the Jackita Ridge trail. The alternate "trail" is some 4 miles from junction to junction, shorter than the main route and infinitely scenic, but is so sketchy, rough, and tricky it is recommended strictly for experienced cross-country travelers.

From the unmarked junction at 8¾ miles, the main route ascends a shoulder, switchbacks 800 feet down a slate scree to a rocky basin, rounds another shoulder and drops 300 feet into another open basin, climbs 500 feet to a third shoulder, drops 1000 feet through meadows and forest to the North Fork Devils Creek, and ascends very steeply upstream ½ mile to the 5500-foot junction with the trail to Anacortes Crossing — which is some 1500 feet and 1 mile from here, and another compulsory sidetrip. Main-route distance to this junction, 13¼ miles.

The trail traverses sweeping gardens of Jackita Ridge, up some and down more, to Devils Pass, 15¼ miles, 5800 feet. The best camping is at Devils Pass Shelter, several hundred feet and ½ mile below the pass in a pretty meadow, reached via the Deception Pass trail and then a sidetrail.

From Devils Pass the way turns west on the Devils Ridge trail, going through open woods near and on the ridge top, then climbing a lush basin to Skyline Camp, 18 miles, 6300 feet — a lovely spot for a campfire and a star-bright sleep, but with no water after the snows are gone.

A flower-and-blueberry traverse and a short ridge-crest ascent lead, at 20 miles, to the 7000-foot site of the demolished Devils Dome Lookout, the highest elevation of the main-route trail.

Now down into a basin of waterfalls and boulders and blossoms and around the flowery slopes of Devils Dome, with time out for a compulsory, easy-walking, off-trail roaming to the 7400-foot summit and wide horizons. At 21½ miles is a ¼-mile sidetrail to 6000-foot Bear Skull Shelter, the first possible camp if the loop is being done in the reverse direction and a long day — 5½ miles and 4500 feet — above Ross Lake.

At last the highlands must be left. The trail goes down the crest a short bit to Dry Creek Pass, descends forests and burn meadows to the only dependable creek (important for refilling canteens when coming up this way!) at 28 miles, enters young trees (hot and grueling to climb in sunny weather) of an old burn, crosses the East Bank Trail and ¼ mile later, at 27 miles, ends at the lakeside camp of Devils Dome Landing.

To return to the start, either hike the East Bank Trail (Hike 20) or, by prearranged pickup, ride back in a boat of Ross Lake Resort (Hike 22).

22 Desolation Peak

Round trip from Desolation Landing
  9 miles
Hiking time 7 hours
Allow 2-3 days
High point 6085 feet
Elevation gain 4400 feet
Best mid-June to September
One day (from the lake) or backpack
USGS Hozomeen Mtn.
Park Service backcountry permit required

A forest fire swept the slopes bare in 1926, giving the peak its name. The lookout cabin on the summit gained fame in literary circles after being manned for a summer by the late Jack Kerouac, "beat generation" novelist and sometime Forest Service employee; some of his best writing describes the day-and-night, sunshine-and-storm panorama from the Methow to Mt. Baker to Canada, and especially the dramatic closeup of Hozomeen Peak, often seen from a distance but rarely from so near. Since Kerouac, the lookout frequently has been manned by poets. The steep trail is a scorcher in sunny weather; carry lots of water.

The start of the Desolation Peak trail can be reached by walking 18 miles on the East Bank Trail (Hike 20) or by riding the water taxi. For the latter, drive State Highway 20 eastward from Colonial Creek Campground 3.8 miles to the parking lot of the Ross Dam trailhead, elevation 1800 feet. But before this, from home or while driving up the Skagit Valley, telephone Ross Lake Resort, 397-4735 (when calling long distance this goes through the Mount Vernon operator) and arrange for boat service. Then, from the trailhead, drop 200 feet to the dam and boat dock opposite the resort, which will ferry you to your destination and return to pick you up at a prearranged time.

The trail starts steep and stays steep, climbing 1000 feet a mile. For such a desolate-appearing hillside there is a surprising amount of shade, the way often tunneling through dense thickets of young trees. This is fortunate, because the sun can be unmerciful on the occasional barren bluffs.

Views come with every rocky knoll. In ½ mile see a small grove of birch trees. In 2 miles refill canteens from a spring — which may, however, dry up in a rainless summer. At 3 miles the trail enters steep, open meadows and at 4 miles is the ridge crest. A high bump remains to be climbed over before the lookout is sighted. The flower fields include some species, sunflowers (balsam root) and erigonum, which properly "belong" on the east slopes of the Cascades.

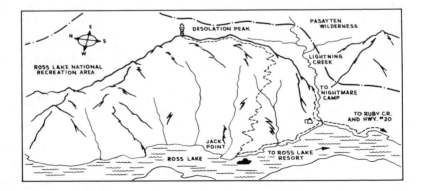

Jack Mountain, left, and Ross Lake from Desolation Peak

The horizons are broad and rich. Only Mt. Baker stands out distinctly among the distant peaks, though those who know them can single out Shuksan, the Pickets, Colonial, Snowfield, Eldorado, and scores of other great mountains. Closer in, the spectacular glacier of 8928-foot Jack Mountain dominates the south. To the north rise the vertical walls of Hozomeen, the south peak so far climbed by but a single route, with many virgin cliffs remaining to tempt the experts. West across Ross Lake are the deep valleys of Noname Creek, Arctic Creek, and Little Beaver Creek. East are the high, meadow-roaming ridges of the Cascade Crest and the Pasayten country.

The fjord-like Ross Lake reservoir, dotted by tiny boats of fishermen, is the feature of the scene. Unfortunately, from fall to spring miles of dreary mudflats are exposed as the reservoir is drawn down; plan the trip for summer, when the full reservoir adorns rather than desecrates the Ross Lake National Recreation Area.

There is a designated campsite in the trees just below the high meadows; water is from snowfields only and usually rare or non-existent by late July. Because of boat schedules, the best plan for a weekend trip is to travel the first day to Lightning Creek Camp, stay there overnight, and do the climb the second day.

SKAGIT RIVER—ROSS LAKE

23 Beaver Loop

Loop trip 27 miles
Allow 3-5 days
High point 3620 feet
Elevaton gain about 3500 feet,
   including ups and downs
Best June through October
USGS Hozomeen Mtn., Mt. Spickard,
   Mt. Challenger, Mt. Prophet,
   and Pumpkin Mtn.
Park Service backcountry permit required

This loop hike from Ross Lake to close views of the Picket Range and back to Ross Lake offers perhaps the supreme days-long forest experience in the North Cascades. The 27-mile trip up the Little Beaver valley and down the Big Beaver passes through groves of enormous cedars, old and huge Douglas firs and hemlocks, glimmery-ghostly silver fir, lush alder, young firs recently established after a fire, and many more species and ages of trees as well. And there are brawling rivers, marshes teeming with wildlife, and awesome looks at Picket glaciers and walls.

However, hikers planning to do the loop should be aware of stringent restrictions on camping. Except at the lakeshore the loop has only five permitted camps, each with a very limited capacity. If each party consisted of just one or two members, the loop could be "full up" with a mere three or four dozen people.

Travel by car and trail to Ross Lake Resort (Hike 22) and arrange for taxi service up the lake and a pickup at trip's end. The loop trip (or day or weekend hikes) can begin at either end; the Little Beaver start is described here.

After a scenic ride up Ross Lake, debark at Little Beaver Landing; a campground here, elevation 1600 feet. The trail starts by switchbacking 800 feet to get above a canyon, then loses most of the hard-won elevation. At 4½ miles is Perry Creek Shelter, an easy ford-or-footlog crossing of several branches of the creek, and a passage along the edge of a lovely marsh. At 9 miles is Redoubt Creek; scout around for a footlog. At 11½ miles, 2450 feet, is a junction.

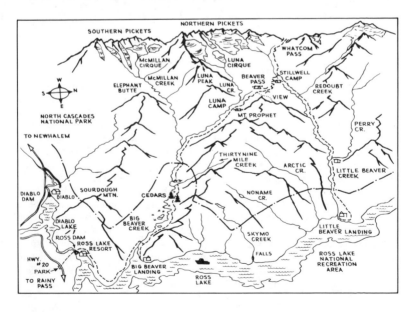

Big Beaver valley. If Seattle City Light is allowed to raise Ross Dam, this part of the valley will be flooded.

The Little Beaver trail goes upstream 6 miles and 2800 feet to Whatcom Pass (Hike 12). Take the Big Beaver trail, which crosses Little Beaver Creek, passes a sidetrail to Stillwell Camp, and climbs a steep mile to Beaver Pass, 3620 feet. The trail goes nearly on the level a mile to designated campsites at Beaver Pass Shelter, the midpoint of the loop, 13½ miles from Little Beaver Landing and 13 miles from Big Beaver Landing.

An hour or three should be allowed here for an easy off-trail sidetrip. Pick a way easterly and upward from the shelter, gaining 500-1000 feet through forest and brush to any of several open slopes that give a staggering look into rough-and-icy Luna Cirque; the higher the climb the better the view.

Passing Lunn Camp on the way, descend steeply from Beaver Pass into the head of Big Beaver Creek; two spots on the trail offer impressive glimpses of Luna Cirque. At 6 miles from Beaver Pass Shelter (7 miles from Big Beaver Landing on Ross Lake) the Big Beaver tumbles down a 200-foot-deep gorge; a good view here of Elephant Butte and up McMillan Creek toward McMillan Cirque. The moderately up-and-down trail crosses recent avalanches which have torn avenues through forest, passes enormous boulders fallen from cliffs above, and goes by a marsh.

At 8 miles from Beaver Pass (5½ from Ross Lake) cross Thirtyninemile Creek; campsite. The way now enters the glorious lower reaches of Big Beaver Creek, a broad valley of marshes and ancient trees, including the largest stand of western red cedar (some an estimated 1000 years old) remaining in the United States. Seattle City Light plans to flood the lower 6 miles of the valley by raising Ross Dam; this absolutely must not be allowed to happen.

Passing one superb marsh after another, one grove of giant cedars after another. At 3 miles from Ross Lake the trail for the first time touches the banks of Big Beaver Creek, milky-green water running over golden pebbles. Finally the trail reaches Big Beaver Landing, from which a ¼-mile trail leads left to Big Beaver Camp.

There are two ways to return to Ross Dam. One is by hiking the 6-mile Ross Lake trail, which branches right from the Big Beaver trail at a junction ¼ mile before the landing. The second is to arrange in advance with Ross Lake Resort to be picked up at Big Beaver Landing.

24 Easy Pass— Fisher Creek

Round trip to Easy Pass
7 miles
Hiking time 7 hours
High point 6500 feet
Elevation gain 2800 feet
Best mid-July through September
One day or backpack
USGS Mt. Arriva and Mt. Logan
Park Service backcountry permit
required

One way from Colonial Creek
Campground to Easy Pass 19 miles
Allow 3-4 days
Elevation gain 5300 feet

Dramatic are the views, but the trail definitely is not easy. Prospectors found this the easiest (maybe the only) pass across Ragged Ridge, and thus the name. However, the tread is rough, at times very steep, in spots muddy, and if that's not enough, progress is blocked almost at the start by a raging creek. Finally, the pass area is very small, extremely fragile, and camping is not allowed.

Drive the North Cascades Highway 21.5 miles east from Colonial Creek Campground or 6.2 miles west from Rainy Pass to an unmarked spur road and parking area, elevation 3700 feet.

In a short ¼ mile the trail blanks out on the bank of swift, cold Granite Creek. If available footlogs are too scary, or not there anymore, the alternatives are to risk the ford — or choose another destination.

From the far bank the trail climbs 2 miles in woods to the edge of a huge avalanche fan, 5200 feet, under the rugged peaks of Ragged Ridge. It now may become elusive, buried in snow or greenery. (Make very sure not to lose the path: cross-country exploration here is agonizing.) The way goes over the avalanche fan and Easy Pass

Western anemone on way to Easy Pass

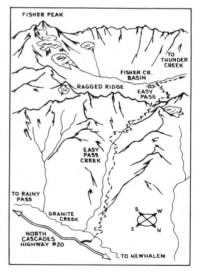

Douglas Glacier and Mt. Logan from Easy Pass. Glacier-carved Fisher Creek valley in foreground

Creek and begins a long, steep ascent along the south side of the valley to the pass. Flower gardens. Small groves of trees. Watercourses. Boulder fields. Up, always up. The route crosses Easy Pass Creek twice more and at about 6100 feet comes within a few feet of a gushing spring, the source of the creek. Tread shoveled from a steep talus slope leads to the 6500-foot pass, a narrow, larch-covered saddle.

For the best views wander meadows up the ridge above the pass and look down 1300 feet into Fisher Basin and out to glaciers and walls of 9080-foot Mt. Logan.

To continue to Diablo Lake, descend 1½ miles to a designated no-fire camp in Fisher Basin, 5200 feet. At 5½ miles is Cosho Camp and, just beyond, an often tricky and dangerous wading or footlog crossing of Fisher Creek. At 10½ miles is Junction Camp, where is met the Thunder Creek trail (Hike 19), which leads to Colonial Creek Campground at 19 miles from the pass.

CASCADE RIVER

25 Lookout Mountain— Monogram Lake

Round trip to Lookout Mountain 10 miles
Hiking time 9 hours
High point 5719 feet
Elevation gain 4500 feet
Best mid-July through October
One day or backpack
USGS Marblemount

Round trip to Monogram Lake 10 miles
Hiking time 9 hours
High point 5400 feet
Elevation gain 4200 feet in,
** 600 feet out**
Best mid-July through October
One day or backpack
Park Service backcountry permit
** required**

Take your pick: a fire lookout with a commanding view of North Cascades peaks and valleys, or a cirque lake, a fine basecamp for roaming, nestled in the side of a heather-covered ridge.

Drive State Highway 20 to Marblemount and continue east 7½ miles on the Cascade River road to the 1200-foot trailhead between Lookout and Monogram Creeks.

The trail climbs steeply in a series of short switchbacks along the spine of the forested ridge between the two creeks, gaining 2400 feet in the 2½ miles to a campsite at the first dependable water, a branch of Lookout Creek at 3600 feet. At 2¾ miles is a junction, elevation 4200 feet.

Lookout Mountain: Go left from the junction, shortly emerging into meadow and switchbacking relentlessly upward. The tread here may be hard to find and difficult to walk. In 1½ miles from the junction, gaining 1500 feet, the 5719-foot summit is attained.

Flowers all around — and views. Look north and west to the Skagit River valley, southeast and below to the Cascade River. Mountains everywhere, dominated by giant Eldorado Peak. About ¼ mile below the summit, in a small flat, is a spring that

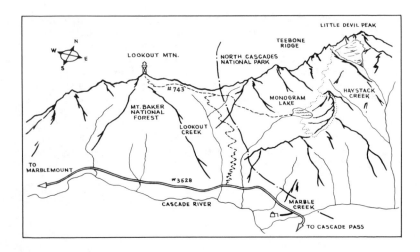

runs most of the summer; magnificent camps here for enjoyment of the scenery in sunset and dawn — but disaster camps in a storm.

Monogram Lake: Traverse right from the junction, the way at spots indistinct, on a steep, lightly-timbered hillside. In about 1 mile from the junction the trail leaves trees for meadow and in another mile crosses a creek, climbs to a 5400-foot crest with broad views, and descends to 4800-foot Monogram Lake, usually snowbound through July. Designated no-fire campsites around the meadow shores.

The lake is a superb base for wanderings. For one, climb open slopes to the southeast and then follow the ridge northerly to a 5607-foot knoll looking down into Marble Creek and across to the splendor of 8868-foot Eldorado — a closer and even better view of the peak than that from Lookout Mountain. Continue on the ridge for more flowers, then drop through gardens to the lake. For a more ambitious tour, ascend meadows on the southern extension of Teebone Ridge and ramble to the 6844-foot south summit of Little Devil Peak, with looks down to small glaciers. Climbers can continue on and on along the rocky-and-snowy ridge, but hikers must stop when the terrain gets too rough for party experience.

Eldorado Peak from Lookout Mountain

26 Hidden Lake Peaks

Round trip to Sibley Creek Pass
  6 miles
Hiking time 5 hours
High point 6100 feet
Elevation gain 2700 feet
Best mid-July through October
One day or backpack
USGS Eldorado Peak and
  Sonny Boy Lakes

Round trip to Hidden Lake
  Lookout 8 miles
Hiking time 8 hours
High point 6890 feet
Elevation gain 3500 feet
Best August through October
One day or backpack
Park Service backcountry permit
  required at Hidden Lake

Flower fields, heather meadows, ice-carved rocks, and snow-fed waterfalls on an alpine ridge jutting into an angle of the Cascade River valley, providing an easy-to-reach viewpoint of the wilderness North Cascades from Eldorado on the north through the Ptarmigan Traverse to Dome Peak on the south.

Drive State Highway 20 to Marblemount and continue east on the Cascade River road 9½ miles (2 miles past the Marble Creek bridge) to Sibley Creek road No. 3503. Turn left 4.2 miles to road-end (the way rough but passable to suitably small and spry cars) in a logging patch, elevation 3400 feet.

Trail No. 745 begins on bulldozer track, entering forest in ¼ mile and switchbacking upward 1 mile. The way then emerges from trees into lush brush and crosses Sibley Creek. (Some years avalanche snow may linger in the creek bottom all summer, in which case look for obvious trail cut through very steep sidehill greenery.) The trail switchbacks up alder clumps and deep grass and flowers to a re-crossing of Sibley Creek at 2½ miles, 5200 feet. Note, here, the abrupt and striking transition from metamorphic to granitic rocks, the first supporting richly-green grassy-type flora, the other dominated by heather. Just past the crossing is a minimal campsite.

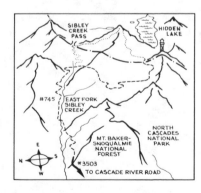

Clark's nutcracker

Snow-covered Hidden Lake and (left to right) Forbidden Peak, Boston Peak, Sahale Peak, Cascade Pass, and Mt. Johannesburg

Sibley Creek Pass: Leave the trail at the second crossing and follow your nose upward, scrambling very steep and slippery, then easy meadows ½ mile to 6100-foot Sibley Creek Pass on the exact boundary of the North Cascades National Park. The view is down to Cascade River forests and up the valley to Cascade Pass and out everywhere to alpine magnificence.

The pass is the recommended destination for short-trippers and hikers lacking experience in snow travel. The views are at least as glorious as those elsewhere on the ridge and the route is free of tricky snowfields much earlier in the summer. From the pass, a moderate rock scramble leads to the 7088-foot highest summit of the Hidden Lake Peaks.

Hidden Lake Lookout: From the second crossing the trail traverses wide-open heather-and-waterfall slopes (several nice good-weather camps), then rounds a corner and climbs. One snow-filled gully may be too treacherous for hikers lacking ice axes. If so, don't attempt to cross, but instead go straight uphill to find a safe detour, or turn back and visit Sibley Creek Pass. The trail may be snowcovered at other points but by proceeding straight ahead the tread can be picked up. At 3½ miles is a tiny basin, a lovely non-storm campsite. The abandoned lookout cabin can now be seen atop cliffs. Continue a short way, usually on a gentle snowfield, to the 6600-foot saddle and look down to Hidden Lake and out to a world of wild peaks.

Though it's only ½ mile and 300 feet from the saddle to the broader views of the 6890-foot lookout, parts of the trail may be lost in extremely-dangerous snow, suited only for trained climbers. Even without snow the final section of trail is airy.

From the saddle an easy walk over loose boulders leads to the 7088-foot peak. Or descend rough talus to the 5733-foot lake, ordinarily snowbound through most of the summer. Designated no-fire campsites on benches near the outlet.

27 Kindy Ridge— Found Lake

Round trip from slide to Kindy Ridge
viewpoint about 10 miles
Hiking time 11 hours
High point 5791 feet
Elevation gain 4700 feet in,
300 feet out
Best July through October
One day
USGS Sonny Boy Lakes and
Snowking Mtn.

Round trip to Found Lake about 14 miles
Hiking time 15 hours
High point 4800 feet
Elevation gain 3600 feet in,
1100 feet out
Best mid-July through October
Backpack
Forest Service wilderness
permit required

A close view of seldom-approached Snowking Mountain, high meadows to explore, and six alpine lakes for camping and prowling. **However, this is an off-trail route, not easy,** recommended only for experienced cross-country travelers.

Drive State Highway 20 to Marblemount and continue east 14½ miles on the Cascade River road. Turn right on Kindy Creek road No. 354 over the Cascade River to road No. 354A. As of 1979, this was blocked by slides at an elevation of 1500 feet. If and when it's reopened, drive on, but until then walk some 4 miles to the road-end in the clearcut of the salvage logging after a 1950s fire. Elevation, 2200 feet.

Follow the road grade across the clearcut; look carefully for a trail angling back to the left toward the corner of the uncut timber. This trail follows, then crosses a creek before starting ever steepening switchbacks up the ridge. Be prepared for a very steep scramble near the ridge top.

Memorize the trail intersection on the ridge in order to find the way when returning. Don't clutter up the forest with plastic markers. Daniel Boone got around without them.

The trail follows the ridge crest to the top of a 5116-foot wooded knoll. From the knoll, drop down on the trail 300 feet to the saddle, leave the trail, and climb 1000 feet to the 5791-foot viewpoint. Trees are few so the way is obvious; generally trend right for the easiest grade.

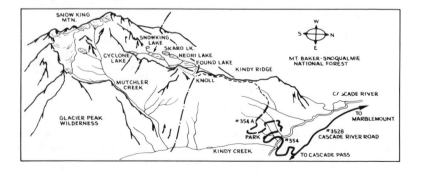

Snowking Mountain and Snowking Lake from Kindy Ridge

To see all the view, move about the broad summit — being careful of fissures, some of them deep, that split the rock. Snowking Mountain and its glaciers are the big reward but there are dividends in all directions — Eldorado, Boston, Formidable, and Resplendent. Four beautiful lakes lie below. Two of them — Neori, the lower, and Skare, the upper — are clear blue water. Snowking Lake, the largest, and a nameless pond above it are a striking turquoise. The other two lakes, Found and Cyclone, are out of sight.

Kindy Ridge is a splendid day hike but waterless and thus campless. For basecamps, since the country is of the kind that cries out for exploration, pick up the Found Creek trail at the 4800-foot saddle between the two knolls and descend 1 mile to 4000-foot Found Lake, gateway to the other lakes and the slopes of Snowking Mountain.

CASCADE RIVER

28 Middle and South Forks Cascade River

Round trip to South Fork trail
   end 6 miles
Hiking time 3 hours
High point 2200 feet
Elevation gain 500 feet
Best June through October
One day or backpack
USGS Sonny Boy Lakes and
   Cascade Pass
Forest Service wilderness permit required

Round trip to Spaulding Mine Trail
   end 7 miles
Hiking time 5 hours
High point 3200 feet
Elevation gain 1500 feet
Best June through October
One day or backpack

Standing on a high summit, looking out to horizons and down to valleys, expands the spirit. Standing in a low valley, looking up from forests to summits, gives humility. To know the North Cascades a person must walk low as well as high. The Middle Fork Cascade valley is one of the "great holes" of the range, an excellent place to learn respect. The companion South Fork is one of the grandest wilderness valleys in the range, giant trees rising high — but not so high as the giant, glaciered peaks all around.

Drive State Highway 20 to Marblemount and continue east 16½ miles on the Cascade River road. Turn right on South Fork Cascade River road No. 3404, extremely rough; some people prefer to walk the 1½ miles to the start of South Cascade River trail No. 769, elevation 1800 feet.

The first ½ mile is up and down along the river bottom to a junction. The South Fork trail goes straight ahead, crosses the Middle Fork, climbs a bit, and enters the Glacier Peak Wilderness. With modest ups and downs the way proceeds through magnificent forest to the end of maintained trail at 3 miles from the road, at about 2200 feet. Good camps along the path. An extremely arduous climbers' route continues another 6 miles to Mertensia Pass, 5000 feet.

Back at the junction, the left fork, the Spaulding Mine Trail, climbs as steeply up along the Middle Fork as its cascades are falling down, sometimes seen and always heard. At the 2400-foot lip of the hanging valley the way gentles out in a superb stand

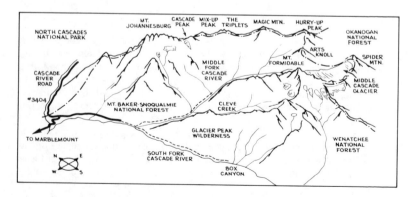

Puffball mushrooms growing in South Cascade River trail

of big trees. At 2 miles is a small creek; leave the trail here and walk several hundred feet down to the riverbank for a look up avalanche-swept Cleve Creek to a glacier on the west ridge of Mt. Formidable. Back on the trail, continue upstream in sometimes forest, sometimes avalanche greenery, to the trail end somewhere around 3 miles, 3200 feet. By following gravel bars of the river upstream, or gravel washes of tributary torrents up the slopes of Johannesburg, enlarged views can be obtained of the Middle Cascade Glacier, cliffs of Formidable, and the summits of Magic, Hurryup, and Spider. Camps abound along the river.

This magnificent valley is in neither the adjoining Glacier Peak Wilderness nor the adjoining North Cascades National Park, a situation that cries out to be rectified.

29 Boston Basin

Round trip to first high moraine 7 miles
Hiking time 8 hours
High point 6200 feet
Elevation gain 3200 feet in,
  600 feet out
Best July through October
One day or backpack
USGS Cascade Pass,
  Forbidden Peak
Park Service backcountry permit required

One of the most spectacular alpine meadows in the Northwest, the flower fields surrounded by rugged peaks and topped by a vigorous glacier. However, the trail is hard to find, in poor condition, and recommended only for experienced hikers. (A new trail probably will be built ultimately, date unknown.)

Drive to the Cascade River road-end (Hike 30), elevation 3600 feet. Climb the new Cascade Pass trail about 17 switchbacks, roughly 1 mile, to a junction with the old, historic, and abandoned Cascade Pass trail at an elevation of about 4400 feet. Go left about ½ mile down the old trail, shortly crossing Soldier Boy Creek, then losing hard-won elevation to about 3800 feet. Watch carefully for a faint path, going right and uphill from the trail.

Follow the boot-built track up and along steep woods, across a large boulder field, over logs and through brush. In about ½ mile of rough, slippery walking look down to

Mt. Johannesburg from Boston Basin

garbage of the Diamond Mine; soon thereafter intersect the old Boston Basin trail. (An alternate and much superior way to get here is to park at the fork 1½ miles below the road-end, walk 1 steep mile up the miners' road to the Diamond Mine, and continue upward on a climbers' path. However, as of 1979 this is still private property and though hikers have a theoretical right to walk through, the miners may question it.)

From the intersection things improve; old but good tread leads through a short bit of woods and then across a ½-mile-wide swath of avalanche greenery, down which roar Midas Creek and Morning Star Creek. Next come switchbacks in deep forest to a broken-down mine cabin; bad-weather campsites here, no scenery.

About ¼ mile from the wrecked cabin the trail emerges from timber and swings around the foot of an open moraine to a raging torrent; boulder-hop across and climb to a viewpoint atop the moraine. Look up to the fearsome cliffs and spires of Forbidden Peak and Mt. Torment, and to the nameless glacier falling from Boston and Sahale Peaks, and across the valley to the mile-high wall of Johannesburg and its finger-like hanging glaciers.

For one exploration of Boston Basin, traverse and climb westward over moraines and creeks to rich-green, marmot-whistling flower fields and beyond to waterfalls pouring down ice-polished buttresses under Mt. Torment.

For another exploration, look for intermittent tread of an old miners' trail that ascends a moraine crest to tunnels and artifacts close under Sharkfin Tower, right next to the glacier falling from Boston Peak.

And a spectacular for the experienced highland rambler only: climb moraines and meadows to Sahale Arm and descend to Cascade Pass; those capable of doing the tour need no further clues.

Enough said; there's a world of private wandering in Boston Basin. However, Park Service regulations severely limit the number of campers — don't expect to stay overnight unless you get permission far in advance.

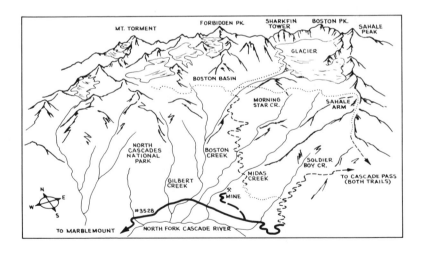

Cascade Pass and Eldorado Peak

CASCADE RIVER

30 Cascade Pass— Sahale Arm

Round trip to Cascade Pass 7 miles
Hiking time 5 hours
High point 5400 feet
Elevation gain 1800 feet
Best mid-July through October
One day
USGS Cascade Pass

Round trip to Sahale Arm 11 miles
Hiking time 10 hours
High point 7600 feet
Elevation gain 4000 feet
Best mid-July through October
One day

An historic pass, crossed by Indians from time immemorial, by explorers and prospectors for a century, and recently become famous as one of the most rewarding easy hikes in the North Cascades. But the beauty of the pass is only the beginning. An idyllic ridge climbs toward the sky amid flowers and creeklets of sparkling water and views that expand with every step. Note: This is now solely a day-use area; Park Service regulations no longer permit camping anywhere between the Cascade River road-end and Cottonwood Camp on the Stehekin River.

Drive State Highway 20 to Marblemount and continue east 25 miles on the Cascade River road to road-end parking lot and trailhead, 3600 feet.

The trail, at an almost-flat 10 percent grade, was designed to accommodate the masses. In some 33 switchbacks the "highway" climbs forest about 2 miles, then makes a long, gently-ascending traverse through parkland and meadows to Cascade Pass, 3½ miles, 5400 feet. Spectacular as the scenery is from road-end, the hiker runs out of superlatives before reaching the pass. The 8200-foot mass of Johannesburg dominates: hardly an hour goes by that a large or small avalanche doesn't break loose from its hanging glacier; several times a summer a huge section of ice roars all the way to the valley floor.

Cascade Pass retains its famous vistas, but during years of overuse the meadows were loved nearly to death. The Park Service is seeking to rehabilitate the flower gardens and thus camping and fires are forbidden.

One sidetrip from the pass, easy and quick, is the wandering way south up the meadow crest of Mixup Arm. Another is to Trapper Lake (Hike 31).

To explore the sky, climb north on a steep and narrow trail through meadows; find the start a few feet over the east side of the pass below a rock outcrop. In 1 mile and 800 feet the trail reaches the ridge crest and a junction. The right fork descends heather 800 feet in 1 mile to 5385-foot Doubtful Lake, a great hike in its own right.

However, Sahale Arm calls. Walk the old prospectors' trail up and along the gentle ridge of flowers, and up some more. Look down to the waterfall-loud cirque of Doubtful Lake and east into the Stehekin River valley. Look west to Forbidden Peak and the huge Inspiration Glacier on Eldorado. Look south to nine small glaciers on the first line of peaks beyond Cascade Pass. Walking higher, see range upon range of ice and spires, finally including the volcano of Glacier Peak.

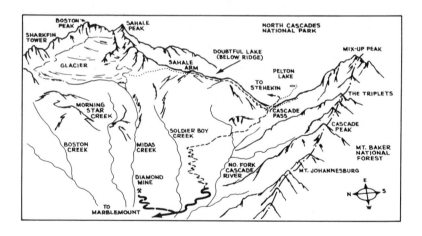

31 Trapper Lake

Round trip from Cascade Pass
  to lake 8 miles
Hiking time 7 hours
High point 5700 feet
Elevation gain 1200 feet in,
  2400 feet out
Best mid-July through September
Backpack
USGS Cascade Pass and Goode Mtn.
Park Service backcountry permit required

An alpine jewel: a deep lake of blue-green water beneath tall cliffs of high and wild peaks, fed by a glacier whose snout nearly reaches the shore.

There are two approaches, one difficult, the other worse. The latter is from the Stehekin River trail, fording the lusty stream about ¼ mile above Cottonwood Camp and climbing 1400 feet of tough brush on a faint, unmarked, straight-up track beaten by hardy and hungry fishermen to a designated campsite at the lake outlet. The former, from Cascade Pass, is described here, being probably the most popular and most scenic.

Descend east from Cascade Pass (Hike 30) about ½ mile. Leave the trail just before it enters forest and drop down a boot-built path to Pelton Creek. Cross the creek and follow the water to tiny Pelton "Lake," 4600 feet. Climb open slopes to the east (on the north side of Pelton Peak), finding a faint and intermittent path up heather to a 5400-foot ridge. From the crest see a very steep green ridge, 300 feet higher, connecting Pelton Peak and a 5973-foot knob. This is the next objective. Where the hillside is the steepest there is an ancient and narrow but quite adequate trail. (Actually, two trails can be seen contouring from the first crest. Take the lower, more obvious one; the upper is difficult.)

The view from the 5700-foot ridge is tremendous, dominated by 7530-foot Trapper Mountain and a far-below corner of 4200-foot Trapper Lake. For most walkers the viewpoint is enough of a trip — especially when they think of the strenuous upward return should they go farther. Round-trip time from Cascade Pass to here is about 4 hours.

However, the sparkling water is enticing. The way to the lake is down a super-steep green wall. Be careful — flowers and heather can be as slippery and treacherous as snow, especially when wet. The route moderates a bit, enters a jungle of mountain

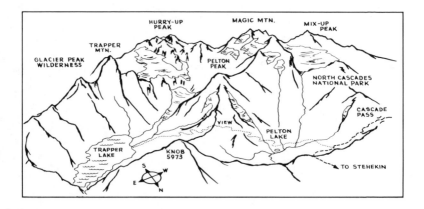

ash, and steepens again. Several paths are beaten through the brush. Be sure to find one — otherwise the thicket is impassable.

Bushes end abruptly at the valley bottom and all is easy to the lakeshore and a designated campsite at the inlet. Not much further exploring is available to a hiker: a steep slope of hard snow effectively prevents circling the lake to the right and dense brush makes the left side unpleasant.

Hurry-Up Peak from trail to Trapper Lake

NORTH FORK STILLAGUAMISH RIVER

32 Round Mountain

Round trip 4 miles
Hiking time 4 hours
High point 5400 feet
Elevation gain 1900 feet
Best early June through October
One day or backpack
USGS Round Mountain and Fortson

Not what you'd call a pristine wilderness experience, not with clearcuts all around and close, but a charming Swiss-type view of the Stillaguamish valley. Look down on farm pastures which from this distance seem as tiny as any in the Alps. Watch ant-sized cars creep along the highway. Trace meanders of the Stillaguamish River beneath the towering, glacier-hung peaks of Whitehorse and Three Fingers. The trail will be kept in a primitive condition with minimum maintenance as a hikers-only route.

Drive Highway 530 east from Arlington to 5 miles west of Darrington. Turn north on Swede Heaven Road (387th N.E.), cross the river, and go downvalley a short bit. Turn right on the first forest road angling upward, road No. 3403, and continue 12½ miles to a junction with spur road No. 3403E. Find (perhaps with difficulty) the unmarked trailhead near the end of this spur, elevation 3500 feet.

The trail contours through woods, passing above several logging patches, and comes to Coney Pass, a saddle in a ridge with an old clearcut on the north slope. The way follows the fire line along the narrow ridge crest to a high point, drops a few feet, goes by some ancient trail signs, and starts up a steep hillside. In some places the path is completely overgrown with huckleberry and young fir trees. If tread is lost, return to the last for-sure spot and try again — once off the route, progress becomes hopeless.

After traversing the high-angle mountainside from east to west, climbing steadily, at about 1 mile the way heads sharply up, gaining a tough 300 feet; open meadows close above offer inspiration. With an abrupt transition from steep forest to rolling heather slopes, the trail enters a large basin and disappears beside a small creek and possible campsite, 4900 feet.

Rosy twisted stalk

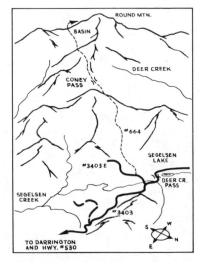

Glacier Peak, in distance, from Round Mountain

Some hikers will be content with a picnic by the stream and a good viewpoint at the basin edge. Others will want to scramble the last ½ mile and 500 feet to the summit. Just about any line of ascent works, but be careful of small cliffs. The best route is up the creek bed, then left to the skyline and on to the approximately 5400-foot summit.

Views, views, views: Darrington and farms of the Stillaguamish, Whitehorse Mountain, Three Fingers Mountain, Glacier Peak, Dome Peak, Mt. Baker, and countless more.

Whitehorse Mountain

NORTH FORK STILLAGUAMISH RIVER

Round trip 7 miles
Hiking time 7 hours
High point 4400 feet
Elevation gain 3600 feet
Best July through September
One day
USGS Silverton

33 Whitehorse Mountain

Built in the early 1900s by Mat Neiderprum as access to his limestone claims, this trail doesn't go anywhere near the top of Whitehorse Mountain. But it sure goes a long way up in the sky, to a little meadow with close views of a glacier and airplane-wing views to the Stillaguamish valley, where cows graze the green pastures and logging trucks rumble through the town of Darrington. Mr. Neiderprum expended minimum effort on such frivolities as switchbacks — his trail is among the steepest in the Northwest, gaining 3600 feet in 3½ miles. Maintenance is now skimpy — some log-crawling and bushwhacking must be expected. And not much water. Many hikers may well prefer to do this in spring, going only to the first good views, turning back when snow grows deep.

Drive State Highway 530 from Arlington 24 miles toward Darrington. Where Swede Heaven Road goes left, turn right on Mine Road 2 miles, on pavement and then gravel, passing several houses, to the trailhead, signed "Neiderprum Trail No. 653." Elevation, 800 feet.

Though cruelly steep, for the first mile the trail is wide and smooth. In the second mile the tread is so-so (still steep). Then it becomes less a trail than a gully gouged by boots proceeding directly in the fall-line, but not always the same line; watch out for branches that deadend. At about 3 miles additional entertainment begins to be provided by logs, mountain ash, huckleberry, salmonberry, and devils club.

At length the way enters a brushy meadow and follows a stream bed, the first and last water. At roughly 3½ miles, 4400 feet, is a tilted meadow. The alert eye can spot flats excavated for Neiderprum's cabin and toolshed. To the left is a rocky knoll, a really delightful place to nurse wounds and enjoy the view down to the pastoral scene of the valley, out to peaks of the North Cascades, and up to the summit icefield of Whitehorse. Hikers stop here. Climbers, properly equipped and trained, traverse steep snow slopes to the left and cross Lone Tree Pass.

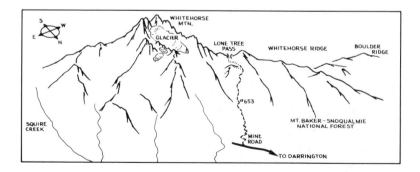

NORTH FORK STILLAGUAMISH RIVER

34 Squire Creek Pass

Round trip to pass 9 miles
Hiking time 6 hours
High point 4000 feet
Elevation gain 2000 feet
Best June through October
One day or backpack
USGS Silverton

Hike through lovely forest to a 4000-foot pass with a dramatic view of the seldom-seen cliffs of Whitehorse, Three Fingers, and Bullon — some of the steepest and grandest walls in the western reaches of the Cascades. Rambles and scrambles from the pass lead to meadowland and more scenery.

From the business section of Darrington drive 5 miles on Squire Creek road No. 3203 to the roadend at a creek. Hike ¼ mile on abandoned road, then follow the trail, which ascends the forested valley to its end and then switchbacks steeply to the pass, 4000 feet, 3½ miles from the road.

A steep trail leads 2 miles from Clear Creek to the pass but is badly overgrown and very difficult to find.

The unlogged, unroaded portions of Squire Creek and Clear Creek are proposed by conservationists for inclusion in a Three Fingers-Whitehorse Wilderness which would also protect the magnificent Boulder River valley. Because of the spectacular peaks, the low-altitude forest and its long hiking season, and the quick access from population centers, this superb — but threatened — wilderness will surely become extremely popular if it is not crisscrossed with multiple-use roads and motorbike trails like the west side of Three Fingers and the valley of Crystal Creek. Only Wilderness classification will do the job.

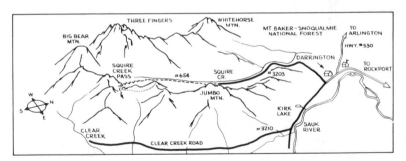

Three Fingers Mountain from Squire Creek Pass

35 Green Mountain

Round trip 8 miles
Hiking time 6 hours
High point 6500 feet
Elevation gain 3000 feet
Best late June through October
One day or backpack
USGS Downey Mtn.

The name of the peak may seem banal, but probably no one has ever looked up its slopes from the Suiattle River valley without exclaiming, "What a **green** mountain!" The trail climbs through these remarkable meadows to a lookout summit with magnificent views to every point of the compass.

Drive north from Darrington or south from Rockport to the Suiattle River road and continue 19 miles to the Green Mountain road. Turn left 5 miles to road-end in a logging patch, elevation about 3500 feet. Find the trail sign above the road several hundred yards before the road-end.

The trail climbs a rather steep mile in mossy forest to a grubby hunters' camp with a year-around spring, then enters the vast meadow system admired from below. First are fields of bracken fern and other subalpine plants, then, on higher switchbacks, a feast (in season) of blueberries. Views begin — down to Suiattle forests and out to Whitechuck Mountain and Glacier Peak. More meadows, and views of Mt. Pugh and Sloan Peak, seen beyond the intervening ridge of Lime Mountain.

At 2 miles, 5300 feet, the trail rounds a shoulder and in ½ mile traverses and drops 100 feet to a pair of shallow ponds amid gardens. Pleasant camps here, and all-summer water. Wood is scarce so carry a stove.

A short way above the pond basin the trail enters a larger, wide-open basin (great camps, but no water in late summer). The lookout cabin, manned in high-danger periods, can now be seen directly above, and also Glacier Peak. Climb in flowers to the ridge and along the crest to the 6500-foot summit, 4 miles. A few yards below the summit ridge on the east is a small rocky-and-snowy basin; delightful and scenic good-weather camps with water but no wood.

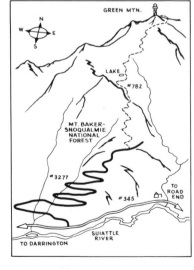

Columbine

Suiattle valley and Glacier Peak. Cabin was built during World War II when the lookout was manned the year-around for airplane watching. Since the picture was taken, the building was accidently burned down.

Look north along the ridge to the nearby cliffs and glaciers of 7311-foot Buckindy (experienced highland travelers can wander there). Look up Downey Creek to peaks of the Ptarmigan Traverse from Dome north to Formidable. Look up Milk Creek to the Ptarmigan Glacier on Glacier Peak. Look to other peaks in all directions, too many to name.

**Round trip to Bachelor Meadows
  23½ miles
Allow 2-3 days
High point 6000 feet
Elevation gain 4600 feet
Best mid-July through September
USGS Downey Mtn. and Dome Peak
Forest Service wilderness permit required**

36 Bachelor Meadows

A pleasant hike through virgin forest along Downey Creek to 6 Mile Camp. For those with the energy and ambition, and experience in traveling rough wilderness, it's a tough climb some 5½ miles farther to meadows under 8264-foot Spire Point, with views of deep and blue Cub and Itswoot Lakes, Dome Peak, Glacier Peak, and other icy mountains.

Drive the Suiattle River road (Hike 35) 19½ miles to Downey Creek Campground and the trailhead, elevation 1450 feet.

The first mile climbs steadily, then the way levels into easy ups and downs amid tall firs, hemlocks, and cedars, crossing small streams, sometimes coming close to the river. At 6¼ miles, 2400 feet, the trail crosses Bachelor Creek. If an overnight stop is wanted here, cross Downey on a log jam to 6 Mile Camp.

For Bachelor Meadows, proceed onward, and now upward, initially on well-graded trail and then, at 7½ miles, on a route trampled out by boots, climbing over roots and plunging through gooey bogs. The worst windfalls have been cut but there are plenty of problems. In about 2 miles cross Bachelor Creek. The track becomes hard to follow through a boulder-strewn meadow deep in ferns and flowers. Views appear of Spire Point at the head of the valley. At about 3½ miles are a succession of good campsites; choose one under trees, away from fragile heather.

Now the trail climbs a short but steep mile and at 5400 feet abruptly leaves forest and enters an improbable little valley at a right angle to the main valley and just under Spire Point. Water and flat campsites here in a scenic meadow.

For broader views continue up the trail ½ mile through heather, following the small valley south to a 6000-foot pass. The trail drops ½ mile to 5338-foot Cub Lake and on down to 5015-foot Itswoot Lake.

Rather than descend, walk ¼ mile westward from the pass along a narrow ridge to a superb view of Dome Peak and the glistening Dome Glacier. A stone's throw below are the two lakes. South is Glacier Peak. By camping either on the ridge or at Itswoot Lake, one can explore meadow slopes eastward to a 6200-foot ridge with an even more complete view of Dome. Take pity on Cub Lake and don't camp there — its shores have been mangled by too much use by fishermen and climbers.

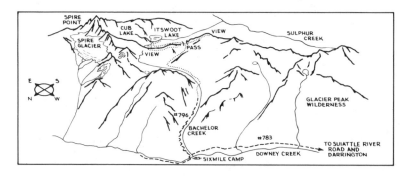

Cub Lake and Dome Peak

37 Milk Creek— Dolly Creek— Vista Creek Loop

Loop trip 33 miles
Allow 3-5 days
High point 6000 feet
Elevation gain 4400 feet
Best mid-July to mid-October
USGS Glacier Peak
Forest Service wilderness permit required

A section of the Pacific Crest Trail climbing high on the north flanks of Glacier Peak. Massive flower fields and close-up views of the mountain. Plan to spend an extra day, at least, roaming alpine ridges.

Drive the Suiattle River road (Hike 35) 23 miles to the end, elevation 1600 feet.

Walk the former road 1 mile to a Y at the former road-end; take the right fork. The Milk Creek trail drops a few steps, crosses the river on a bridge, and enters the Glacier Peak Wilderness. The way begins in glorious forest; at a mile or so is an awesome grove of ancient and huge cedars, hemlocks, and Douglas firs. Going somewhat level, sometimes uphill, passing cold streams, the path rounds a ridge and enters the valley of Milk Creek.

The trail enters a broad field of greenery at 3 miles, 2400 feet, with a stunning look up to the ice, a satisfying reward for a short trip. A pleasant campsite in the forest by the river ½ mile before the field.

From here the trail ascends gently, then steadily, passing campsites in the woods, and meets the Pacific Crest Trail at 7½ miles, 3900 feet. A short bit before the junction, under an overhanging rock, is Whistle Pig Camp — a nice spot on a rainy night, though with room for only several sleepers. Other small camps have been squirmed into the brush at and near the junction, purely from desperation.

Turn left at the junction and plod upward on a series of 36 switchbacks (growing views of Glacier Peak and toward Mica Lake and Fire Mountain) to the crest of Milk Creek Ridge at 11½ miles, 6000 feet. The climbers' route to the summit of Glacier leaves the trail here; hikers can explore higher in flowers for hours before difficulties turn them back.

The trail traverses the flowery basin of the East Fork Milk Creek headwaters, crosses a ridge into the source of Dolly Creek, and at 14 miles comes to Vista Ridge and a camp, 5500 feet.

Flower gardens spread in every direction and views are grand north to Miners Ridge, Plummer Mountain, Dome Peak, and beyond. Glacier Peak is too close and

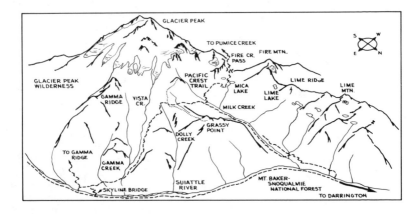

Glacier Peak and Milk Creek valley

foreshortened to be seen at its best. The trip schedule should include one or more walking-around days from the Vista Ridge camp. Wander up the crest to a 7000-foot knoll. Even better, hike north in meadows to 6500-foot Grassy Point, offering impressive views up and down the green valley of the Suiattle River, but especially a mind-blasting spectacle of the white-glaciered volcano.

From the ridge the trail descends a long series of switchbacks into forest. At 20 miles, 3000 feet, is a campsite by the crossing of Vista Creek. At 21¼ miles is a junction with the Suiattle River trail and at 22 miles, 2700 feet, is a camp beside the Suiattle River. Here the trail crosses Skyline Bridge and proceeds 11 miles down the valley, in 33 miles reaching the road-end and completing the loop.

SUIATTLE RIVER

38 Image Lake

Round trip to Image Lake 32 miles
Allow 2-4 days
High point 6050 feet
Elevation gain 4400 feet
Best mid-July through October
USGS Glacier Peak and Holden
Forest Service wilderness permit required

A 2-mile-high volcano, the image of its glaciers reflected in an alpine tarn. Meadow ridges for dream-walking. The long sweep of Suiattle River forests. Casting ballots with their feet, hikers have voted this a supreme climax of the alpine world of the North Cascades and the nation. Incredibly, Kennecott Copper Corporation may take advantage of a serious flaw in the Wilderness Act and dig a monstrous open-pit mine here, in the very heart of the Glacier Peak Wilderness.

Drive the Suiattle River road (Hike 35) 23 miles to the end, elevation 1600 feet.

Walk the former road 1 mile to the former road-end and a Y; go left on the Suiattle River trail, largely level, partly in ancient trees, partly in young trees, sometimes with looks to the river, crossing small tributaries, to Canyon Creek Shelter, 6½ miles, 2300 feet. At about 9½ miles, 2800 feet, is a creek with small campsites on both sides; be sure to fill canteens. Just beyond is a trail junction; go left on Miners Ridge trail No. 785. The forest switchbacks are relentless and dry, but with occasional glimpses, then spectacular views, out to the valley and the volcano. At 12½ miles are two welcome streams at the edge of meadow country, and at 13 miles, 4800 feet, is a junction; campsites here.

Miners Cabin trail No. 795, leading to Suiattle Pass, goes straight ahead from the junction; take the left fork to Image Lake. Switchback up and up, into blueberry and flower meadows with expanding views, to a junction atop Miners Ridge, about 15 miles, 6150 feet. A ¼-mile trail leads left to Miners Ridge Lookout, 6210 feet. The main trail goes right ¾ mile, traversing, then dropping a bit, to 6050-foot Image Lake.

Don't come to Image Lake expecting privacy; for that, one must seek out other nooks and corners of the area. Indeed, over-use of the lake threatens its integrity and rules out any chance of lonesomeness. To protect especially fragile qualities, the Forest Service has prohibited camping in the basin and bans swimming in the lake — which is the water supply. Horses should be prohibited within ½ mile of the lake, but they are still allowed to contaminate the water. Below the lake ¼ mile is a hikers' camp. A mile away at Lady Camp are accommodations for horses and mice.

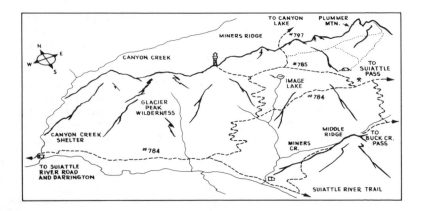

Glacier Peak and Image Lake, a small jewel in an emerald setting

Exploring the basin, climbing the 6758-foot knoll above, visiting the fire lookout, walking the Canyon Lake trail into the headwaters of Canyon Creek — thus one may fill memorable days. By no means omit the finest wandering of all, along the wide crest of Miners Ridge, through flower gardens, looking north to Dome Peak and south across Suiattle forests to Glacier Peak. Experienced scramblers can ascend steep heather to the 7870-foot summit of Plummer Mountain and wide horizons of wild peaks.

Also, hike the grassy trail east 1 mile to lovely Lady Camp Basin. Here is the west edge of the ½-mile-wide open pit mine Kennecott wants to dig; this blasphemy has been prevented so far by violent objections from citizen-hikers but can only be stopped for good and all by your letters to congressmen and senators urging them to exercise the right of eminent domain and purchase the patented mining claims. From Lady Camp the trail drops some 500 feet in ½ mile to a junction with the Suiattle Pass trail, which can be followed 1¾ miles back to the Image Lake trail junction.

39 Suiattle River to Lake Chelan

One-way trip 29½ miles
Allow 5-7 days
High point 6438 feet
Elevation gain about 5000 feet
Best mid-July through September
USGS Glacier Peak, Holden, Lucerne
Forest Service wilderness permit required

A rich, extended sampler of the Glacier Peak Wilderness, beginning in green-mossy westside trees, rising to flowers of Miners Ridge and views of Glacier Peak, crossing Suiattle and Cloudy Passes, descending parklands of Lyman Lake to rain-shadow forests of Railroad Creek and Lake Chelan. The traverse can be done in either direction; the west-to-east route is described here.

Drive to the Suiattle River road-end, 1600 feet, and hike 13 miles on the Suiattle River trail, to the 4800-foot junction with the Image Lake trail (see Hike 38).

Continue straight ahead on Miners Cabin Trail, climbing 1¾ miles to a second junction with the Image Lake trail, 5500 feet. (The lake can — and should, if time allows — be included in the trip by taking the lake trail, which is 4½ miles long from end to end, thus adding some 3 extra miles and about 600 feet of extra elevation gained and lost.) In trees just past the junction is a miners' shack belonging to Kennecott Copper and a spring, a bad-weather campsite. The way now contours, crossing one huge and many small avalanche paths, entering open slopes with grand

Lyman Lake

views to Fortress, Chiwawa, and other peaks at the head of Miners Creek, passing more miners' junk in a small flat, and at 17 miles reaches Suiattle Pass, 5983 feet. A bit before the pass and below the trail is a pleasant camp on a meadow bench.

The trail drops some 300 feet into headwaters of South Fork Agnes Creek (the drop can be avoided by taking a rough hiker-only alternate path) and climbs to the most spectacular views and gardens of the trip at 6438-foot Cloudy Pass, 19 miles. (From here, easy meadows demand a sidetrip to 7915-foot Cloudy Peak and along the ridge to 8068-foot North Star Mountain.)

Descend magnificent flowers, then subalpine forest, to 5587-foot Lyman Lake, 21 miles. Beautiful as is the lake, its shores fringed by greenery, the campground, on a short spur trail west, is marshy; camps above, under Cloudy Peak, have better views and fewer bugs. (From the lake, a steep path, rather obscure at the start, climbs 500 feet to Upper Lyman Lake, alpine camps, and a mandatory sidetrip to the toe of the Lyman Glacier. See Hike 70.)

The trail drops past the outlet creek of Lyman Lake, where frothy water pours down long, clean granite slabs, and switchbacks into forests of Railroad Creek; views of Crown Point Falls and Hart Lake. After boggy walking and many bridges, at 24½ miles, 3989 feet, is Rebel Camp and at 25½ miles is Hart Lake. Good camping at both.

The last portion of the route is over blocks of rock under a tall cliff, past tumbling waterfalls, occasional views of high peaks, to beaver bottom and green jungle, and finally a jeep track and baseball field to the abandoned mining town of Holden 29½ miles, 3200 feet.

Holden, now owned by the Lutheran Church and used for various religious activities, is 12 miles by road from Lucerne, on the shores of Lake Chelan. Though not particularly pleasant, the road can be walked (a parallel trail is planned for future construction). In June-July-August a station wagon (capacity 6 passengers) from Lucerne Resort makes one trip daily from Holden to the lake, leaving just before noon, in time to catch the **Lady of the Lake,** which provides transit downlake from Lucerne to Chelan, from where bus connections can be made home (Hike 76). (If the Lucerne taxi is full up, the extra hikers must either walk the road or wait until next day.)

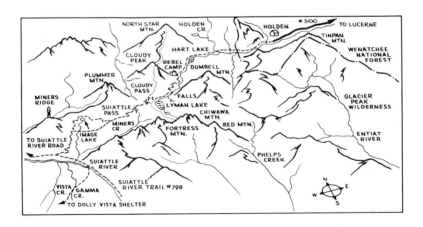

SUIATTLE RIVER

40 Around Glacier Peak

One-way trip 51 miles
Allow 5 days minimum
High point 6409 feet
  (Little Giant Pass)
Elevation gain 9800 feet
  To: Buck Creek Pass 4100 feet
    Little Giant Pass 3800 feet
    Boulder Pass 1550 feet
Best late July through September
USGS Glacier Peak and Holden
Forest Service wilderness permit required

Mount Rainier National Park has the renowned Wonderland Trail; the Glacier Peak Wilderness offers an equally-classic around-the-mountain hike. The 96-mile circuit with an estimated 15,500 feet of climbing includes virgin forests, glacial streams, alpine meadows, and ever-changing views of the "last wild volcano."

The complete trip requires a minimum 10 days, and this makes no allowance for explorations and bad-weather layovers. However, the loop breaks logically into two sections which can be taken separately. Perhaps the ideal schedule is to do the entire circuit on a single 2-week jaunt, keeping packs to a reasonable weight by arranging to be met midway with additional supplies.

North and East Section

Begin at Suiattle River road-end. Hike 9 miles along the Suiattle River on trail No. 784 to a junction. Go right on trail No. 785 1¼ miles to Middle Ridge trail No. 2000 and climb 9½ miles to Buck Creek Pass.

(Two partial alternate routes can be taken; each adds a day and many extra rewards. One is the Milk Creek-Dolly-Vista trail (Hike 37), which starts at Suiattle

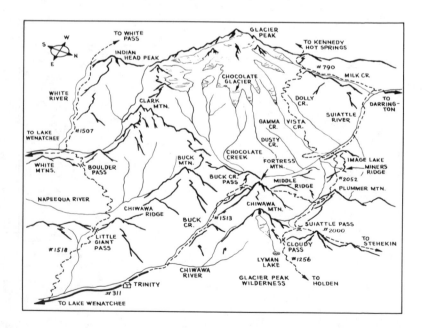

River road-end and rejoins the main route near the 10-mile marker; this alternate adds 12 miles and 3200 feet of elevation gain to the total. The other is the Image Lake-Miners Ridge trail (Hike 38), which leaves the main route at 9½ miles and rejoins it 6 miles below Buck Creek Pass; this alternate adds 8 miles and 1700 feet of elevation gain. The two alternates can be combined on a single trip; first do the Milk Creek-Dolly-Vista trail, then backtrack 1 mile to begin the Image Lake-Miners Ridge trail.)

Descend 9½ miles from Buck Creek Pass to Trinity (Hike 71) and walk 5½ miles down the Chiwawa River road to Little Giant trail No. 1518. Climb 4¾ miles to Little Giant Pass (Hike 69) and descend 1¾ miles into the Napeequa River valley and a junction with Boulder Pass trail No. 1562. Climb 6½ miles over the pass and down to the White River trail (Hike 67). If the trip is to be broken at this point, hike 3½ miles downriver to the White River road.

A possible itinerary (excluding the alternates) would be: Day One, 10 miles and a 1150-foot climb to Miners Creek Shelter; Day Two, 9½ miles and a 3200-foot climb to Buck Creek Pass; Day Three, descend 3350 feet in 15 miles to Maple Creek; Day Four, climb 3900 feet, descent 2300 feet, in the 6½ miles to Napeequa River; Day Five, 10 miles to White River road-end, a climb of 1550 feet and a descent of 3350 feet. However, frequent campsites along the route allow shorter days or different days.

Ptarmigan in summer plumage

Around Glacier Peak (Cont'd.)

One-way trip 43 miles
Allow 5 days minimum
High point 6450 feet (Red Pass)
Elevation gain 5700 feet
  To: White Pass 3700 feet
    Red Pass 700 feet
    Fire Creek Pass 2000 feet
Best late July through September
USGS Glacier Peak and Holden
Forest Service wilderness permit required

South and West Section

Begin at White River road-end. Hike 14¼ miles on White River trail No. 1507 to an intersection with the Pacific Crest Trail. Continue north on the crest 2 miles to White Pass (Hike 66).

From White Pass contour and climb to Red Pass in 2 miles, then descend the White Chuck River (Hike 43) 7 miles to a junction. For the main route, climb right on the Pacific Crest Trail, crossing headwaters of Kennedy Creek, Glacier Creek, Pumice Creek, and Fire Creek and reaching Fire Creek Pass in 8 miles (Hike 42).

(For an inviting alternate, go 1½ miles from the junction downriver to Kennedy Hot Springs, enjoy a hot bath, then continue a short ½ mile to the Kennedy Ridge trail (Hike 42) and climb to rejoin the main route; this alternate adds 1¼ miles and 800 feet of elevation gain to the total.)

From Fire Creek Pass, the snowiest part of the entire circuit, descend a valley of moraines and ponds, past the magnificent cold cirque of Mica Lake, reaching the Dolly-Vista trail junction in 4 miles. Continue 7½ miles down Milk Creek trail to the Suiattle River road-end (Hike 38).

A possible itinerary would be: Day One, 9 miles and climb 800 feet to Lightning Creek; Day Two, 9¼ miles, a gain of 2100 feet and a loss of 1000 feet, to Glacier Peak Shelter (the shelter is gone but the campsite remains); Day Three, drop 1700 feet and climb 2250 on the 9½ miles to Pumice Creek; Day Four, 500 feet up and 900 feet down on 4¼ miles to Mica Lake; Day Five, 11 miles and 3800 feet down to Suiattle River road. Again, frequent campsites allow shorter or different days.

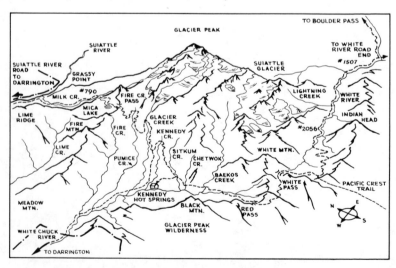

Indian Head Peak from White Pass

WHITE CHUCK RIVER

41 Meadow Mountain

Round trip to 5800-foot viewpoint
  16½ miles
Hiking time 9 hours
High point 5800 feet
Elevation gain 3300 feet
Best July through October
Backpack
USGS Pugh Mtn. and Glacier Peak

One-way trip from Meadow Mountain
  road-end to White Chuck River
  road-end 20 miles
Allow 2-4 days
High point 5800 feet
Elevation gain 4400 feet, including ups
  and downs
Best July through October
Forest Service wilderness permit required
  beyond 5800-foot viewpoint

Meadows laced with alpine trees, views to White Chuck forests and Glacier Peak ice, and a long parkland ridge for roaming, with sidetrips to cirque lakes.

Drive from Darrington on the Mountain Loop Highway 10½ miles to the White Chuck River road. Turn left 5½ miles to Straight Creek road No. 327, shortly beyond the crossing of the White Chuck River. Turn left 2 miles, climbing and switchbacking, following "Meadow Mountain" signs at all junctions, to a gate and parking area 2500 feet.

Walk 5 miles on a road, now driven only by loggers, to the end, 3400 feet, and views of Glacier Peak, White Chuck Mountain, and Mt. Pugh.

The trail climbs a steep 1¼ miles (but in deep, cool forest) to the first meadow. Cross a bubbling brook in an open basin and then choose either of two destinations, both offering splendid views down to the green valley and out to the peaks. For the easiest, follow a faint way trail 1 mile westward to a high knoll, about 5600 feet. For the best, and with the most flowers, hike the main trail 2 miles eastward, climbing to a 5800-foot spur ridge from Meadow Mountain.

For one of the great backpacking ridge walks in the Glacier Peak Wilderness, take the up-and-down trail traversing the ridge east toward Fire Mountain. Earlier camps are possible, but the first site with guaranteed all-summer water is Hunter's Camp at 9 miles, ½ mile beyond the 5800-foot viewpoint, in a bouldery basin to which the trail drops to avoid cliffs of Meadow Mountain.

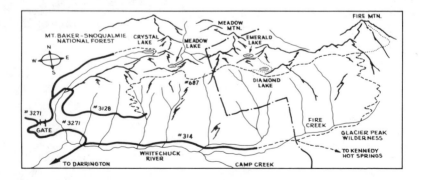

Flower fields on Meadow Mountain. Glacier Peak in distance

Going up, then down, then up again, at 10¼ miles the trail touches the 5850-foot ridge crest. From here, descend 1 mile northwest on a much-used but easily-lost path to 5300-foot Diamond Lake. From the east side of the lake climb a wide gully up the low ridge and descend extremely-steep slopes (no trail) to Emerald Lake, 5200 feet. Good camps at both; stay 100 feet from the shores.

The main trail continues along the ridge to a low saddle at about 11 miles. The path proceeds east through patches of trees, grassy swales, sidehill flowers, and views.

At 12½ miles is a magnificent camp in a cliff-walled basin and at 14 miles, beneath Fire Mountain, are charming garden camps near the site of long-gone Fire Chief Shelter. From this area experienced off-trail travelers can find an easy but not obvious route to the summit of 6591-foot Fire Mountain; if the terrain gets steep and scary, you're on the wrong route — turn back.

The trail descends an old burn to Fire Creek forests, joining the White Chuck River trail at 18½ miles, 1½ miles from the White Chuck River road. By use of two cars, one parked at each road-end, hikers can enjoy a 20-mile one-way trip along the full length of the ridge trail; a 3-day schedule allows for sidetrips, but more days could easily be spent exploring.

42 Kennedy Ridge and Hot Springs

Round trip to Kennedy Hot Springs
11 miles
Hiking time 5 hours
High point 3300 feet
Elevation gain 1000 feet
Best May through November
One day or backpack
USGS Glacier Peak

Round trip to Kennedy Ridge moraine
18 miles
Hiking time 8-10 hours
High point 6200 feet
Elevation gain 4000 feet
Best July through October
One day or backpack
Forest Service wilderness permit required

Two hikes which can be done separately or combined. A short-and-low trip leads through tall old trees, beside a roaring river, to a tingling bath in volcano-warmed waters — the most mob-jammed spot in the Glacier Peak Wilderness. A long-and-high trip climbs to alpine flowers with a close look at icefalls tumbling from Glacier Peak.

Drive from Darrington on the Mountain Loop Highway 10½ miles to the White Chuck River road. Turn left 11 miles to the road-end parking area and campground, elevation 2300 feet.

The wide, gentle White Chuck River trail has become — deservedly — the most popular valley walk in the Glacier Peak area. The way goes through virgin forest always near and sometimes beside the ice-fed river, beneath striking cliffs of volcanic tuff, crossing the frothing tributaries of Fire, Pumice, and Glacier Creeks. At 5 miles, 3300 feet, is a junction with the Kennedy Ridge trail.

Kennedy Hot Springs: In 1976 a monster flood obliterated the White Chuck River trail above Kennedy Creek. The new route goes up Kennedy Ridge trail to cross the creek. Upon intersecting the old trail, descend right on it ¼ mile to the guard station, hot springs, and camp, 3300 feet. Cross the river on a bridge, turn left past the trail to Lake Byrne (Hike 45), and in a few yards come to steaming, mineralized waters seeping from the earth. A tub-like pool about 5 feet square and 5 feet deep has been dug, just big enough for three or four people. The water is not as hot as the Japanese like it, but the

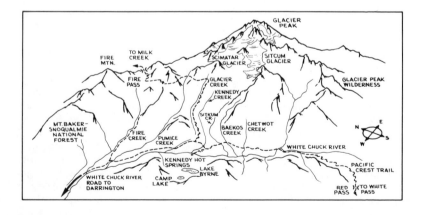

Glacier Peak and Scimitar Glacier on right, from Kennedy Ridge trail

idea is the same — submerging to your chin and letting the bubbling heat relax your muscles. The water is usually a yellowish-reddish murk, but never mind; to clean away the iron oxide, one can always plunge into the icy river, several yards away. (This is the way the Finns like it — hot, then cold.)

Summer is not the best time for a bath; the trail remains superb in all seasons, but 2,500 people signed the Kennedy register in 1977, which means the waiting line gets long in good weather. For leisurely and private soaking, make an overnight trip in April or May, when weather is poor and the high country (and perhaps the trail too) is deep in snow.

Kennedy Ridge: From the junction at 5 miles, just before crossing Kennedy Creek, climb left on the Kennedy Ridge trail. (Fill canteens before starting up.) The steep forest way, with occasional glimpses of ice, joins the Pacific Crest Trail at 2 miles, 4150 feet. The Crest Trail switchbacks through cliffs of red and gray andesite, then along heather parklands on a moraine crest, swinging left to reach the welcome wet splash (and campsite) of Glacier Creek at 5650 feet, 4 miles from the White Chuck River trail.

Leave the trail and climb open subalpine forests on the old moraine, then in ½ mile step suddenly out onto raw boulders of a much newer moraine. See the Kennedy and Scimitar Glaciers tumbling from the summit of the volcano. See glacial debris and cataracts below the ice. See valley forests, peaks beyond.

It's a shame to turn back at the edge of so much good highland roaming. Just 1 mile from Glacier Creek, over Glacier Ridge, are the splendid meadows and camps of Pumice Creek, and in 3½ miles more is Fire Creek Pass. With a schedule of 3 or more days, these and other delights can be enjoyed.

WHITE CHUCK RIVER

43 White Chuck Glacier

**Round trip to White Chuck Glacier
28 miles
Allow 4 days minimum
High point about 6500 feet
Elevation gain 4200 feet
Best late July through September
USGS Glacier Peak
Forest Service wilderness permit required**

Begin beside a loud river in deep forest. Walk miles through big trees, climb to little trees and wide meadows. Roam flowers and waterfalls and moraines to a broad glacier. Wander gardens and ridges. In the opinion of some experts, this is the supreme low-to-high tour of the Glacier Peak Wilderness.

Drive to the White Chuck River road-end, 2300 feet, and hike 5½ miles to 3300-foot Kennedy Hot Springs (Hike 42).

Ascend steeply then gently to join the Pacific Crest Trail at Sitkum Creek, 3850 feet, 7 miles from the road; camping space is available here when Kennedy is full-up, as it often is. The Crest Trail continues along the valley, passing the avalanche track and meadow-marsh of Chetwot Creek, fording Baekos Creek, and at 9½ miles, 4000 feet, crossing a high bridge over the rocky chasm and thundering falls of the White Chuck River.

Now the trail climbs a valley step. Trees are smaller and so is the river, assembling itself from snow-fed tributaries. A little meadow gives promise of what lies above. More subalpine forest. Then the way enters the tremendous open basin of Glacier Peak Meadows. At 12 miles, 5400 feet, is the site of the long-gone Glacier Peak Shelter, and magnificent campsites everywhere around.

As a base for easy hiker-type explorations, this highland valley of flowers and creeks and snowfields is unsurpassed in the North Cascades.

First off, if your hike is mid-August or later, visit the ice; before that it is covered with snow. Climb meadows around the valley corner east, taking any of many appealing routes to a chilly flatland of moss and meanders, to moraines and meltwater, and finally the White Chuck Glacier. The white plateau is tempting, but only climbers with rope and ice ax should venture on its surface.

For another trip, investigate the intriguing White Chuck Cinder Cone, remnant of a volcano smaller and newer than Glacier Peak. Scramble meadows higher to the 6999-foot summit of Portal Peak.

If your visit is in late July or early August it is flower time on White Mountain. Therefore, hike the Crest Trail 2 miles up a wintry, rocky basin to 6450-foot Red Pass; from here,

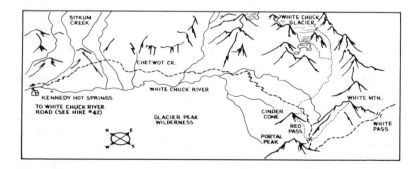

Glacier Peak from White Mountain

continue on the trail to White Pass (in early July be careful of the steep snow slopes) or leave the trail in about ½ mile and follow the flower crest to the summit of 7030-foot White Mountain (Hike 46).

Every direction calls. Invent your own wanderings. The minimum trip to the glacier can be done in 3 days but any itinerary of less than a week will leave the visitor frustrated, determined to return soon to finish the job at leisure.

Campsites other than those mentioned above are plentiful along the trail and throughout the high basin. However, as a conservation rule to be followed here and everywhere, camps should be placed in trees adjacent to meadows, not in the actual meadows, which are so fragile that only a few nights of camping can destroy nature's work of decades.

WHITE CHUCK RIVER

44 Mount Pugh

Round trip to Stujack Pass 7½ miles
Hiking time 6-7 hours
High point 5500 feet
Elevation gain 3600 feet
Best mid-July through October
One day, possibly backpack
USGS Pugh Mtn., White Chuck Mtn.

Round trip to Mt. Pugh 10 miles
Hiking time 10-12 hours
High point 7201 feet
Elevation gain 5350 feet
Best August through October
One day, possibly backpack

A strikingly high and imposing peak, considering its position so far west from the main mountain mass; the height and the detachment make for an exceptional viewpoint. See out to Puget Sound lowlands. See the North Cascades from Baker to Eldorado to Dome to Bonanza. See nearby Glacier Peak standing magnificently tall above White Chuck River forests. Closer, see the superb horn of Sloan and the sharp peaks of the Monte Cristo area. A rare panorama indeed, but not for everyone — the upper portion of the trail once led to a fire lookout but has long been abandoned and now is climbers' terrain. However, hikers can go most of the way and see most of the horizons.

Drive from Darrington on the Mountain Loop Highway 14 miles to Mt. Pugh road No. 3131. Turn left 1 mile to Mt. Pugh trail sign, elevation 1900 feet.

The steep trail climbs cool forest 1½ miles to tiny Lake Metan, 3180 feet, and the first outward looks. Just before the lake are springs providing the last dependable all-summer water; fill canteens. Relentless switchbacks ascend to meadows, 3 miles, beyond which point the trail is not maintained. The only decent camps on the route are here, but water may be gone by late summer.

Three Fingers and Whitehorse appear beyond valley forests as the trail switchbacks up talus and flowers to the notch of Stujack Pass, 3¾ miles, 5500 feet. Inexperienced travelers should have lunch and turn back, content with a full bag of scenery.

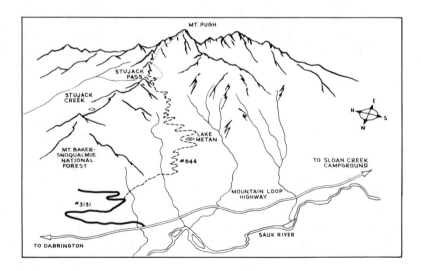

Mt. Pugh from Meadow Mountain

Those who go beyond Stujack must be trained and equipped for steep snow travel (early summer) and for rock scrambling (all summer). The abandoned trail climbs abruptly from the pass to a knife-edge rock ridge, then picks a delicate way along cliffs above a glacier trough, perhaps vanishing occasionally in snowfields. Part of the trail was dynamited from rock to provide access to the summit lookout; the first cabin was destroyed by lightning, and its successor was burned several years ago. (Note old lumber and ironware, remnants of a "tramway" used to haul building materials to the top.) Steep heather and rock slabs lead to the summit, 5½ miles, 7201 feet.

The summit views are worth the effort for travelers who can use ice ax, hands and feet, and perhaps rope, and thus manage the upper "trail" in safety. The views short of the summit are also worthwhile; be sure to stop, satisfied, when the going gets scary.

45 Lost Creek Ridge—Lake Byrne

Round trip to Round Lake viewpoint
   10 miles
Hiking time 6-8 hours
High point 5550 feet
Elevation gain 3550 feet
Best July through October
One day or backpack
USGS Sloan Peak

Round trip to Lake Byrne 24 miles
Allow 3 days minimum
High point 6000 feet
Elevation gain about 6500 feet, including
   up and downs in and out
Best August through October
USGS Glacier Peak and Sloan Peak
Forest Service wilderness permit required

A long ridge of green meadows, alpine lakes, and wide views of peaks near and far — one of the most memorable highland trails in the Glacier Peak region. The ridge can be ascended from either end for day trips or overnight camps, or walked the full length on an extended backpack. However, the middle section of the route is strictly cross-country travel, with no trail ever built and none planned; particularly in the fog, hikers must be careful not to get lost on Lost Ridge.

Drive from Darrington on the Mountain Loop Highway 17 miles to North Fork Sauk River road No. 308. Turn left 3 miles to a small parking area and trail sign, elevation 2000 feet.

The trail goes gently along the valley ½ mile, then climbs steeply through open woods, with occasional views of impressive Sloan Peak, to 4425-foot Bingley Gap, 3 miles. The way continues some 2 miles up and along the ridge to meadows and a 5550-foot saddle overlooking Round Lake, 5100 feet. (A steep sidetrail descends to the lake and good camps.) Scramble up the grassy knoll east of the saddle for more views of Sloan and a look at Glacier Peak. Here is the place for day-trippers to have

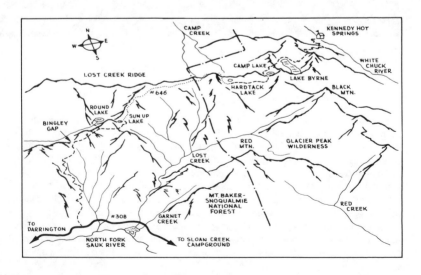

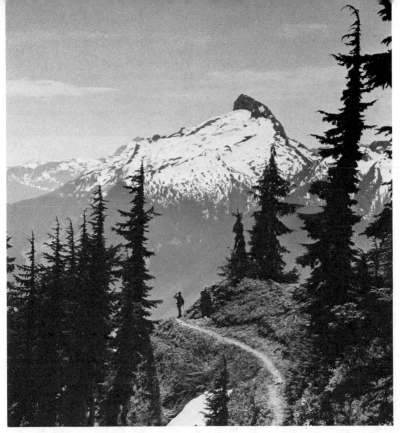

Sloan Peak from Lost Creek Ridge trail

lunch, soak up the scenery, and return home; generally the trail is reasonably snow-free by early July.

Beyond this point the up-and-down trail is sketchy, very snowy until late July, and requires careful routefinding. (The section from ¾ mile past Sunup Lake to Hardtack Lake is only partly a "constructed" trail and is more of a high route with scattered sections of good tread and boot-built or hoof-built track.) However, the going is easy and glorious — always near or on the crest, mostly in vast meadows, through open basins, near small lakes, with constant and changing views, and a choice of delightful camps. At 11 miles, the trail now good, is 5650-foot Camp Lake, set in a cliff-walled cirque. From here the trail climbs to a 6000-foot knob, drops a few feet to the rocky basin of "Little Siberia," then descends to famous Lake Byrne, 12 miles, 5550 feet. Flowers and rocks and waterfalls of the basin and adjoining ridges demand leisurely exploration, ever dominated by the tall white volcano rising beyond White Chuck River forests.

From the lake the trail abruptly drops 2250 feet in 2 miles to Kennedy Hot Springs (Hike 42), 5½ miles from the White Chuck River road. If Lake Byrne is the primary goal, the quickest route is from this road, gaining 3200 feet in 7½ miles for a very long day or reasonable weekend. If transportation can be arranged, such as by use of two cars, a 19-mile one-way trip can be done from one road to the other; allow 3 days or more.

NORTH FORK SAUK RIVER

46 White Pass— Red Pass

**Round trip to White Pass 18 miles
Allow 3 days
High point 5904 feet
Elevation gain 3700 feet
Best late July through October
USGS Glacier Peak
Forest Service wilderness permit required**

A cool, green forest for an easy afternoon stroll. Or vast meadows, attained by a grueling climb, for days of wandering flowers and views, always dominated by the grandeur of Glacier Peak.

Drive from Darrington on the Mountain Loop Highway 17 miles to North Fork Sauk River road No. 308. Turn left 7 miles to Sloan Creek Campground, elevation 2200 feet.

North Fork Sauk River trail No. 649 begins gently in rain forest, entering the Glacier

Yakbid Shelter, named for an Indian guide who led early surveyors through the region. Since this picture was taken, the shelter was destroyed by heavy snow.

Peak Wilderness at ½ mile. Ancient trees and a rusty-red mineral spring slow the pace. Day-trippers may turn back at about 1 mile, where the trail crosses a wide avalanche track and bouldery creek with a fine look at the north wall of Sloan Peak.

More forests and avalanche swaths lead to a campsite at Red Creek, 3¾ miles, 2800 feet, and onward to Makinaw Shelter, 5 miles, 2950 feet.

Now begins a stern 3000-foot climb. Fill canteens at the last dependable creek, 5½ miles. If the day is clear, the water will be badly wanted on the interminable switchbacks up an old burn regularly swept clean by avalanches, the whole south-facing slope open to the blazing sun. Flowers appear, and endless alpine meadows, and broad views, but no all-summer water.

However, at 5950 feet, 8½ miles, is a junction with the Pacific Crest Trail; shortly before or after there is water, a grand relaxation from the supreme effort, and full enjoyment of the hard-won scenery.

Two destinations, or a combination of both, now are offered.

For White Pass, go right in meadows an up-and-down ½ mile to the 5900-foot pass. The greenery is magnificent in every direction. Walk south along the Crest Trail. Wander northwest on sheep tracks to a 6500-foot saddle with staggering views of the White Chuck Glacier and Glacier Peak. Camps at the site of now-gone Yakbid (White Pass) Shelter and nearby.

For Red Pass, go left from the junction, traversing steep meadows 1½ miles to the 6500-foot pass. Look down into headwaters of the White Chuck River (Hike 43) and across to Glacier Peak.

For the best views, hike partway (about ½ mile) toward Red Pass, leave the trail at a point where upward progress is obviously easy, and scramble meadows to the west ridge of White Mountain. Follow the flowery crest to the 7030-foot summit, then descend the south ridge to White Pass. If the ridge is hiked in late July, there is a double reward: the view and the fields of flowers, including many, many white or cream-colored paintbrush.

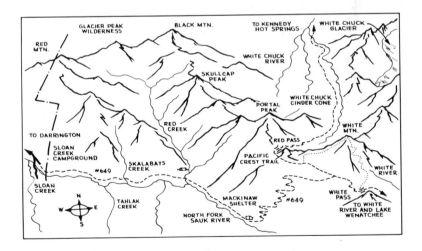

NORTH FORK SAUK RIVER

47 Pilot Ridge— Blue Lakes

Round trip to Blue Lakes 21 miles
Allow 3 days
High point 6200 feet
Elevation gain 5000 feet in and
 800 feet out
Best August through October
USGS Bench Mark Mtn., Glacier Peak,
 and Sloan Peak
Forest Service wilderness permit required

A lonesome hikers-only trail along a high ridge, through meadows and all-directional views, to a grassy summit and alpine lakes. Connections can be made for loop trips and cross-mountain trips. Prime country for the experienced highland rambler seeking solitude and a bit of adventure.

Drive from Darrington on the Mountain Loop Highway 17 miles to North Fork Sauk River road No. 308. Turn left 7 miles to Sloan Creek Campground, elevation 2200 feet.

Walk the North Fork Sauk River trail (Hike 46) 2 miles to Pilot Ridge trail No. 652. Go right from the 2450-foot junction, crossing the river on a footlog. The next 3 miles are why the ridge is so lonesome — the trail gains 3000 feet in a series of short switchbacks. Be sure to fill canteens before starting the climb, which has drinking water at only two places, and these undependable.

Reaching the ridge crest, then traversing its slopes, at 6 miles the trail approaches a 5600-foot high point. Now the trees give way to meadows with views of Sloan Peak and glaciers falling from the Monte Cristo peaks into Pride Basin. Sometimes the track traverses around knobs, sometimes it goes over the tops. If the tread is lost, follow the ridge crest — you can't go wrong. On the trail or off, views of Glacier Peak are tremendous.

For the first good campsite, leave the trail at 8 miles, climb over the saddle east of a 6265-foot knob, and drop to a small 6159-foot tarn on the north side of the ridge.

The trail abandons the crest to traverse a cirque on the west slopes of Johnson Mountain to an old lookout site. At 10 miles is a sidetrail climbing in 1 mile to the 6721-foot summit of the meadowy mountain, a splendid viewpoint to Red Pass, White Pass, and Ten Peaks — not to forget the omnipresent Glacier Peak. A party can make Johnson Mountain its destination, omitting the remainder of the ridge.

The main trail continues around a spur of the mountain and drops to a junction at 10½ miles. The left fork leads in a few hundred feet to upper Blue Lake, 5500 feet. Some camps by the cliff-walled lake, which usually is frozen until mid-August; better

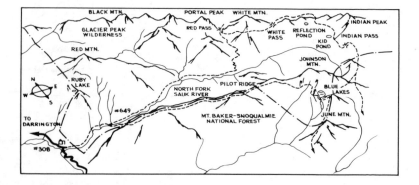

Johnson Mountain and Pilot Ridge

camps at lower Blue Lake, reached on the right fork, ½ mile beyond the junction.

The right fork is the main trail, which ends at June Mountain, 13 miles from the road, at a junction with the Bald Eagle trail. A two-ridge loop trip is possible if transportation can be arranged from one road to another.

The Bald Eagle trail can be followed 2½ miles to Dishpan Gap and a junction with the Pacific Crest Trail. However, if Dishpan Gap is the goal, a shorter route is available, going steeply up and down 1 mile (no real trail) from Upper Blue Lake to the Crest Trail at a point ¾ mile south of the Gap. Distance from upper Blue Lake to the Gap via the Bald Eagle alternate, about 4½ miles; via the shortcut, about 2 miles.

For a splendid loop with no extra transportation needed, go 6¾ miles on the Crest Trail (Hike 66) from Dishpan Gap to White Pass, then 9 miles down the North Fork Sauk River trail (Hike 46). Total distance 28 miles; allow 3 days.

Or, one can cross the Cascade Crest and descend to the Little Wenatchee River road-end on the east side of the range (Hike 65).

SOUTH FORK STILLAGUAMISH
   RIVER

48 **Goat**
    Flats

Round trip to Goat Flats 9 miles
Hiking time 6 hours
High point 4700 feet
Elevation gain 2000 feet
Best early July through October
One day or backpack
USGS Granite Falls and Silverton

The rock spires and icefields of Three Fingers Mountain stand near the west edge of the North Cascades, rising above lowlands and saltwater, prominent on the skyline from as far away as Seattle. On a ridge of the mountain are the lovely alpine meadows of Goat Flats, the most beautiful in the Verlot area. Once upon a time a great network of trails linked the North and South Forks of the Stillaguamish River. Now most of the forest land is chopped up by logging roads, the trails ruined or abandoned or neglected. The hike to Goat Flats follows a small remnant of the old pedestrian network.

Drive the Mountain Loop Highway 6½ miles east from Granite Falls to Forest Service road No. 320 and turn left 1½ miles to a major junction. Go left on road 320, passing several side-roads and also the Meadow Mountain trail (an alternate but longer route). At 17 mles from the Mountain Loop Highway turn right on road No. 320B and in ¼ mile find the trailhead, elevation 2800 feet.

The trail climbs along the forested side of the ridge 2 miles and emerges into subalpine meadows of 3800-foot Saddle Lake. Just before the lake outlet is a three-way junction. The right leads to Meadow Mountain, a tree-covered hill. Straight ahead are campsites and a shelter on the far side of the lake. Take the left fork to Three Fingers and Goat Flats.

From the lake the trail ascends steep slopes above Saddle Creek forests and in 1 mile enters rolling meadows with acres and acres of blueberries and heather. The meadows are broken by groves of alpine trees and dotted with ponds — one in particular, several hundred feet below the trail, offers an excellent camp.

Some 2½ miles from Saddle Lake the trail reaches the meadow plateau of 4700-foot Goat Flats. Near the center is a very old and decrepit log shelter once used as a patrol cabin. Sad to say, the heather and huckleberries are being trampled to death by hikers who refuse to stay on the trail; leaving the trail to pick berries or enjoy viewpoints is expected, but otherwise parties should keep to the beaten path. The meadows also are taking a terrible beating from over-camping. Certainly no fires should be built here and it would be far better for campers to use sites a bit before, a bit beyond, or off to the side of the Flats.

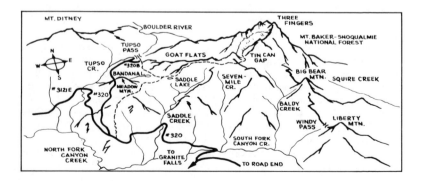

Fogbound Goat Flats

For most hikers the Flats are far enough, offering a close-up view of the cliffs and ice of Three Fingers, looks south to Pilchuck, north to Whitehorse and Mt. Baker, west to saltwater ways and the Olympics. Campers get the best: sunsets on peaks and valleys, farm and city lights in the far-below lowland night, a perspective on megalopolis and wildness.

For hikers who want more, the trail goes on, traversing meadows and then climbing steeply up a rocky basin to 6400-foot Tin Can Gap, above the Three Fingers Glacier. From here a climbers' route weaves along an airy ridge to the foot of the pinnacle of the 6854-foot South Peak of Three Fingers, atop which is perched a lookout cabin built in the 1930s. The pinnacle once was mounted by a series of ladders, long since rotted away. In order to build the cabin, the Forest Service dynamited a platform on the summit; tradition says the original summit never was climbed before it was destroyed. Tradition also says one lookout was so stricken by vertigo he had to telephone Forest Service supervisors to come help him down the ladder. Hikers will not want to go beyond Tin Can Gap.

SOUTH FORK STILLAGUAMISH RIVER

49 Mount Forgotten

Round trip to meadows 8 miles
Hiking time 7 hours
High point 5200 feet
Elevation gain 3100 feet
Best mid-June through October
One day or backpack
USGS Bedal

A valley forest, a waterfall, a small alpine meadow, and views of the impressive wall of Big Four Mountain and the white volcano of Glacier Peak. Come early for flowers, come late for blueberries.

Drive from Verlot on the Mountain Loop Highway 15 miles to Perry Creek road No. 3010, about 1 mile beyond Big Four Picnic Area and just after the crossing of Perry Creek. Turn left 1 mile to the cramped parking area at road-end, elevation 2100 feet.

The trail traverses a steep hillside, now in forest, now in a grand display of ferns and flowers, boulder-hops a frenzied creek, and at 2 miles climbs above Perry Creek Falls. Pause to look over the top of the falls — but don't trust the handrail. A few feet farther the way crosses Perry Creek on boulders. A campsite here.

Elevation is gained steadily to a small field of heather and lupine dotted by alpine trees. The trail switchbacks up forests on the slopes of Mt. Forgotten, enters lush, fragile meadows, and disappears at about 5200 feet, 4 miles.

Novice hikers should turn back here, well-rewarded by views of Glacier Peak, seen at the head of the long valley of the White Chuck River, and closer views of Big Four, Twin Peaks, Mt. Dickerman, and the long ridge of Stillaguamish Peak.

Experienced off-trail travelers can continue onward and upward a mile, climbing very steep heather slopes, then scrambling broken rock, to the 6005-foot summit of the peak and more views.

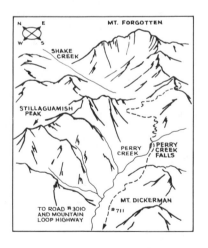

Oak ferns

White Chuck valley and Glacier Peak from Mt. Forgotten

Round trip 8 miles
Hiking time 8-9 hours
High point 5723 feet
Elevation gain 3800 feet
Best July through October
One day
USGS Bedal

50 Mount Dickerman

All too few trails remain, outside Wilderness Areas and National Parks, which begin in valley bottoms and climb unmarred forests to meadows. The way to Dickerman is strenuous, but the complete experience of life zones from low to high, plus the summit views, are worth every drop of sweat.

Drive from Verlot on the Mountain Loop Highway 16½ miles to a small parking area and easily-overlooked trail sign, elevation 1900 feet, about 2½ miles beyond Big Four Picnic Area.

The trail doesn't fool around: switchbacks instantly commence climbing up and up and up through lovely cool forest; except perhaps in late summer, several small creeks provide pauses that refresh. Tantalizing glimpses through timber give promise of scenery above. A bit past 2 miles lower-elevation trees yield to Alaska cedars and alpine firs. Then the forest thins as the trail traverses under towering cliffs onto flatter terrain. Near here, in a sheltered hollow to the west, is a little lakelet reached by a faint path; camping is possible but the water purity is questionable after the season of gushing snowmelt.

The next ½ mile ranks among the most famous blueberry patches in the Cascades; in season, grazing hikers may find progress very slow indeed; in the fall, photographers find the blazing colors equally obstructive. Now, too, the horizons grow.

The final mile is somewhat steeper, switchbacking meadows to the broad summit, as friendly a sackout spot as one can find.

Abrupt cliffs drop toward Perry Creek forests, far below. Beyond are Stillaguamish Peak and Mt. Forgotten. To the east rise Glacier Peak and the horn of Sloan Peak and all the Monte Cristo peaks. And across the South Fork Stillaguamish River are rugged Big Four Mountain and the striking rock slabs of Vesper Peak. But this is only a small part of the panorama which extends in every direction.

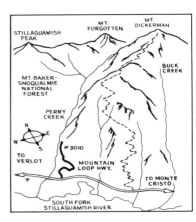

Picking huckleberries

*October snowfall on Mt. Dickerman.
Del Campo Peak in distance*

SOUTH FORK SAUK RIVER

51 Goat Lake

Round trip 10 miles
Hiking time 5 hours
High point 3162 feet
Elevation gain 1250 feet
Best mid-June through October
One day or backpack
USGS Sloan Peak and Bedal

A subalpine lake beneath cliffs and glaciers, a popular destination with hikers of all ages. Wander beside clear, cold water, investigate artifacts of long-ago mining, and admire snowfed waterfalls frothing down rock walls. The trail (foot travel only) partly traces the route of a wagon road dating from the late 19th century.

Drive from Verlot on the Mountain Loop Highway 19½ miles to Barlow Pass, then north about 4 miles to Elliott Creek road No. 309. Turn right 1 mile to a gate, parking area, and trailhead, elevation 1900 feet.

The recently-abandoned road can be walked but is a mile longer and not as pretty as the trail, which mainly follows an ancient wagon road, mostly in forest, in sight and loud sound of cascade-roaring Elliott Creek. At 3½ miles pass the end of the abandoned logging road and continue gently climbing. At 4½ miles the trail leaves the wagon road, steepens, and switchbacks upward, rejoining the road just before the lake outlet at 5 miles, 3162 feet.

For an interesting sidetrip, at about the 4¼-mile mark the wagon road diverges rightward from the trail and crosses Elliott Creek to decrepit remains of a mining settlement. The road then switchbacks and in roughly ½ mile recrosses the creek on risky remnants of a bridge to meet the trail.

Enjoy the views of Foggy Peak. Prowl relics of what was, some 75 years ago, a busy mining town. In summer sunshine, take a brisk swim.

Beyond the outlet is a nice spot to picnic. The trail continues left around the shore, eventually disappearing in alder and vine maple. On a rocky knoll before the brush begins is a particularly fine place to sit and stare and eat lunch before going home.

Because campers have overused the lakeshore areas, these are now restricted to picnicking. Camping is permitted only at the old hotel site on a knoll above the outlet.

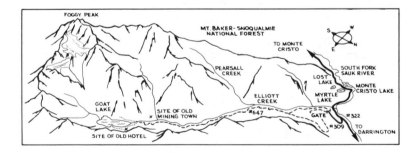

Goat Lake and shoulder of Foggy Peak

Round trip to basin entrance 6 miles
Hiking time 7 hours
High point 5000 feet
Elevation gain 2600 feet
Best late July through October
One day or backpack
USGS Monte Cristo

52 Gothic Basin

A glacier-gouged basin designed for wandering. Rounded buttresses polished and scratched by ice, sparkling ponds in scooped-out rock, an Arctic-barren cirque lake, loud waterfalls, meadow nooks, old mines, ore samples, and views of Monte Cristo peaks. The miner-built trail is steep from start to end, and often extremely steep, but mostly in reasonably decent shape.

Drive from Verlot on the Mountain Loop Highway 19½ miles to Barlow Pass. Go straight ahead on the Monte Cristo road 2 miles; ¼ mile beyond the bridge over the South Fork Sauk River, park in a small lot, elevation 2400 feet. A sign marks the beginning of the route.

From the sign, follow boot tracks downstream on gravel several hundred feet to get around an alder patch. Proceed to the river at a point a few yards below the mouth of Weden Creek. Here is a large, time-bleached footlog, chopped flat on top for easy crossing — but unfortunately it may no longer reach the far bank. Newer footlogs, if any, may be so high in the air acrophobics may prefer to go upstream to just above Weden Creek and ford — but in high water this is virtually impossible. The river crossing is the toughest part of the hike and effectively stops casual walkers. However, in late summer the wade is ordinarily safe and easy. Tread starts beyond the footlogs.

The sturdy miners didn't waste effort on switchbacks and the trail is steep all the way. The first 1½ miles are waterless, but luckily shaded by superb big trees. At 1½ miles is a series of three streams rushing down slot gorges; here too are flowers, a mine, and views across Weden Creek to Silvertip Peak.

The gorges may be snowfilled and dangerous until early August; if so, the hiker without ice ax should turn back, content. Beyond, the trail enters brush, the tread gets skimpy and requires some careful walking, and the grade is at least as grueling as ever. A magnificent waterfall, "King Kong's Showerbath," demands a halt amid unpleasantness. Another mine invites a sidetrip to inspect rusted garbage. After an especially straight-up and rock-scrambling stretch, the way emerges into a final ½ mile of heather and flowers, traversing the valley wall on meadow shelves, gradually nearing the ridge crest.

At 3 miles, 5000 feet, the trail cuts through the ridge into Gothic Basin and ends in a meadow among buttresses. A good campsite here and many others throughout the basin.

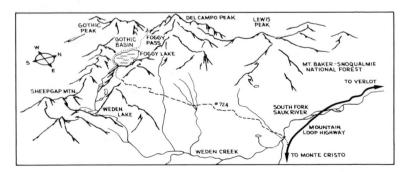

Sheep Gap Mountain from Gothic Basin

Now explorations. In the lower basin are flower gardens, artifacts of oldtime mining, waterfall gorges, and views down to Weden Creek and across to the Monte Cristo group. Especially fascinating are the rocks: limestone, sandstone, conglomerate, granite, and iron-red mineralized zones, all plucked and polished by the ice, the dominant brownish limestone weathered into oddly-beautiful forms. Follow the stream bed or the buttress crest 300 feet higher to Foggy (Crater) Lake, in a solemn cirque under Gothic Peak and Del Campo. Scramble slabs and talus and blossoms to the ridge of gothic, or to 5500-foot Foggy Pass between Gothic and Del Campo, or to the ridge east of the lake, for higher views of the Monte Cristos, Sultan Basin, Sloan Peak, and more.

SOUTH FORK SAUK RIVER

53 Poodle Dog Pass

Round trip to Poodle Dog Pass 3 miles
Hiking time 4 hours
High point 4350 feet
Elevation gain 1600 feet
Best July through October
One day
USGS Monte Cristo

A deep alpine lake in a cirque of cliffs, waterfalls, and meadows, especially beautiful during fall colors. Because of private land dating back to the 1890s, when Monte Cristo was a roaring mining town, the trail is poor much of the way. However, the difficulties are worth it, as thousands of hikers testify with their feet each summer.

Drive from Verlot on the Mountain Loop Highway 19½ miles to Barlow Pass. Go straight ahead on the Monte Cristo road 4 miles to the entrance to Monte Cristo, now a privately-owned resort. Either park well off the side of the road or drive ¼ mile into the resort, where a per-person fee is charged. Find the trailhead, signed "Silver Lake," in front of the pay booth, elevation 2800 feet. There is also a feeder trail from the resort.

The first ½ mile of trail, partly on abandoned truck road, then in a 1960s clearcut, is very poor; don't blame the Forest Service — this is private land. At last the way enters unmolested trees and ascends steeply in the fashion of no-nonsense miners intent on gaining elevation with minimum fuss. The trail becomes a small creek during rainy spells and is always rocky, rough, and slippery.

At 1½ miles from Monte Cristo is Poodle Dog Pass, 4350 feet. Views of Wilmon Spires through subalpine trees; a good spot for lunch before going home. However, trails beckon beyond the four-way junction at the pass.

The main trail, an historic but abandoned miners' route, descends Silver Creek to Mineral City. A sketchy way trail, easy to lose in fog, goes left from the pass 3

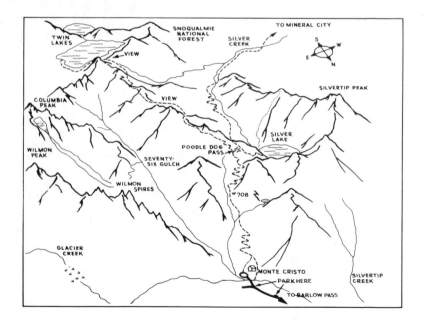

Silver Lake and Silvertip Peak

up-and-down miles to 4560-foot Twin Lakes and a wealth of campsites amid a world of alpine roaming.

Most short-trippers choose Silver Lake, descending the right fork from the pass ¼ mile to the 4260-foot shore. Camping is possible by the outlet but the space is cramped and abused.

For the best views and picnics, cross the outlet and climb open slopes 700 feet to a shoulder of Silvertip Peak. Look down Silver Creek toward Mineral City, look beyond Silver Lake to the Monte Cristo peaks. In season, graze blueberries.

SOUTH FORK SAUK RIVER

54 Glacier Basin

Round trip 5 miles
Hiking time 5 hours
High point 4500 feet
Elevation gain 1700 feet
Best July through October
One day or backpack
USGS Monte Cristo and Blanca Lake

Meadows and boulders, flowers and snowfields, cold streams for wading and soft grass for napping, all in a dream basin tucked amid fierce peaks. The miner-built trail, mostly on private land, is extremely steep and rugged, but short.

Drive from Verlot on the Mountain Loop Highway 19½ miles to Barlow Pass. Go straight ahead on the Monte Cristo road 4 miles to Monte Cristo. Disposing of the car is a serious problem that the Forest Service cannot solve — space on public land is too cramped. Park well off the side of the road, taking care not to block the small campground. Back down the road ¼ mile are a few more spaces. It may be best to drive into the resort and pay the per-person parking fee. Elevation, 2800 feet.

Begin by walking an abandoned mining road 1½ miles, much of the way through clearcuts on private land, to the start of the true trail, which ascends at a moderate grade through open greenery, then enters alders and Alaska cedars and becomes steep. Stop for a rest on a rock outcrop above a loud waterfall. The next stretch is the worst, blistering hot in sunny weather, and the straight-up "trail" eroded to a deep rut by years of snowmelt and boots. The rock slabs and mud slopes are slippery, often requiring use of alder handholds. Going down is even messier than going up. But in ½ mile unpleasantness is over, the track easing out on remnants of an old mining road and entering a gulch filled with talus, snow, and whistling marmots.

Below the waste rock and rusted garbage of a mine, the trail divides. Avoid the low route beside the creek; it's on snowfields in early summer, through mud and brush patches later on. Take the high route: walk beyond the mine a few yards and climb about 50 feet on dirt and boulders to a rock causeway carrying a large pipe — formerly the water supply for the mine.

With startling abruptness the way opens into the basin — the meandering creeks, the flat fields of grass and blossoms, and the cliffs and glaciers of Cadet and Monte Cristo and Wilmon Peaks, the sharp thrust of Wilmon Spires.

What to do now? Sit and look, have lunch, watch the dippers. Or roam among boulders and wade sandy creeks and maybe organize a snowball fight. Or climb scree slopes to explore old mines. Or take a loitering walk to Ray's Knoll (named for climber Ray Rigg) and views over the basin and down the valley. Scramblers can continue up an easy gully to a higher cirque with glaciers, moraines, waterfalls, and broader views.

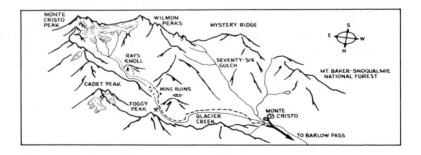

Glacier Basin and Monte Cristo Peak

But please be kind to the fragile basin meadows, already mauled by tents and boots. Walk softly. And camp not in the flower flats but either up on Mystery Ridge or on Ray's Knoll. No fires!

131

SKYKOMISH RIVER —
SOUTH FORK STILLAGUAMISH
RIVER

One-way trip about 9½ miles
Hiking time 6 hours
High point 4500 feet
Elevation gain about 2800 feet from
  Stillaguamish, 1500 feet from Sultan
Best July through October
One day or backpack
USGS Silverton and Index

55 Bald Mountain

A new trail built by the state Department of Natural Resources, so new (1976) it's not shown on federal maps, traverses the 7-mile ridge dividing Sultan Basin from the Stillaguamish. Walk the complete high way, partly in views of valleys, lakes, and peaks, and partly in gorgeous deep forest. Or just visit the scenic climax in huckleberry-heather meadows near the summit of 4851-foot Bald Mountain. This climax can be attained from either end: the distance is less from the Sultan start but the access road is atrocious; the road is good to the Stillaguamish start but the way is long, with some ups and downs.

Stillaguamish start

Drive the Mountain Loop Highway from Granite Falls to 5 miles past the Verlot Ranger Station and turn right on road No. 3015, signed "Bear Lake Trail" and "Bald Mountain Trail." At 2.7 miles from the highway turn right on road No. 3015B, signed "Bald Mountain." At 4.3 miles go uphill left. Stay right at the next Y and at a bit more than 5 miles reach a large DNR sign and parking lot, elevation 2100 feet.

Walk a steep cat road up a few hundred feet to the trail, which proceeds from old clearcut into old virgin forest, much of the way on puncheon. At ¾ mile pass a sidetrail to Beaver Plant Lake and in a scant mile reach a Y. The right fork goes a short bit to Upper Ashland Lake and camps. Keep left.

The trail climbs around the end of Bald Ridge in grand forest, at 3 miles topping a 3950-foot saddle with views of Three Fingers, the Stillaguamish, and Clear Lake, directly below. For bigger views, on the subsequent contour leave the trail and climb to a 4250-foot peak above Island Lake. Discouraged words may be uttered at about 4 miles, where the trail, to pass under rugged cliffs, switchbacks down and down 500 feet into the head of Pilchuck Creek. As some compensation, here is the first water since the lakes area. The lost elevation is regained and at about 6½ miles is a 4400-foot saddle under the highest peak of Bald. Here begin those promised meadows, easily followed to the top.

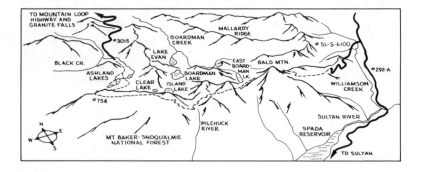

Bald Mountain

Sultan start

Drive US 2 to the east end of Sultan and turn north on the Sultan Basin road. At 13 miles enter the Sultan Basin watershed at Olney Pass. Take the middle of three forks and at 19.6 miles from Sultan turn left on Williamson Creek road No. 292A. Stay at creek level, dodging sideroads, and at 22.5 miles turn left on road No. SL-S-6100. Cross Williamson Creek and start climbing. But maybe not on wheels — deterioration of the grade is often progressive once the Sultan Basin road is left, frequently ruling out the family sedan; when the going gets too tough for machines, try your feet. Logging spurs are numerous; alertness and luck are needed to stay on the proper road. At 1.7 miles from Williamson Creek keep left; at 2 miles leave SL-S-6100 and go right; at 2.6 miles go left; at 3.3 miles go straight; and at 3.4 miles (about 26 from Sultan) reach the road-end and trailhead, elevation about 3600 feet.

Bulldozer track soon yields to trail and forest, and in 1 mile to heather-and-huckleberry parkland. At 2 miles the way tops a 4500-foot ridge and drops to broad meadows above several lakelets with campsites. From here the summit of Bald is a stroll. The trail contours on beneath the peak toward Ashland Lakes.

Air view of Lake Blanca and Kyes Peak. Glacier Peak on right

56 Lake Blanca

Round trip to lake 8 miles
Hiking time 6-8 hours
High point 4600 feet
Elevation gain 2700 feet in,
   600 feet out
Best July through October
One day or backpack
USGS Blanca Lake

The rugged cliffs of Kyes, Monte Cristo, and Columbia Peaks above, the white mass of the Columbia Glacier in the upper trough, and the deep waters of ice-fed Lake Blanca filling the lower cirque. A steep forest climb ending in a grand view, with further explorations available to the experienced off-trail traveler.

Drive US 2 to Index junction and turn left on the North Fork Skykomish River road 14 miles to Garland Mineral Springs. At a junction ½ mile beyond the springs, turn left on road No. 2901 the 2 miles to Lake Blanca trail sign and parking area, elevation 1900 feet.

The trail immediately gets down to the business of grinding out elevation and never neglects that assignment, relentlessly switchbacking up and up in forest, eventually with partial views out to Glacier Peak. At 3 miles the way reaches the ridge top at 4600 feet, the highest point of the trip. In a few hundred yards is shallow little Virgin Lake, amid meadows and trees of a saddle on the very crest. Acceptable camping here for those who don't wish to carry packs farther.

Now the trail goes down, sidehilling through trees with glimpses of blue-green water, dropping 600 feet in 1 mile and reaching the 3972-foot lake at the outlet. Relax and enjoy the wind-rippled, sun-sparkling lake, ¾ mile long, the Columbia Glacier, the spectacular peaks. Where the trail hits the lake, and across the outlet stream on the west shore, are a number of overused but fairly decent campsites. Don't expect to find any easy wood; carry a stove.

Experienced hikers can explore along the rough west shore to the braided stream channels and waterfalls and flowers at the head of the lake. Those with proper mountaineering background and equipment can climb the Columbia Glacier to the col between Columbia and Monte Cristo Peaks and look down to Glacier Basin. The descent into the basin is not technically difficult, but strictly for parties skilled in use of the ice ax.

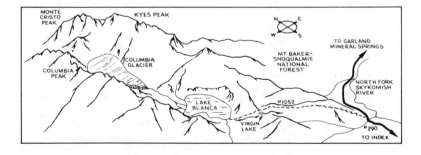

North wall of Baring Mountain

57 Barclay and Eagle Lakes

Round trip to Eagle Lake 8½ miles
Hiking time 6 hours
High point 3888 feet
Elevation gain 1700 feet
Best late June through October
One day or backpack
USGS Baring

For many years Barclay Lake ranked among the most popular low-elevation hikes In the Cascades, passing through pleasant old forest to the base of the tremendous north wall of Mt. Baring, a trip good in early spring and late fall when higher country was deep in snow. The wall remains, and the lake, but not much forest. Tragically, the walk to Barclay Lake no longer deserves, by itself, inclusion in this book. However, there is still Eagle Lake, amid trees, meadows, and peaks, and offering a staggering cross-valley look at the north wall of Baring, a legend among climbers and to date ascended only once.

Drive US 2 some 6 miles east from Index junction. Turn left at Baring on 635 Place NE, cross railroad tracks, and go 4.3 miles to the somewhat-hard-to-see trailhead, elevation 2200 feet.

The trail, with minor ups and downs and numerous mudholes, meanders through what remains of the forest of Barclay Creek, in 1½ miles reaching Barclay Lake, 2422 feet, and at 2¼ miles ending near the inlet stream. Camping at several spots along the shore and also a neck-stretching look up and up the precipice of 6123-foot Mt. Baring.

At the lakehead, just where the trail leaves the water by a small campsite with a well-hidden toilet, find a meager path climbing 1000 feet straight up steep forest. For a bit the way is on rockslide, then briefly levels and resumes climbing beside another rockslide. The grade abruptly flattens at a viewpoint above Stone Lake and contours to 3888-foot Eagle Lake.

By the shore is a private cabin, kept locked; the owner maintains a campsite for public use near the outlet. It would be nice indeed did not a few slobs leave garbage strewn around — twice they've burned down shelters.

For more views, and for meadows, wander up the easy slopes of 5936-foot Townsend Mountain or from the outlet roam downstream through the lovely forest, heather, and marsh of Paradise Meadow.

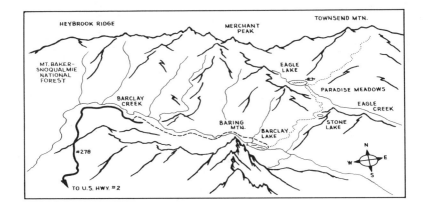

58 A Peach, A Pear, and a Topping

Round trip to Pear Lake 15 miles
Allow 2 days
High point 5300 feet
Elevation gain 3200 feet in,
   500 feet out
Best July through October
USGS Captain Point and Benchmark Mtn.

Savor flower and heather gardens ringing three alpine lakes and a spatter of ponds along the Pacific Crest Trail. And if all these sweet things seem to call for whipped cream, stroll to a peak for a panorama of a horizonful of valleys and mountains.

To approach from the east, drive road No. 2713 from the Little Wenatchee River (see Hike 64) and at 4 miles past the junction with road No. 2801 find Top Lake trail No. 1506. From the more popular west, drive US 2 to Skykomish and just east of town turn north on Beckler River road No. 280. At 7 miles turn right on Rapid River road No. 270. At 11.4 miles is the start of Meadow Creek trail No. 1057. (In 1979 the sign gave only the number.) Elevation, 2100 feet.

Beginning amid the ravages of the 1960s Evergreen Mountain fire and subsequent salvage logging, the trail (a goshawful goo from churning by horses, which also have ruined hillside tread) gains almost 1000 feet switchbacking out of Rapid River valley. At about 1 mile the burn is left, forest entered, and the grade moderates and contours into Meadow Creek drainage, crossing Meadow Creek at 3 miles hopping boulders (there aren't really enough). At 3¾ miles recross the creek to a junction with an abandoned trail to Cady Ridge. The way climbs steeply from Meadow Creek into Cady Creek drainage. At 6.5 miles the Crest Trail is reached at the lower of the two Fortune Ponds, 4700 feet.

Walk the Crest Trail south. At 7¾ miles cross 5200-foot Frozen Finger Pass between Cady Creek and Rapid River and drop to Pear Lake, 8 miles, 4809 feet. No camping within 100 feet of the shores here or at Fortune Ponds. Peach Lake, at the same elevation over the ridge south, is best reached by contouring off-trail around the ridge end and below cliffs, passing narrow Grass Lake. Top Lake is attained via ½ mile more on the Crest Trail and another ½ mile on trail No. 1506. For the promised land of views, leave the trail at Fortune Ponds and ascend Fortune Mountain, 5903 feet.

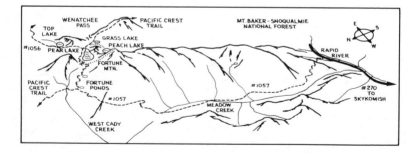

Upper Fortune Pond. Monte Cristo peaks in background

Bear tracks at upper Fortune Pond

NASON CREEK

59 Lake Valhalla

Round trip 11 miles
Hiking time 6 hours
High point 5100 feet
Elevation gain 1100 feet
Best mid-July through October
One day or backpack
USGS Labyrinth Mtn.

North from Stevens Pass the Pacific Crest Trail roams by a splendid succession of meadowy alpine lakes. First in line is Lake Valhalla, set in a cirque under the cliffs of Lichtenberg Mountain.

Drive US 2 to Stevens Pass, elevation 4061 feet, and park in the lot at the east end of the summit area. Find the trail beside the PUD substation.

The way begins along the original grade of the Great Northern Railroad, used when trains went over the top of the pass; the right-of-way was abandoned upon completion of the first Cascade Tunnel (predecessor of the present tunnel) early in the century.

From the open hillside, views extend beyond the pass to ski slopes and down Stevens Creek to Nason Creek and far east out the valley. Below is the roar of highway traffic. In 1½ miles the gentle path rounds the end of the ridge and enters the drainage of Nason Creek. Here a sidetrail drops east ½ mile to the old Cascade Tunnel, now employed as a research station by University of Washington geophysicists.

The main trail descends a bit to cross a little stream, climbs a ridge, and at 3½ miles enters a basin of meadows and marsh. Staying east and below the Cascade Crest, the way ascends easily to a 5100-foot spur, then drops to the rocky shore of the 4830-foot lake.

Heavily-used and frequently-crowded camps lie among trees near the outlet; wood

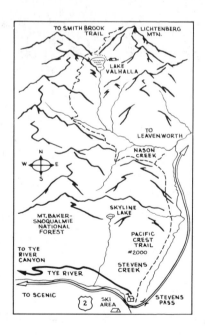

Pipsissewa or princess pine

Lake Valhalla from Crest Trail near Lichtenberg Pass

is hard to come by, so carry a stove. For explorations, climb heather meadows to the summit of 5920-foot Lichtenberg and broad views, or continue north on the Pacifc Crest Trail (Hike 101) as far as time and energy allow.

A much shorter (5 miles roundtrip) but less scenic approach is via the Smith Brook trail (Hike 60) which joins the Pacific Crest Trail at Union Gap ½ mile from the road. The Crest Trail leads south from the Gap 2 miles to Lake Valhalla.

NASON CREEK

60 Lake Janus and Grizzly Peak

Round trip to Grizzly Peak 15 miles
Hiking time 6-8 hours
High point 5597 feet
Elevation gain 2200 feet in,
 800 feet out
Best mid-July through October
One day or backpack
USGS Labyrinth Mtn. and Captain Point

A strikingly-beautiful alpine lake and a long ridge trail, sometimes in Western Washington and sometimes in Eastern Washington and sometimes straddling the fence. An easy but spectacular stretch of the Pacific Crest Trail. The trip can be done in a day but at least a weekend should be planned — the lake is inviting and "looking around the next corner" is bound to be irresistible.

Drive US 2 east 4½ miles from Stevens Pass and turn left on Smith Brook road. Cross Nason Creek bridge, turn left, and follow the road 3½ miles toward Rainy Pass to the Smith Brook trailhead, elevation 3800 feet. There is no space for cars so drop passengers and packs here and return ¼ mile to the last switchback for parking.

Climb a long ½ mile on trail No. 1590 to 4680-foot Union Gap and the junction with the Pacific Crest Trail. Turn right, dropping 700 feet down the west side of the crest to round cliffs of Union Peak, then regaining part of the elevation before reaching 4146-foot Lake Janus, 2½ miles from the Gap. The trail goes through pleasant forest with the far-off sound of Rapid River. Though the grade is gentle, the tread is badly water-eroded in places from years of heavy use.

The lake is everything an alpine lake should be — sparkling water surrounded by meadows and tall trees and topped by the bright green slopes of 6007-foot Jove Peak. Numerous camps are available, including a mountain memorial cabin that has not been treated kindly. Wood is scarce so carry a stove.

From the lake the trail enters forest on smooth and easy tread, climbs 1100 feet in 1½ miles to the Cascade Crest, contours around the Eastern Washington side of a small hill and then ducks around a corner back into Western Washington, a process repeated frequently on the way to Grizzly Peak.

Every turn of the crest-wandering trail offers new views. Look east down into Lake Creek and Little Wenatchee River drainage and across to nearby Labyrinth Mountain.

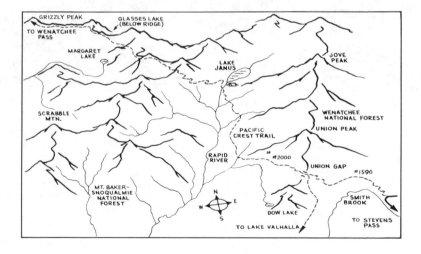

Lake Janus

Look north to Glacier Peak. Look west down to the Rapid River and out to peaks above the Skykomish. At 2 miles from Lake Janus is a glimpse of Margaret Lake, some 400 feet below the trail. A short ½ mile beyond is a view down to Glasses Lake and larger Heather Lake; this is a good turnaround point for day hikers.

At about 4½ miles from Lake Janus the trail climbs within a few feet of the top of 5597-foot Grizzly Peak and more panoramas — but unfortunately not of Glacier Peak, cut off by a nameless peak ½ mile north. The trail also goes close to the summit of the nameless peak, with a view of Glacier Peak; succumbing to this temptation will lead to further temptations, on and on along the Pacific Crest Trail.

61 Nason Ridge

Round trip to Rock Mountain 9 miles
Hiking time 7 hours
High point 6852 feet
Elevation gain 3100 feet
Best August through October
One day or backpack

Round trip to Alpine Lookout 8 miles
Hiking time 6 hours
High point 6200 feet
Elevation gain 1700 feet
Best August through October
One day
USGS Wenatchee Lake and Labyrinth Mtn.

A prime tour for experienced navigators is the magnificent journey along the full length of Nason Ridge, 26 miles through wide-sky highlands from near the Cascade Crest to near Lake Wenatchee. Most hikers, though, sample the high delights on day or weekend hikes via four access trails, the two most popular of which are described here.

Snowy Creek to Rock Mountain: For this pleasant way to Nason Ridge through cool forest, by many small creeks, drive 6 miles from the Little Wenatchee River road (Hike 63) on the Rainy Creek road. Starting at 3800 feet, climb 1¼ well-graded but sketchily-maintained miles on trail No. 1531 to the 4640-foot junction with the trail from Rainy Pass.

Mountain goats at Alpine Lookout

In 1 mile east from this junction is a 3800-foot campsite in a large, level meadow below cliffs of Rock Mountain. Tread vanishes in the meadow but reappears halfway across, on the left. The next 2 miles are grueling, entering trees and leaving them, climbing 1800 feet to the ridge of Rock Mountain. From the junction on the ridge it's ⅓ mile to the 6852-foot summit, formerly site of a lookout cabin. (From the junction the way drops ¾ mile to the 6200-foot intersection with the Rock Mountain trail, which climbs in 4 miles and 3500 feet from US 2 at a point 9 miles east of Stevens Pass.)

Alpine Lookout: Drive US 2 east from Stevens Pass about 17 miles to a Highway Department rest area. A few hundred feet beyond, turn left on Butcher Creek road No. 2717. Cross Nason Creek, avoid spur roads, turn right at 2½ miles, and drive almost to road-end. Find the trailhead (Round Mountain trail No. 1529) at 4100 feet. Climb 1000 feet in 1½ miles to the junction with the Nason Ridge trail and continue climbing west 2½ miles to the lookout, 6200 feet.

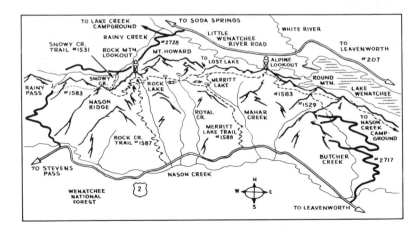

Wenatchee Lake and meanders of the Little Wenatchee River from Dirtyface

LAKE WENATCHEE

62 Dirtyface Peak

Round trip 9½ miles
Hiking time 7 hours
High point 6193 feet
Elevation gain 4300 feet
Best mid-June through October
One day or backpack
USGS Wenatchee Lake

A stiff climb, cruelly hot in summer, to an airy view over Lake Wenatchee and into the Glacier Peak Wilderness. The last 2½ miles are dry so carry lots of water. For hikers who don't mind a few small snowpatches, this is a fine mid-June trip.

Drive US 2 east from Stevens Pass 19 miles and turn left to Lake Wenatchee. Pass the state park road, the roads to Plain and Fish Lakes, and continue to Lake Wenatchee Ranger Station. Turn right to the small campground behind the station; just before the first campsite is the trailhead, elevation 1900 feet.

The trail is mostly in very good shape, wide and smooth, but steep, very steep, gaining about 1000 feet a mile. (The trail sign says the peak is 4 miles, but the distance is definitely 4½ miles or more.) In the first mile are several creeks. At 1½ miles is an abandoned logging road. Follow it a short ½ mile to its end and pick up the trail again. Here is a good campsite in the woods, and also the last water.

The way relentlessly climbs 70 switchbacks (we counted them) to the summit ridge. At about switchback 45 the trail leaves tall Ponderosa pine and enters alpine trees and flowers — and glorious views of the lake. Near the ridge crest is a small sign pointing to "Last Water." Ignore it; the water is over the ridge and down the other side. From the crest it is almost ½ mile and 11 more switchbacks (for a total of 81) to the 6193-foot summit.

Enjoy views west to Nason Ridge, north up the Napeequa River to Clark Mountain, Chiwawa Ridge, and the Chiwawa valley, and east to endless hills. Below to the left is Fish Lake and directly beneath, Lake Wenatchee. At the head of the latter note the vast marshes and the meandering streams: at one point the White River comes within a few feet of the lake but snakes back another ¼ mile before entering. (All this magnificence of marshland and meanders, all the wildlife range, would be endangered if a dam now being plotted is allowed to materialize.) Ant-size boats can be seen on the lakes, and cars on the highways.

In early July the summit is a striking rock garden of blossoming phlox. In late summer and fall the upper trail offers blueberries to sate a perhaps gigantic thirst.

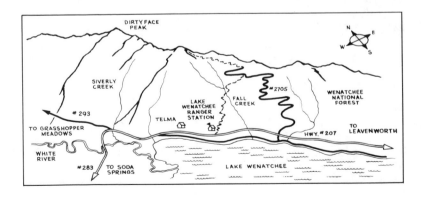

Round trip to Minotaur Lake 7 miles
Hiking time 5 hours
High point 5550 feet
Elevation gain 2000 feet
Best mid-July through October
One day or backpack
USGS Labyrinth Mtn.

63 Minotaur Lake

Minotaur Lake lies in a Grecian setting. Above and beyond are the rock walls of 6376-foot Labyrinth Mountain. Below is Theseus Lake. Heather meadows and alpine firs complete the mythological scene. No longer are seven girls and seven boys annually given in sacrifice to Minotaur, but each year visitors pay (in season) a tribute to the gods as the bugs take a libation of blood.

Drive to Lake Wenatchee Ranger Station (Hike 62) and continue 1½ miles to a junction. Turn left on Little Wenatchee River road No. 283 the 6 miles to Rainy Creek road first on No. 2714 then on No. 2728. Turn left 8 miles to road No. 2728B and 1 mile more to the trailhead, elevation 3800 feet, a couple hundred feet after crossing a small creek.

The first 1½ miles are on North Fork Rainy Creek trail No. 1517, maintained but muddy. The trail switchbacks up a hill, drops to cross an unnamed creek, and follows this stream ¾ mile. The North Fork trail goes on, but at about 2 miles find an unmaintained fisherman's path shooting straight up. There is no formal tread, only the groove pounded by many boots. The route gains 1500 feet in the next 2 miles. The track is well-marked and has plenty of water; views are limited to a few glimpses out through trees. At the end of the long, steep ascent the trail turns downvalley ½ mile, losing 100 feet, then turns again and heads up Minotaur Creek. Forest gives way to highland meadows and at 3½ miles is 5550-foot Minotaur Lake.

Around the shores are several good campsites. Cross the outlet and walk a few

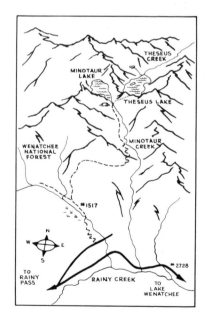

Cow parsnip

Theseus Lake

yards northeast to see 5060-foot Theseus Lake; a very steep path leads down to its shores and more good camps.

For broader views of mountains west to Stevens Pass, north to Glacier Peak, and east beyond Lake Wenatchee, scramble easily to open ridges above the lakes and wander the crests.

LITTLE WENATCHEE RIVER

64 Heather Lake

Round trip to Heather Lake 6½ miles
Hiking time 4 hours
High point 3953 feet
Elevation gain 1300 feet
Best July through October
One day or backpack
USGS Labyrinth Mtn. and Captain Point

Waters of the ½-mile-long lake-in-the-woods reflect rocks and gardens of Grizzly Peak. A family could be happy here for days, prowling about from a comfortable basecamp. So could doughty adventurers seeking more strenuous explorations.

Drive Little Wenatchee road No. 283 (Hike 63) 6 miles, turn left on road No. 2714, and at 6.5 miles keep right on road No. 2713. At 11.3 miles turn left on Lake Creek road No. 2801. At 13.6 miles the road ends at the start of hikers-only Heather Lake trail No. 1526, elevation 2700 feet.

The trail is a constant (nearly) joy, the minor ups and downs of the first 1½ miles, netting only 100 feet, easing muscles into their task. Having done so, it turns stern, crossing Lake Creek on a bridge and heading up seriously, leaving no doubt why machines and horses are forbidden. At 2½ miles, after gaining 900 feet, the grade relents and joy resumes in the last ¾ mile to Heather Lake, 3953 feet, with fine camps and a cozy privy.

The bare schist near the lake outlet, studded with tiny garnets, displays the grinding done by the glacier that scooped out the lake basin. Once these slabs were smooth, but eons of erosion have eaten away the polish, leaving only the grooves.

Attractive to the ambitious navigator with USGS map and compass, a way trail rounds the left side of the lake. At the far end follow a small stream south, climbing 700 feet in ½ mile to Glasses Lake, 4626 feet, so named because from neighboring peaks it looks like a pair of eyeglasses.

For more exercise, try Lake Louis and/or Grizzly Peak. From Heather Lake backtrack down the trail some 500 or 800 feet and climb wooded slopes to the left. Cliffs must be avoided and brush wrestled, but perseverance and clean living lead to the crest of the prominent ridge forming the north end of the Heather Cirque. As the ridge narrows a faint path appears. Soon Lake Louis can be seen to the right, 400 feet below, accessible via steep heather slopes studded with little cliffs. If Grizzly Peak is the choice, continue up the ridge to broad, heathery slopes, the 5770-foot summit, and panoramas from Mt. Rainier to Mt. Baker. (The USGS map shows Grizzly as a lesser point, only 5597 feet, ½ mile south. That has to be a mistake.)

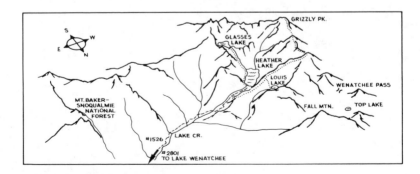

Glasses and Heather Lakes. Glacier Peak in distance

65 Meander Meadow— Kodak Peak

Round trip to Meander Meadow
12 miles, Kodak Peak 16 miles
Allow 2-3 days
High point (Kodak Peak) 6121 feet
Elevation gain 2000 feet to Meander
Meadow, 3100 feet to Kodak Peak
Best mid-July through October
USGS Poe Mtn. and Bench Mark Mtn.

A forest-and-meadow valley floor, a steep-and-hot struggle, and finally a superb little basin of grass and flowers and slow, deep meanders of the headwater stream. Above lie parklands of the Cascade Crest and endless easy wandering with views to everywhere.

Drive Little Wenatchee River road (Hike 63) 14½ miles to the end at Little Wenatchee Ford Campground and trailhead, elevation 3000 feet.

In ¼ mile the trail passes a junction with the Poe Mountain trail, which climbs steeply right in about 2½ miles to a 6015-foot summit of "Poet Ridge," a good day hike.

Meander Meadow

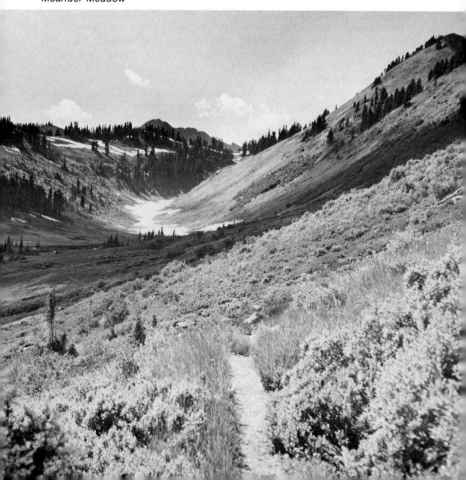

The first 4 miles of the valley trail are gently up and down, with a net gain of only 700 feet, alternating between forest and glade and frequently crossing creeks. The easy part ends at the edge of a vast meadow; here are a small creek and a campsite. The next 2 miles, gaining 1300 feet, may require courage and fortitude when the sun is blazing and flies are biting, especially if the sheep have been here recently. The way climbs grass and brush, becoming confused in a maze of sheep paths through sometimes-soggy greenery; look sharp to stay on the track. Once above the last meadow, in mixed trees and avalanche paths, the tread is distinct but steep. Fortunately there is a spring just where needed most. And views grow with every step. At 6 miles the trail drops a short bit into the basin of 5000-foot Meander Meadow; the camps are splendid and so are the hours of flower walking.

The trail crosses a meandering highland fragment of the Little Wenatchee River and climbs another open mile and 500 more feet to a ridge and trail fork. Go either way — north or south of a small hill — to the Pacific Crest Trail at 5450-foot Sauk Pass.

The junction with the Crest Trail gives the first view of Glacier and marks the boundary of the Glacier Peak Wilderness. Walk the trail north ½ mile to a 5630-foot saddle above Meander Meadow, on the east ridge of 6121-foot Kodak Peak. Climb blossoms ½ mile to the summit panorama and start cranking film through the Kodak.

For a loop trip, two alternate routes can be taken back down to Little Wenatchee Ford:

Cady Pass: See Hike 66.

Cady Ridge: From the junction with the Pacific Crest Trail at Sauk Pass, go 2 miles south and turn left on Cady Ridge trail. Tread is often lost in meadows, but the way climbs and contours rather obviously to the south of the highest point on the ridge and then follows ups and downs of the crest 2½ miles before starting a long, steep, dusty descent. There is no water on the ridge, which is not recommended for an up-hike. Total distance from the Crest to the road, about 5 miles.

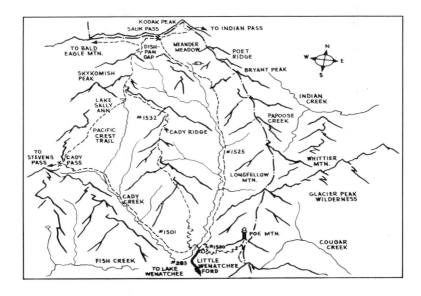

LITTLE WENATCHEE RIVER

66 Cady Pass to White Pass

Round trip 31 miles
Allow 4-6 days
High point (White Pass) 5900 feet
Elevation gain about 4000 feet in,
about 1200 feet out
Best late July through September
USGS Bench Mark Mtn.,
Poe Mtn., and Glacier Peak
Forest Service wilderness permit required
beyond Kodak Peak

Some argue this is the most beautiful segment of the entire Pacific Crest Trail in the Cascades. Certainly it offers one of the longest gentle meadow walks anywhere in the range, wandering at and above timberline a dozen miles.

Any part of the route is worth a visit but the best plan is to do the whole walk on a single trip.

Drive to Little Wenatchee Ford Campground, elevation 3000 feet (Hike 65). Park here and walk back down the road a short bit to the trailhead.

The trail drops to a bridge over the Little Wenatchee River. In ¼ mile more keep left at the junction with the Cady Ridge trail and follow Cady Creek 5 miles, gaining 1700 feet (including ups and downs), to wooded and waterless 4300-foot Cady Pass. Turn right on the Pacific Crest Trail, climbing 1300 feet in 2 miles to break out above timberline on the divide between Cady Creek and Pass Creek. Now the way goes around this side or that of one small knoll after another, alternating between Eastern and Western Washington. Then comes a traverse along the east slope of 6368-foot Skykomish Peak. At 2½ miles from Cady Pass (8 miles from the road) is 5479-foot Lake Sally Ann, a charming little tarn amid cliff-bordered meadows; this is the first dependable campsite on the trip, and badly overused.

Less than ½ mile north from the lake is an intersection with the Cady Ridge trail (Hike 65); another camp here in a broad meadow. Climb a waterfall-sparkling basin to 5680-foot Wards Pass and roam parkland atop and near the crest to 5600-foot Dishpan Gap at about 4¼ miles from Cady Pass. Here is a junction with access trails from the west (Hike 47).

The Crest Trail contours on in picturesque alpine trees and heather meadows to 5450-foot Sauk Pass, 5½ miles from Cady Pass, and two junctions with the little Wenatchee River trail (Hike 65). Traverse the green slopes of Kodak Peak to a 5630-foot saddle above the flat basin of Meander Meadow, take off for the short sidetrip to the 6121-foot summit of Kodak.

A descent across a gorgeous alpine basin and down forest leads to mostly-wooded

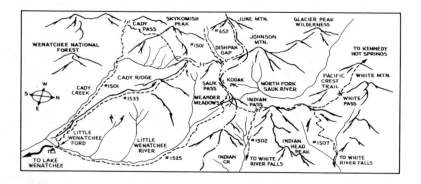

Sauk River valley from Crest Trail on side of Indian Head Peak

Indian Pass, 5000 feet, 7 miles from Cady Pass, and the junction with Indian Creek trail. Pleasant campsites in the pass — but usually no potable water except in early summer.

Climb forest, climb gardens around the side of Indian Head Peak to tiny Kid Pond and beyond to 5378-foot Lower White Pass, 8½ miles from Cady Pass, and the junction with the White River trail.

The final 1½ miles are the climax, past Reflection Pond into flower fields culminating at 5904-foot White Pass, 10 miles from Cady Pass, 15½ miles from the start.

For dramatic views of Glacier Peak and the White Chuck Meadows, walk the trail west to Red Pass or climb 7030-foot White Mountain. (For details, see Hike 46.)

If transportation can be arranged, a party can continue out to civilization via the North Fork Sauk River (Hike 46) or the White Chuck River (Hike 43).

67 Napeequa Valley via Boulder Pass

Round trip to Napeequa ford 28 miles
Allow 3-7 days
High point (Boulder Pass) 6250 feet
Elevation gain 4250 feet in,
   2000 feet out
Best mid-July through October
USGS Holden and Glacier Peak
Forest Service wilderness permit required

The Napeequa is the fabled Shangri La of the Cascades. As in the story, the only entries are high, rocky-snowy passes, below which lie lush green meadows surrounded by towering cliffs topped by glaciers. However, there are at least two differences from the valley described by James Hilton in his novel: no beautiful Chinese girls in a monastery; instead, there are, in season, swarms of vicious huge bugs to bedevil the poor pilgrim.

Drive to Lake Wenatchee Ranger Station (Hike 62) and continue 1½ miles to a junction. Keep right on the White River road to the end and trailhead, elevation 2200 feet.

Hike the White River trail 4 pleasant virtually-level miles through lovely virgin forest to the Boulder Pass trail, 2470 feet. Subsequent mileages are calculated from this junction.

The well-graded trail climbs steadily to Boulder Pass. In about 2½ miles is a

Napeequa River

crossing of Boulder Creek. At 4 miles is 5000-foot Basin Camp, under the walls of 8676-foot Clark Mountain. This is a logical and splendid spot to end the first day — and also a grand base for an extra day exploring a very faint path west to a 6150-foot saddle overlooking the White River. To find the path, cross the creek from camp to a point just under a slab of red rock on the opposite side of the valley. Even without tread the going would be fairly easy up open meadows.

From Basin Camp the trail climbs 2½ miles to 6250-foot Boulder Pass, the meadowy saddle to the immediate south of Clark Mountain. Look down into the Napeequa valley and over to Little Giant Pass (Hike 69). The hike to here, 10½ miles from the road, makes a strenuous but richly-rewarding 2-3-day trip.

To continue into Shangri La, descend monotonous switchbacks 3½ miles to the valley floor. This is the new-style Forest Service 10 percent-grade concept at its very worst, with switchbacks so flat (designed for fat dude horses, not true mountain horses, much less hikers) they invite shortcutting; even so, please resist the temptation, since each shortcut eventually becomes an erosion gully.

The trail reaches the valley floor — and trouble — at 4340 feet. The Forest Service is unable to keep a bridge across the swift-flowing Napeequa River, which can be forded at this point in late August but in high water is very treacherous.

If you can manage to cross, explorations are limited only by the time available. Follow the trail up the wide, green valley floor, probably the floor of an ancient lake, 5 or 6 miles; good camps are numerous. In ½ mile look to glaciers on Clark Mountain. In 2 miles pass under the falls of Louis Creek. Wander on and on, higher and higher, better and better, to trail's end in the moraines and creeks of Napeequa Basin, a deep hole half-ringed by dazzling glaciers, one of which tumbles nearly to the basin floor. Experienced off-rail travelers can find meager sidetrails into the hanging valleys of Louis Creek and High Pass Creek and climb to Louis Basin or 6876-foot High Pass.

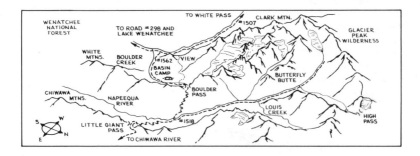

CHIWAWA RIVER

68 Mad River

Round trip to Blue Creek Guard
Station 11 miles
Hiking time 6 hours
High point 5400 feet
Elevation gain 1250 feet
Best late June through October
One day or backpack
USGS Sugarloaf, Chikamin, and
Silver Falls

Miles and miles of easy, pleasant roaming in the Entiat Mountains. Trails follow noisy creeks through picturesque glades, trails cross vast meadows of brilliant flowers, trails round shores of little lakes, and trails climb a mountain — all in all, a grand area for a weekend or for a week-long family vacation. Unfortunately, however, though there are 150 square miles here of wilderness (unprotected), the Forest Service permits motorcycles on the trails after they dry out in mid-July.

Some hikers may prefer to climb to the highlands via trail from the Entiat River road to avoid the poor access road from the Chiwawa; nevertheless, the latter approach is described — it's a horror for great big family sedans but not too bad for small and agile cars.

From Highway 2 between Stevens Pass and Leavenworth turn east on Highway 207 toward Lake Wenatchee State Park. Pass the park and at 4 miles, just past the Wenatchee River bridge, go straight ahead on a paved county road. Stick with this road, dodging sideroads to Fish Lake and the Chiwawa River road, and at 10½ miles cross the Chiwawa River in the middle of a vacation-home development. Turn north on the old Chiwawa River road No. 2746 for 1.6 miles and turn right on road No. 2722. At 7.3 miles from the bridge, after a final steep and narrow 2 miles that only a jeep or beetle could love, is Maverick Saddle. An even rougher road, probably best walked, leads .3 mile to the trailhead, signed "Mad River trail 1409." Elevation, 4250 feet.

The trail goes downriver 15 miles to Pine Flat on the Entiat River. It also goes upriver, your way to go. In ¾ mile pass the Hiyu Trail and at 1 mile cross a bridge over the Mad River — at this point really just a pretty creek. At 1½ miles is Jimmy Creek trail, first of three routes to the summit of 6719-foot Cougar Mountain. At 3 miles is an intersection with a trail that goes right to the top of Cougar, left to Lost Lake. At 4 miles cross Mad River on a driftwood log and at 4½ miles recross near a junction with Whistler Pig Creek trail, the third way up Cougar. At 5 miles is a broad meadow and at 5½ miles Blue Creek Guard Station, a splendid spot for a basecamp.

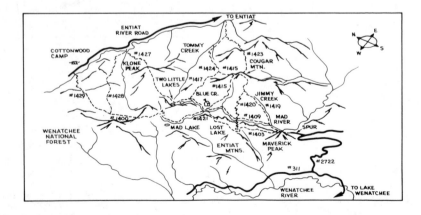

Mad River near Blue Creek Patrol Cabin

Many loops attract the explorer. One is to two little lakes named Two Little Lakes, with a short sidetrip up 6834-foot Klone Peak and a return past Mad Lake, set in an enormous meadow which in early summer dries out and becomes solid blue-red with lupine and paintbrush. Other loops are to Lost Lake and around Cougar Mountain. Pleasant alternative returns from the guard station are via Lost Lake.

CHIWAWA RIVER

69 Napeequa Valley via Little Giant Pass

Round trip to the pass 13 miles
Hiking time 9 hours
High point 6409 feet
Elevation gain 4200 feet in,
  300 feet out
Best mid-July through September
One day or backpack
USGS Holden
Forest Service wilderness permit required
  beyond the pass

Climb to the famous view of the fabled Napeequa Valley. Look down on the silvery river meandering through green meadows of the old lakebed. See the gleaming ice on Clark Mountain and Tenpeak, glimpse a piece of Glacier Peak. But you gotta really want it. Strong mountaineers turn pale at memories of Little Giant in sunshine and flytime. However, though more grueling than the Boulder Pass entry (Hike 67), the trail is 5 miles shorter and has no fearsome ford of the Napeequa to face. Ah, but it does have a fearsome ford of the Chiwawa River. But that's at the very beginning, so you get the bad news in time to choose another destination should the flood be boiling halfway up your Kelty.

Drive US 2 east from Stevens Pass 19 miles and turn left toward Lake Wenatchee. A short distance past the Wenatchee River bridge keep right at a Y and go 1½ miles. Turn left on paved road No. 311. Follow this road crossing the Chiwawa River on a concrete bridge. Proceed upvalley on the Chiwawa River road, about 19 miles. Spot a barricaded sideroad left, signed "Bridge Out." Park here, elevation 2600 feet.

Inspect remains of the bridge taken out by a flood in 1972. If the wade looks safe, do it, and follow roads through abandoned Maple Creek Campground, heading straight toward the mountainside. Just short of a little tin cabin cross a footbridge over a wash to the right and pretty soon pick up the trail. The old straight-up sheep driveway of evil reputation has been replaced (and the sheep are long gone from here, too) by a nicely-graded trail climbing the valley of Maple Creek in pretty pine forest, crossing a saddle, and dropping to South Fork Little Giant Creek at about 3¼ miles from the river, elevation 4000 feet. Campsites on both sides.

Now the way steepens and at about 4¾ miles half-scrambles up a broad rib of bare schist that splits the valley in two and on a sunny day will fry your boots. But shortly

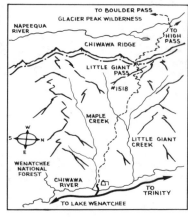

Glacier lilies

Napeequa River from Little Giant Pass. Clark Mountain on left

above, creeks begin, and camps that get progressively better, the last on a scenic meadow knoll at 5½ miles. A last lovely mile in greenery and marmots leads to the 6409-foot pass and the boundary of the Glacier Peak Wilderness, 6½ miles from the river.

Better views can be obtained by scrambling up the knobs on either side of the pass, which in addition to being a sensational grandstand is a glory of flowers.

The trail down to the Napeequa is sufficiently maintained for hikers — but not for horses or sheep, and bleached bones prove it. Watch your step — at spots a misstep could add you to the casualty list. The distance to the 4200-foot valley floor is 3 miles, and if the views don't have you raving the blossoms will. Or, in season, the flies. The trail proceeds upvalley 2 miles to the site of the bridge that is gone and the ford that remains to cross the river to the Boulder Pass trail (Hike 67). The best camps hereabouts are on gravel bars.

CHIWAWA RIVER

70 Spider Meadow and Pass

Round trip to upper Spider Meadow
  12½ miles
Hiking time 8 hours
High point 5100 feet
Elevation gain 1700 feet
Best mid-July through October
One day or backpack
USGS Holden

Round trip to Spider Pass 16 miles
Allow 2-3 days
High point 7100 feet
Elevation gain 3600 feet
Best late July through September
USGS Holden
Forest Service wilderness permit required

A glorious valley-bottom meadow in a seeming cul-de-sac amid rugged peaks. Yet the trail ingeniously breaks through the cliffs and climbs to a little "glacier" and a grand overlook of Lyman Basin and summits of the Cascade Crest. For hikers trained in use of the ice ax, this can be merely the beginning of a long and classic loop trip.

Drive about 22 miles on the Chiwawa River road (Hike 69) to the Phelps Creek road. Turn right 2 miles to the end and trailhead, elevation 3500 feet.

Miners of ages past built a wagon road up Phelps Creek and until the 1960 creation of the Glacier Peak Wilderness the track was used by jeeps. Nature is now reclaiming its own, but the walk begins on old ruts.

The gentle grade goes up and down in forest, passing the Carne Mountain trail in ¼ mile, Box Creek in 1 mile, and Chipmunk Creek in 1¾ miles. At 3½ miles, 4175 feet, are the crossing of Leroy Creek, the junction with Leroy Creek trail, a campsite, and the end of the old road.

The way continues through forest interspersed with flower gardens. At 5¼ miles, 4700 feet, is the spectacular opening-out into Spider Meadow. Red Mountain shows its cliffs and snows; the views include other walls enclosing Phelps headwaters — no way can be seen to escape the valley, an apparent deadend. A mile of flower walking leads to the crossing of Phelps Creek, 6¼ miles, 5000 feet. A bit beyond are ruins of a miner's cabin. Good camps here and throughout Spider Meadow. Hikers with only a day or a weekend may turn back here, well content.

But there is much more. A faint path extends to ancient prospects in the rocky-snowy-cliffy head of Phelps Creek, impressively stark and barren. The main trail does the unexpected, switchbacking improbably amid trees and rocks into a hanging

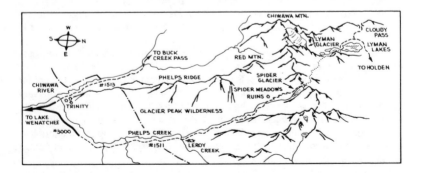

Chiwawa Mountain

valley, ending by waterfalls, larch-dotted knobs, and rocks and flowers at 7 miles, 6200 feet. A splendid if tiny campsite here; no wood but lots of water and long views downvalley to Spider Meadow, Mt. Maude, and Seven-Fingered Jack.

Immediately above is the narrow snowfield of Spider "Glacier." In a short mile, either up the snow-filled gully or along the easy and scenic rock spur to the east, is 7100-foot Spider Pass. Look down to the Lyman Glacier, the ice-devastated upper Lyman Basin, and the greenery of the lower basin.

An old trail ascends ¼ mile from the pass to a mine tunnel. One must marvel at the dogged energy of the man (he also built the cabin in Spider Meadow) who hauled machinery and supplies to so airy a spot. In the end he was injured by a cave-in and for days lay alone and helpless in the tunnel; his wife and children finally came to his rescue — and then insisted he give up mining.

The trail-less route down into upper Lyman Basin, 6000 feet, is partly on steep snow and requires ice axes. If hikers can manage this slope, their way is open to enjoy a 5-9 day loop trip of about 33 miles, one of the finest roamings in the North Cascades: Spider Pass, Lyman Basin, Lyman Lake, Cloudy Pass, Suiattle Pass, Miners Ridge, Buck Creek Pass, and Trinity, ending just 2 miles from the beginning. For route details, see Hikes 39, 40 and 71.

CHIWAWA RIVER

71 Buck Creek Pass

Round trip to pass 19 miles
Allow 2-3 days or more
High point 5800 feet
Elevation gain 3000 feet
Best late July through October
USGS Holden
Forest Service wilderness permit required

In a mountain range full to overflowing with "unique places," two things have given Buck Creek Pass a distinctive fame: an unusual richness of flower gardens rising from creek bottoms to high summits; the exceptional view of the grandest ice streams of Glacier Peak, seen across the broad, forested valley of the Suiattle River.

The trail lends itself to a variety of trips short and long: a day's walk as far as time allows; a weekend at the pass; or the start (or end) of multiday tours — such as over Middle Ridge to Image Lake and the Suiattle River road, or to Miners Ridge and Lyman Basin and Lake Chelan, or the classic loop suggested in Hike 70.

Drive about 24 miles on the Chiwawa River road (hike 70) to the end at Phelps Creek, elevation 2772 feet, next to the old mining town of Trinity.

Cross the Phelps Creek bridge into Trinity and follow trail signs past the buildings. The townsite is privately owned, so don't prowl around without specific permission; however, hikers have legal right of passage through the town. Continue over the valley floor on old roads become trail. At 1¼ miles is a sign announcing entry into the Glacier Peak Wilderness; a nice creek here in forest shade, much appreciated after the mostly-flat but mostly-hot walk thus far. The abandoned road climbs moderately to a junction at 1½ miles: the road leads straight ahead toward mining claims on Red Mountain; the trail turns left.

Tread goes down and up along the Chiwawa River, crosses the foaming torrent on a bridge at 2¾ miles, 3400 feet, and enters the valley of Buck Creek; just beyond the bridge is a campsite in woods.

The trail climbs a valley step, levels out and passes a forest camp in a patch of grass, switchbacks up another glacier-gouged step, and emerges from trees to traverse a wide avalanche meadow at 5 miles, 4300 feet. This is a good turnaround for a day hike, offering a view of the cliffs and hanging glaciers on the north wall of 8573-foot Buck Mountain.

At 7 miles, 4500 feet, is a footlog (maybe) crossing of Buck Creek, and also a camp; look up to eight waterfalls frothing down from hidden cirques. The trail recrosses the creek in ½ mile and crosses again in another ½ mile — both times maybe by footlog or maybe by wading. From the third crossing, 8¼ miles, 4900 feet, the route becomes steep, switchbacking from open valley up and up through trees, then meadows.

In the final ½ mile drop a bit to the green floor of a meandering stream, then climb

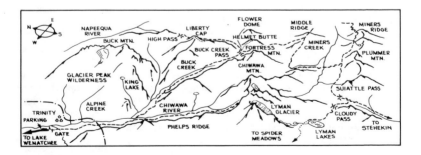

Glacier Peak from Buck Creek Pass

flowers and parkland to Buck Creek Pass, 9½ miles, 5800 feet. Camping has been banned at the pass itself to let mangled meadows recuperate but there are cozy, secluded mountain homes all around, before and beyond the pass.

Explorations? Enough for a magnificent week. First try 6200-foot Flower Dome, an evening's wander from the pass, to see sunset-colored snows of Glacier Peak beyond shadowed green vastness of the Suiattle. Then spend an afternoon on blossom-bright Liberty Cap, 6700 feet and exploring out on the deadend trail toward High Pass. Then the panoramas of 7366-foot Helmet Butte. And if more is wanted, onward to Middle Ridge, Image Lake, and where you will.

72 Duncan Hill

Round trip from road No. 2920
  14 miles
Hiking time 7 hours
High point 7819 feet
Elevation gain 3300 feet
Best mid-July through mid-October
One day or backpack
USGS Lucerne

Round trip via Anthem Creek trail
  16½ miles
Hiking time 12 hours
Elevation gain 4700 feet
One day or backpack

Sweat and pant and grumble to a former lookout site atop 7819-foot Duncan Hill and there be richly rewarded for the suffering with views up and down the Entiat Valley, from golden sagebrush hills to the rock-and-snow giants of Mt. Maude and Seven Fingered Jack. The trail traverses the peak, making possible two quite different routes that can be combined in a superb loop, if transportation can be arranged from one trailhead to another. It is also the opening leg of another fine loop to Milham Pass. To ameliorate the suffering, carry water to compensate for Nature's stinginess.

According to the Forest Service ranger, this trail is so little used by machines or feet you can have a purer wilderness experience here than on the bike-infested Entiat River trail. However, the soft pumice under the Duncan Hill trail has been so sorely grooved by a few motorbike wheels, one must often walk to the side of the trail.

Drive US 97 north from Wenatchee up the Columbia River 16 miles to Entiat. Turn left on the Entiat River road 33 miles (5 miles short of the end at Cottonwood Campground) and near North Fork Campground turn right on road No. 2920. Drive another 6 miles passing some unused (in 1979) side roads. At 5.8 miles stay right at a well traveled intersection, and at 5.9 miles go left a short distance to the trailhead, elevation 4800 feet.

The way sets out along wooded Duncan Ridge, climbing a 5549-foot knob, dropping 100 feet, then climbing again to 5800 feet. The grade moderates and about 3½ miles enters semi-meadows, with water and good camps, at the head of Duncan Creek. At about 5 miles there is a junction; keep right. At 6½ miles is another junction; again keep right and climb to the top of Duncan Hill, 7 miles from the road.

For the second approach, drive all the 38 miles to Cottonwood Campground, elevation 3144 feet. Try this route in May or June — there likely will be too much snow

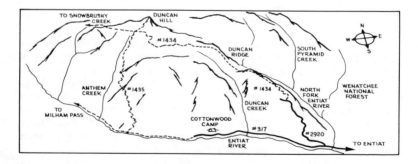

In May, deer are often seen alongside the Entiat River trail.

to reach the summit but the spring flowers are worth it, as is the abundance of does with fawns. (Look and photograph all you want, but never touch.)

Walk Entiat River trail No. 1400 a flattish 2½ miles and turn right, uphill, on Anthem Creek trail No. 1435. Now the fun begins — if your idea of entertainment is endless switchbacks gaining 2400 feet. At 5900 feet, 6 miles from the road, is the junction with Duncan Ridge trail No. 1434. For camping, turn left ¼ mile to water or 1 mile farther to a spot about 500 feet above the crossing of Anthem Creek. For the summit, turn right and climb open scree and flowers; the tread becomes obscure, so watch it. At 7¾ miles is a junction; take the upper trail to the summit, 8¼ miles.

If a party has two cars, or some other ingenious scheme, the two summit approaches make a dandy combination.

For a loop famous for flowers and views, at the 5900-foot junction turn left on Duncan Ridge trail the 6 up-and-down miles to Snowbrushy Creek trail and Milham Pass (Hike 74). Descend to the Entiat River trail and thence to the road.

Upper Larch Lake from trail below Fifth of July Mountain

ENTIAT RIVER

73 Larch Lakes Loop

Round trip (shorter loop) 18 miles
Allow 2-3 days
High point 6500 feet
Elevation gain 3400 feet
Best mid-July through September
USGS Lucerne
Forest Service wilderness permit required

Two clear lakes surrounded by alpine trees and meadows nestled under cliffs of Fifth of July Mountain. An entryway to miles and miles of up-and-down high trails along the Entiat Mountains.

Drive the Entiat River road (Hike 72) to the end, elevation 3144 feet. Hike the Entiat River trail 5 miles to Larch Lakes trail, 3800 feet. The way crosses the Entiat River, goes ¼ mile through stately forest, and then begins a grueling climb of 1900 feet in 2½ miles, switchbacking up a treeless, shadeless, waterless south slope. On a hot day the best plan is to loiter by the river until late afternoon, when sun has left the hillside — or better yet, cook dinner by the river and make the ascent in the cool of evening. Waiting until morning does no good; the hillside gets the first rays of sun.

Before starting up, note the waterfall high on the hillside to the west. Elevation of this falls (which comes from the lake outlet) provides a measure of how much climbing remains to be done.

The tortuous switchbacks abruptly flatten into a traverse along the shores of 5700-foot Lower Larch Lake, leading to a large meadow and acres of flat ground for camping. The trail continues a short ½ mile to Upper Larch Lake, more meadows, and the junction with the Pomas Creek trail. Here is a choice of loop trips.

For the longer of the two, climb north some 700 feet to Larch Lakes Pass, then amble on to 6350-foot Pomas Pass and down Pomas Creek to a junction with the Ice Creek trail, 6 miles from Upper Larch Lake. Go left to Ice Lakes (Hike 75) or right to the Entiat River trail.

For the shorter and more popular loop, follow the trail south around Upper Larch Lake. Tread disappears in meadows and several starts can be seen on the wooded hillside left of Fifth of July Mountain. If the path you select is terribly steep and then vanishes by a small stream, it's the wrong one. Cross the stream and pick up the correct one in a small flat meadow.

The trail climbs steadily more than a mile, with airy views down to Larch Lakes, then contours the mountain to a 6500-foot junction with the Cow Creek trail, the return route via Myrtle Lake.

The ascent of Fifth of July Mountain is a virtual must. Though the north face of the peak is a tall, rugged cliff, there's an easy side. Leave packs at the junction and climb the Garland Peak trail a mile south to 7000-foot Cow Creek Pass (some signs say Fifth of July Pass) and ascend the gentle south slope to the 7696-foot summit and a 360-degree panorama of Glacier, Clark, Maude, Rainier, and other peaks beyond counting.

The Cow Creek trail descends a steep 2 miles to the edge of Cow Meadows, just out of sight of the trail and offering a splendid camp, 5100 feet. Another 2 miles drop to sparkling, motorcycle-loud Myrtle Lake, 3700 feet, ½ mile from the Entiat River trail, reached at a point 3½ miles from the road-end.

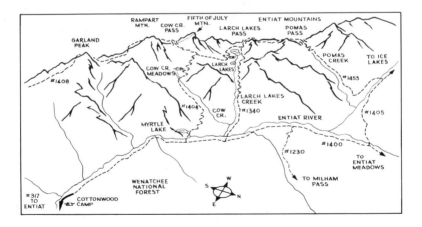

ENTIAT RIVER

74 Milham Pass— Emerald Park

Round trip from road to Milham Pass
25 miles
Allow 2-4 days
One-way trip to Lake Chelan
22½ miles
Allow 2-4 days
High point 6663 feet
Elevation gain 2700 feet
Elevation loss to Lake Chelan 5500 feet
Best mid-July through September
USGS Lucerne

A high pass surrounded by the snowy summits of Pinnacle Mountain and Saska, Emerald, and Cardinal Peaks, all standing well above 8000 feet. If transportation can be arranged, a one-way trip can be made down into the lovely meadows of Emerald Park and out to Lake Chelan. Alternatively, of course, the approach to Milham Pass can begin from the lake.

Drive the Entiat River road (Hike 72) to the end, elevation 3144 feet. Hike the Entiat River trail 6½ miles to the Snowbrushy Creek trail, 3900 feet. A few hundred feet below the junction is an excellent campsite in Snowbrushy Meadow.

The first mile climbs steeply from the Entiat valley into the Snowbrushy valley. Then the way parallels the creek, continuing a steady but reasonable ascent through open forest and large meadows. At about 2½ miles from the Entiat trail is the first decent camp, in trees; beyond are numerous sites in flowers and grass. At 3 miles the trail crosses a 5700-foot meadow under Gopher Mountain, with views of Saska Peak spires at the valley head and back out to Fifth of July Mountain, across the Entiat.

The way passes junctions with the Pyramid Mountain trail, climbing east to high viewpoints, and indistinct 45-Mile Sheep Driveway, climbing northwest over Borealis Ridge and descending to the Entiat River trail — offering a longer but more scenic return route.

From about 4½ miles the grade steepens for the final ascent to 6663-foot Milham Pass, 6 miles from the Entiat trail and 12½ miles from the road. To get the best views, scramble a few hundred feet up the ridge to the south, taking due caution among large and loose boulders on steep sections of the slope. The scramble is rewarded by a look down to the bright green meadow of Emerald Park and out east to peaks beyond Lake Chelan.

To continue to Lake Chelan, follow the Emerald Park Creek trail, which goes along the crest of the pass a few hundred feet north, then drops abruptly. A large snowfield generally covers the tread here until mid-July; descend with care.

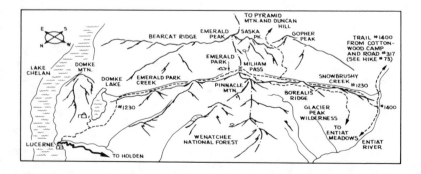

Emerald Park from Milham Pass

About 2 miles below the pass the trail enters the big meadow of Emerald Park, 5400 feet; a fine camp here. The next 6 miles to the Domke Lake trail, in sun-baked brush and scrub, then forest, are steep and rough.

From the Domke Lake junction, 2200 feet, a sidetrail leads a short mile to the 2192-foot lake and a campground. The main trail descends 2 miles from the junction to Lucerne, 10 miles from Milham Pass, on the shores of 1096-foot Lake Chelan. For boat service on the lake, see Hike 76.

75 Entiat Meadows and Ice Lakes

Round trip to Lower Ice Lake 28 miles
Allow 3-5 days
High point (knoll above lower lake)
6900 feet
Elevation gain 4200 feet
Best August through September
USGS Holden and Lucerne
Forest Service wilderness permit required

Round trip to Entiat Meadows 30 miles
Allow 3-4 days or more
High point 5500 feet
Elevation gain 2400 feet
Best July through October

A long trail with many byways to glory and at the two ends a pair of climaxes: a vast meadow under small glaciers hanging on the walls of a row of 9000-foot peaks; two high, remote lakes set in cirque basins close under cliffs of 9082-foot Mt. Maude, with alpine trees standing out starkly in a barren, glaciated landscape reminiscent of Khyber Pass.

Drive to the end of the Entiat River road (Hike 72), elevation 3144 feet.

Hike the Entiat River trail, engineered by the Forest Service the first 4½ miles into a motorcycle raceway; stay alert to avoid being knocked down or run over, especially by unsupervised children. At 3½ miles is the turnoff to the Cow Creek trail and Myrtle Lake, destination of most razzers. At 5 miles is the Larch Lakes trail (Hike 73) and at 5½ miles a campsite by Snowbrushy Creek. At 6½ miles, 3900 feet, is a beautiful camp below the trail in Snowbrushy Meadow; here too is the Snowbrushy Creek trail to Milham Pass (Hike 74). In 8 miles enter the Glacier Peak Wilderness and at 8¼ miles, 4300 feet, reach the split.

Ice Lakes

The Ice Creek trail goes left a short bit to a camp and the site of a bridge that washed out and has not been replaced, because the Entiat Ranger District staff believes wilderness designation precludes bridges; strange reasoning, for outside the wilderness area, the same rangers patrol trails on motorcycles. So, the Entiat River must be waded, easier said than done and often downright dangerous until late summer.

The way climbs gradually in forest the first mile, then drops 400 feet to Ice Creek. At

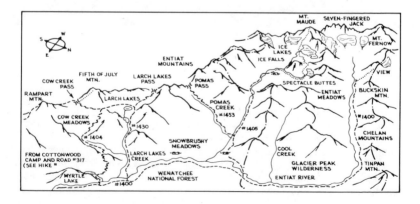

Ice Falls

Entiat Meadows and Mt. Maude

1½ miles, 4300 feet, is a junction with the Pomas Creek trail, an excellent alternate return route via Larch Lakes, as described in Hike 73.

The route goes along the river bottom, alternating between small alpine trees and meadows. At about 3 miles is a crossing of Ice Creek; since a footlog seldom is available and the channel is too wide to jump, be prepared to wade — and find out how well the creek lives up to its name. In another mile is another crossing, but this time the creek can be stepped over on rocks. At some 4½ miles from the Entiat trail, formal tread ends in a rocky meadow and delightful campsite, 5500 feet. The noisy creek drowns the sound of a pretty waterfall tumbling from Upper Ice Lake.

From the trail end a boot-built path follows the rocky meadow north to the valley head, passing the waterfall. Generally keep right of the creek, but cross to the left when the going looks easier there. The valley ends in a steep green hillside; above, in hanging cirques, lie the lakes. From a starting point to the right of the creek, scramble up game traces, crossing the creek and climbing between cliffs to its left. The way emerges onto a rocky knoll 100 feet above 6800-foot Lower Ice Lake, 6 miles from the Entiat trail. Camp on pumice barrens, not the fragile heather; no fires permitted.

Upper Ice Lake is a mile farther. Head southwest in a shallow alpine valley, below cliffs, to the outlet stream and follow the waters up to the 7200-foot lake, beautifully cold and desolate.

Mt. Maude cliffs are impressive from the lakes. However, the long and gentle south ridge of the peak offers an easy stroll. The scramble to the ridge, though, is not a complete cinch; patches of steep snow remain in summer and require an ice ax for safe passage. Maude is the only 9000-footer in the Cascades accessible to hikers, but they must be experienced hikers thoroughly familiar with the ice ax and the rules of safe travel on steep terrain. The summit views extend from Glacier Peak to the Columbia Plateau, from Mt. Rainier to an infinite alpine wilderness north.

Entiat Meadows

The way to the split is principally through forest; the final 7 miles up the Entiat River alternate between trees and meadows. Though sheep have not been allowed in the valley for years, some meadows still show deep rutting from thousands of hooves and some of the native flowers have never grown back.

At 13 miles, having gained only some 2000 feet thus far, the grade steepens a little for a final 12 miles and then, at about 5500 feet, the tread fades out in fields of heather and flowers. The camps are fine throughout the miles-long Entiat Meadows and the views are grand — up the cliffs of the huge cirque to the summits of Fernow, Seven-Fingered Jack, and Maude, all above 9000 feet, and to the remnants of the Entiat Glacier, which in days of glory excavated the cirque and gave the valley its contours.

If ambition persists, scramble up grassy slopes of the ridge to the north and look down into Railroad Creek and the town of Holden.

LAKE CHELAN—STEHEKIN RIVER

76 Chelan Lakeshore Trail

One-way trip from Prince Creek
17½ miles
Allow 2-4 days
High point 2200 feet
Elevation gain and loss
about 2600 feet
Best March through June
(or rainy summer days)
USGS Lucerne, Prince Creek,
Sun Mtn., and Stehekin

One-way trip from Moore 7 miles
Hiking time 4 hours
High point 2200 feet
Elevation gain and loss
about 1500 feet

While cruising along Lake Chelan, have you ever craved to know this unique "fiord" more intimately, in the unhurried way of the trail-tramper? If so, take a spring or early-summer hike, sometimes close to the wind-rippled waters, sometimes on high bluffs with sweeping views. Or try it in fall, for the gorgeous colors. Traverse grass-lands and rock buttresses, swinging into surprising little gorges with bubbling brooks, passing old homestead sites.

Rattlesnakes live here, but don't make a big thing of it. Unless cornered, snakes will run rather than fight.

Drive to Chelan or Twenty Five Mile Creek and board the passenger boat. (1979 schedule. Daily May 15 to September 30: leave Chelan 8:30 a.m., Twenty Five Mile Creek 10 a.m.; leave Stehekin 2:15 p.m. October 1 to May 15, Monday, Wednesday, and Friday only: leave Chelan 8:30 a.m., Twenty Five Mile Creek 9:45 a.m.; leave Stehekin 12:10 p.m.) Since only one daily round-trip is offered at present, overnight camping or hotel accommodations are necessary to do any hiking.

Backpackers can start at Prince Creek and hike the full 17½ miles to Stehekin. Day hikers can start at Fish Creek and have Stehekin overnight gear put off at Stehekin. If the party has reservations at North Cascades Lodge there, send word ahead and the resort people will pick up the baggage. Otherwise baggage will be left at the boat landing — generally safe.

When buying a ticket, tell the boatman where you want off. If you wish to be picked up along the lake, arrange the time and location beforehand. However, if plans

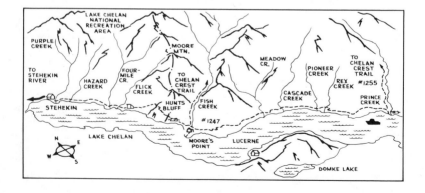

Lake Chelan and McGregor Mountain from Hunts Point

change while on the trail, waving a large white flag from one of the landings will bring the boat.

Because the boat reaches Prince Creek Camp in late morning, some parties prefer to laze away the afternoon on the alluvial fan and hoist packs the next morning. This also gives them time to brood over the crossing of Prince Creek, a cinch in summer and fall but next to impossible in spring snowmelt, a time when other creeks also can be raging horrors, arguing in favor of the fall-color season.

From Prince Creek the trail ascends slopes of grass and yellow pines, passes an old orchard, and goes around cliffy bluffs some 500 feet above the lake. The way descends nearly to the shore to avoid cliffs, then climbs again, entering the cool ravine of rocky Rex Creek at 3¾ miles, and at 4¼ miles the greenery of Pioneer Creek. Traversing high above the lake with views out, the trail crosses Cascade Creek, 6 miles. At 7 miles is Meadow Creek and a trail shelter. Close below and a bit beyond is a resort, Meadow Creek Lodge, a convenient spot to meet or leave the boat.

The trail climbs to an aspen grove and glacier-streamlined rock knobs and switch-backs down to Moore's Point, with deer-grazed pastures and gnarled orchards enclosed by New England-like stone walls. At 11 miles is the bridge over Fish Creek; a bit farther is a trail shelter, but a far pleasanter spot to stay is the campground ¼ mile off the lake trail on the glorious promontory of Moore's Point.

Now the trail climbs 1000 feet to Hunts Bluff, 13 miles, and the climax views. Look down the lake to Lucerne and up the lake to Stehekin, with Castle Mountain on the left and McGregor Mountain up the river valley. Boats below seem to be toys in a big, big pond.

The trail drops to the Lakeshore (Flick Creek) Shelter, 14 miles, and from here to Stehekin never again climbs high, wandering along the base of cliffs and through woods to Flick Creek, Four Mile Creek, Hazard Creek, and finally Stehekin, 17½ miles.

177

77 Chelan Summit Trail

One-way trip from South Navarre
38 miles
Allow 5-9 days
High point 7400 feet
Elevation gain about 8500 feet
Best early July through September
USGS South Navarre, Big Goat Mtn.,
Martin Peak, Prince Creek, Oval Peak,
Sun Mountain, and Stehekin

A miles-and-miles and days-and-days paradise of easy-roaming ridges and flower gardens and spectacular views westward to the main range of the Cascades, beyond the deep trench of Lake Chelan. Snowfree hiking starts weeks earlier, and the weather is much better, than in the main range, which traps and stops nearly all the maritime fogs, mists, and drizzles of summer. The trail generally traverses meadows and parkland at altitudes of 6000-6500 feet. It crosses a number of wide-view shoulders and passes, all about 7000 feet, and at three places dips briefly into forest at low points of some 5500 feet. The peaks (most of them easy walks or scrambles) run to above 8000 feet, climaxing in the Sawtooth group, topped by 8795-foot Oval Peak. Good-to-magnificent camps are spaced at intervals of 2-3 miles or less. Sidetrips (on or off trails) to lakes, passes, and peaks are so many and so appealing that one is constantly tempted to leave the main route and explore; for that reason a party should allow extra days for wandering.

The trail can be sampled by short trips from either end or by intersecting it via feeder trails from Lake Chelan on one side or the Methow and Twisp Rivers on the other. (For examples of the latter, see Hikes 83 and 84.) The perfect dream trip is hiking the whole length from South Navarre to Stehekin. But how, then, does one retrieve the car at the Navarre trailhead? By retracing steps the entire distance? Perhaps by having two cars in the party and leaving the other at the Lake Chelan boat dock? But then, how does one get the car up the atrocious roads to that trailhead? Some years no cars can make it, and some cars never can make it. Most parties thus settle for nearly-perfect dream trips that start on feeder trails from the lake and use the **Lady of**

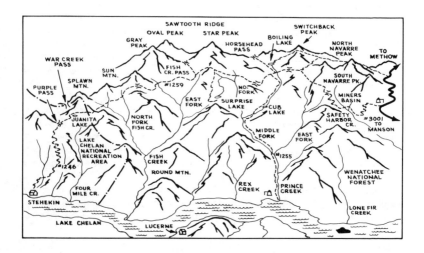

Horsethief Basin

Meadow above Prince Creek

the Lake (see Hike 76 for the schedule) to easily and neatly complete a loop. One of these feeders is noted in the following end-to-end description of the route.

South Navarre is at about the midpoint of an 86-mile loop road of which the last 20 miles on either side of the trailhead are usually passable in summer by jeeps and trucks and agile little cars, but a misery if not impossible for great big heavily-loaded passenger cars. The Grade Creek road ordinarily is the best choice, if open — but it's folly to set out on it without first checking at the Chelan Ranger Station. A longer-way-around alternative, but maybe taking less time, is the Gold Creek road from the Methow Valley (Hike 83), which intersects the loop road at a point only 10 atrocious miles from the main trailhead (8 miles from the hikers-only trailhead).

For the Grade Creek road, drive from Chelan toward Manson on Highway 150. At 2 miles beyond Manson turn right, following signs to Antilon Lake and Grade Creek road No. 3001, which climbs scenically and tortuously high above Lake Chelan to the trailhead at South Navarre Campground, elevation 6400 feet, 40 miles from Chelan.

Actually, there's a better start. Continue on the road 2 more miles to what locals call "Narvie Basin," and there, at 6440 feet, find a hikers-only alternate trail, an ancient sheepherders' route recently reopened. Ascend lovely gardens of the basin (fine camps) and climb to 7850 feet, very nearly to the summit, on wide-view North Navarre Peak. The way continues high on the ridge for more than 2 miles before descending to join the main trail at the 7400-foot pass above Horsethief Basin, at 6 miles from the start. Having no wheels and more scenery, this definitely is the best short trip in the Navarre vicinity, and the best start for a long trip, having about the same distance and elevation gain-loss as the main trail.

The main trail, razzed by motorcycles, begins by sidehilling 1 mile through rock gardens and silver forest of South Navarre Peak, 7870 feet, southernmost high peak of the Chelan Summit (Sawtooth Ridge), then descends over 1000 feet in forests to Safety Harbor Creek, then climbs to meadows of Miners Basin (4 miles) and a ridge crest. A traverse above headwater meanders of Safety Harbor Creek in Horsethief Basin leads to the 7400-foot pass (6½ miles) to East Fork Prince Creek.

The way drops a short, steep bit (snowy in early July) to the broad meadow basin and ascends gently around the base of Switchback Peak (8321 feet) to the 7120-foot pass (8½ miles) to Middle Fork Prince Creek. Down and around another wide parkland, at 10½ miles is the junction with the Middle Fork Prince Creek trail.

(This is the most popular feeder for a neat-and-easy loop, particularly because it leads to the heart of the very best part of the high country. Have the **Lady** drop you at Prince Creek Campground and take the Prince Creek trail, gaining 5500 feet in 11 miles. Camps at 4, 6, and 8 miles from the lake.)

From the junction the trail swings up to the 7050-foot saddle (12 miles) to North Fork Prince Creek, descends to a 5600-foot low point in forest (14½ miles), and climbs to flowers again and the 7400-foot pass (18½ miles) to East Fork Fish Creek. Above the pass is 8690-foot Star Peak, second-highest summit of Sawtooth Ridge. Only now (?) are the motorcycles required to stop, the only flaw northward being the bands of sheep that often chew the flowers and muddy the waters.

A short, steep drop, an up-and-down meadow traverse, and a gentle ascent lead to the 7400-foot pass (22 miles) to North Fork Fish Creek. Then comes a descent to a 5500-foot low point in trees (24½ miles) and a climb through gardens to a 7250-foot pass (27½ miles) to Four Mile Creek. Cairn-marked for a bit, the way descends some and traverses up and down to 6665-foot Lake Juanita (30 miles).

At 30½ miles is 6900-foot Purple Pass, famous for the gasps drawn from all who come here. Below — 5800 feet below — are wind-rippled, sun-sparkling waters of Lake Chelan, seeming close enough to reach in one long dive. However, most folk get down via hundreds of switchbacks descending Purple Creek to Stehekin, 38 miles; there's no danger of boredom, not with constant views of lake and Stehekin valley and the 7000-foot walls of peaks beyond, and watching out for rattlesnakes.

LAKE CHELAN—
STEHEKIN RIVER

78 Agnes Creek

One-way trip to Suiattle Pass
   or Cloudy Pass 18 miles
Hiking time 9 hours
High point (Suiattle Pass) 5983 feet
Elevation gain 4400 feet
Best mid-July through October
USGS McGregor Mtn., Mt. Lyall,
   and Holden
Forest Service wilderness permit required

One of the supreme long-and-wild, low-to-high valleys of the North Cascades. The Pacific Crest Trail gently ascends 18 miles of Agnes Creek forest to Suiattle Pass and connecting trails to Image Lake, Suiattle River, Buck Creek Pass, and a suggested loop trip (which can be done in the reverse direction as well) over Cloudy Pass and down Railroad Creek to Lake Chelan. For much shorter hikes there are trails along Agnes Gorge and into the West Fork Agnes — see below.

Trips from the Stehekin valley require special transportation arrangements. First a party must get to Stehekin, either by boat (for schedule, see Hike 76) or Chelan Air Service, located near the town of Chelan. Then a ride must be obtained to the trailhead. Formerly this was complicated, but now a shuttlebus runs the road on a regular schedule in summer months; fares are moderate.

In any event, a hiking party ordinarily can't get started on the trail until mid-afternoon of the first day, and must be off the trail by late morning of the last day to catch the boat. Any trip from the Stehekin must be planned with these time factors in mind.

Travel to High Bridge Ranger Station, 11 miles from Stehekin. About 500 feet beyond the bridge, on the left side of the road, is the Agnes Creek trailhead, elevation 1600 feet. The trail drops a few feet, crosses Agnes Creek, and commences a long, easy grade. Glimpses ahead of Agnes Mountain and glaciers on Dome Peak; to the rear, McGregor Mountain.

In 5 miles cross Pass Creek to 5 Mile Camp and a junction with the West Fork Agnes trail (see below). Keep left, following the South Fork Agnes. At 6½ miles the way comes to the edge of a deep canyon; to here the Agnes has been constantly heard but seldom seen. The trail stays high on the hillside, only occasionally nearing the river until beyond Swamp Creek.

The valley forest is continuously superb, with notable groves of cedar in the first 5 miles and a fine stand of large hemlock and fir near Swamp Creek. Good campsites at 5 Mile Camp and Swamp Creek, 8 miles.

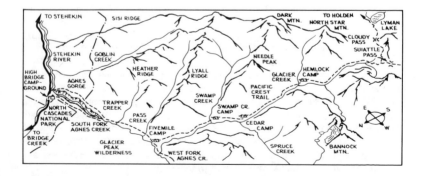

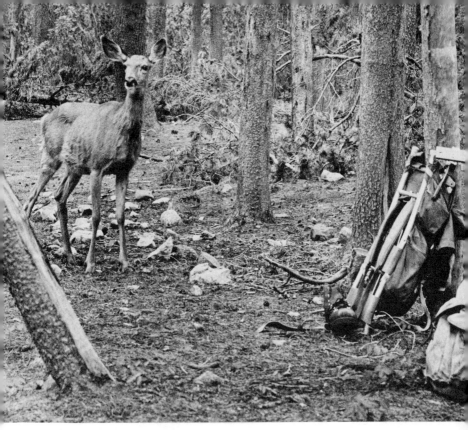

Five Mile Camp

Without ever getting particularly steep, at 17 miles and 5600 feet the trail reaches a timberline junction. The left goes a mile to 6400-foot Cloudy Pass and down Railroad Creek to Holden and Lucerne, as described in Hike 39. The right goes a mile to 6000-foot Suiattle Pass and down to the Suiattle River road, as described in Hike 38 and Hike 39.

The valley offers two shorter trips, each deservedly famous. For one, take the trail on the west side of Agnes Gorge, with awesome looks into the roaring canyon. Find the beginning about 250 feet up the road from High Bridge Campground. The trail deadends in some 1½ miles and there is no possible crossing of Agnes Creek to the main trail. (Once upon a time a bridge spanned the gorge; only the abutments remain — and terrifying it is to think of building a bridge here — or walking it!) This walk can be done as early as mid-May.

For the other, stop overnight at 2300-foot 5 Mile Camp, cross the Agnes on a bridge, and hike 3 miles on the West Fork Agnes trail to its deadend at the edge of grassy Agnes Meadow, 2500 feet, surrounded by towering rock walls topped by glaciers. To get better views, go back down the trail a short bit from the meadow and climb woods to a clearing. This sidetrip can be done in mid-June, a time when the meadow, just melted out of snow, is all one white-and-yellow glow of avalanche lily and spring beauty.

79 North Fork Bridge Creek

LAKE CHELAN—STEHEKIN RIVER

Round trip to cirque 21 miles
Allow 2-3 days
High point 4200 feet
Elevation gain 2000 feet
Best early July through October
USGS McGregor Mtn., and Mt. Logan
Park Service backcountry permit required

The North Cascades are distinguished by tall peaks — and also by deep holes. Among the most magnificent holes in the range is the huge cirque at the head of North Fork Bridge Creek, where breezes ripple meadow grasses beneath the ice-hung precipices of 9160-foot Goode Mountain, 8515-foot Storm King Peak, and 9087-foot Mt. Logan.

Travel to Bridge Creek, 16 miles from Stehekin (Hike 78). Just before the creek is the trailhead, elevation 2200 feet. The trail starts with a short, stiff climb of 400 feet, then goes up and down in woods, emerging to view of Memaloose Ridge and reaching the bridge over Bridge Creek at 2½ miles, 2600 feet. Across the bridge and ¼ mile beyond is a junction; go left on the North Fork trail.

The way ascends steeply a bit and gentles out. From brushy openings in the forest are views of rugged cliffs — a promise of what is to come. At 5½ miles is the last camp in the North Fork permitted by the Park Service, at Walker "Park," 3100 feet. This miserable camp in depressing fly-ridden weeds originally was built by the Forest Service to keep hunting-party horses out of the meadows. Hunters can't get in the basin now — and neither can hikers unless they can do as much walking in a day as a backcountry ranger. At 6½ miles, 3200 feet, are gravel bars of Grizzly Creek, a much pleasanter place for a camp but that is not permitted, in order to protect the fragile gravel. Here the maintained trail ends. The ford of the wide, cold, rushing creek is not really difficult or dangerous except in the high water of early summer of big storms, but neither is it for novice hikers, who may be forced to turn back.

The way leaves woods and wanders along the valley bottom in cottonwood groves, avalanche brush, and patches of grass. Immense views continue — up and up the 6000-foot north wall of Goode to icefalls of the Goode Glacier and towers of the summit.

The grade grows a little less gentle as the valley opens into the North Fork Meadows, at 9½ miles, 3800 feet, formerly the site of famous Many Waterfalls Camp, but that is now banned to protect the fragile boulders and hip-high grass. The scene is glorious with wide fields of grass, with neck-stretching gazes to Goode and Storm King and other views up and down the valley.

The scene is glorious with wide fields of grass, with neck-stretching gazes to Goode and Storm King and other views up and down the valley.

Paths here are confusing; climb the brushy knoll above to a resumption of tread amid

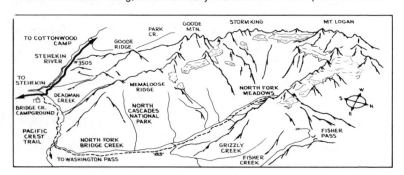

Mt. Goode and upper North Fork Bridge Creek

small and sparse trees. In a stand of old alpine timber which has escaped avalanches is the heather-surrounded wreckage of a miner's cabin. The trail emerges into grass and flowers of the cirque, 10½ miles, 4200 feet, and fades away. The views of Goode are better than ever, and Logan's walls are close above the amphitheater.

Roam upward into moraines and snowfields at the base of the cliffs. Experienced off-trail hikers can find game traces climbing intricately through brush and rocks of the steep slopes north, leading to higher meadows and moraines and an easy ramble to the 7000-foot ridge crest; look down the other side to the vast Douglas Glacier and out to the rough summits of Ragged Ridge and a peak-full horizon beyond.

185

80 Park Creek Pass

Round trip to pass 16 miles
Allow 3-4 days
High point 6100 feet
Elevation gain 3900 feet
Best mid-July through September
USGS Goode Mtn. and Mt. Logan
Park Service backcountry permit required

A wild and alpine pass on the Cascade Crest between the 9000-foot summits of Mt. Buckner and Mt. Logan, dividing snow waters flowing east to the Stehekin River and Lake Chelan and snow waters flowing west to the Skagit River and the inland sea. The pass and its surroundings rank among the scenic climaxes of the North Cascades National Park. A basecamp can be established for roaming, or a one-way trip made over the mountains from lowlands east to lowlands west. In either case, be aware the

Air view of Park Creek Pass. Mt. Buckner, left, Mt. Logan, right

Park Service has eliminated all camping near the pass. From the last permitted camp in Park Creek it is 5 miles, with a 2000-foot climb, over and down to Thunder Basin Camp.

Travel 18½ miles from Stehekin (Hike 78) to Park Creek Campground and trailhead, elevation 2300 feet.

The trail switchbacks steeply from the Stehekin into the hanging valley of Park Creek, then goes along near the stream through forest and occasional open patches with views up to Goode Ridge. At 2 miles, 3200 feet, is a one-site designated camp and a footlog crossing of the creek. Beyond here the grade gentles, continuing mostly in trees but with openings that give looks to Park Creek Ridge. At 3 miles is an obscure junction with a rough-and-sketchy climbers' route to 7680-foot Goode Ridge and broad views; the scramble is for experienced hikers only, but well worth the effort.

Crossing numerous creeks in green avalanche tracks, views growing of high peaks, the trail ascends gradually to 4000 feet, 4½ miles. Now the way leaves the main valley of Park Creek, which falls from the glaciers of Mt. Buckner, and traverses and switchbacks steeply into a hanging side-valley, gradually emerging into parkland. At 7 miles, 5700 feet, the trail flattens out in a magnificent meadow laced by streams and dotted by clumps of alpine trees, the view dominated by the north wall of 8200-foot Booker Mountain.

A final wander in heather and blossoms leads to the rocky, snowy defile of 6100-foot Park Creek Pass, 8 miles from the Stehekin road.

In order to preserve the fragile meadows, camping is not permitted in the area near the pass; however, fair basecamps for exploration are located in the forest at 5 miles and 2 miles west of the pass in Thunder Basin.

For one wandering, with grand views of Buckner, Booker, Storm King, and Goode (tallest of all at 9160 feet, third-highest non-volcanic peak in the Cascades), find an easy flowery route to the ridge southeast of the pass, overlooking the head of Park Creek. For another, descend west from the pass about ½ mile, leave the trail, and contour meadows and moraines to a mind-expanding vista of the giant Boston Glacier and great peaks standing far above the deep valley of Thunder Creek.

If transportation can be arranged, a one-way trip can be made on down Thunder Creek to Diablo Lake. See Hike 19.

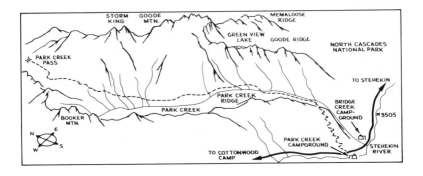

81 Horseshoe Basin (Stehekin)

Round trip from Cascade River road
  18 miles
Allow 3-4 days
Elevation gain 3000 feet in,
  1800 feet out

Round trip from Cottonwood Camp
  8 miles
Hiking time 5 hours
Elevation gain 2000 feet

Round trip from Stehekin trail 4 miles
Hiking time 2½ hours
High point (mine) 4800 feet
Elevation gain 1200 feet
Best July through October
USGS Cascade Pass and Goode Mtn.
Park Service backcountry permit required

Nine or more waterfalls tumble to the meadow floor of this cliff-ringed cirque. Above are glaciers on Sahale and Boston Peaks, both nearly 9000 feet, and the spires of Ripsaw Ridge. Wander the flowers and rocks and bubbling streams. The basin is well worth a visit in its own right, and makes a splendid sidetrip on the cross-mountain journey described in Hike 82.

The basin trail can be reached either from the west side of the Cascades or the east. For the west approach to the junction, ascend to Cascade Pass (Hike 30) and descend 3 miles into the Stehekin valley. For the east approach to the junction, travel to the end of auto road at Cottonwood Camp, 2800 feet, and walk the abandoned mining road 2 miles (Hike 78).

At an elevation of 3600 feet on the Stehekin River trail, the old mining road (dating from the 1950s) switchbacks sharply in a rockslide, climbing around and up the

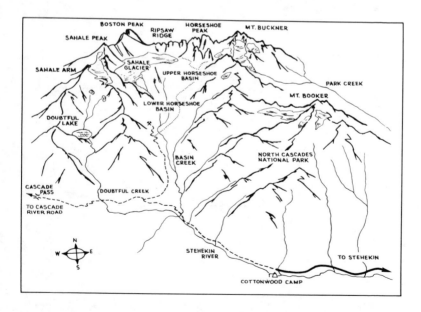

Glory Mountain, left, Trapper Mountain, right, from mine in Horseshoe Basin

mountainside to enter the hanging valley of Basin Creek. At 1½ miles the way emerges from brush and flattens out amid boulder-strewn meadows, 4200 feet. Impressive looks upward from flowery knolls to ice and crags, and a magical view and sound of white water on the glacier-excavated walls.

The old road continues ½ mile upward across the sloping floor of the basin to a mine tunnel at 4800 feet, close under the froth and splash of the falls. No mine is safe, so best just look in. Hours can be spent roaming the basin, enjoying.

Experienced off-trail hikers can go higher. Cross the creek a short way below the mine and scramble brushy slopes, amid small cliffs to the right of the vertical walls, into the upper cirque of Horseshoe Basin. The ascent is not easy, but doesn't require the ropes and other gear of mountain climbers; traces of an old miners' trail may be found, simplifying progress. Once on the high shelf under Mt. Buckner and Ripsaw Ridge, the way is open for extended explorations in heather and moraines, always looking down waterfalls to the lower basin and out to peaks beyond the Stehekin.

LAKE CHELAN—
STEHEKIN RIVER

82 Lake Chelan to Cascade River

One-way trip from Cottonwood Camp
  to Cascade River road 9 miles
Hiking time 6 hours
High point (Cascade Pass) 5400 feet
Elevation gain 2600 feet
Best mid-July through mid-October
USGS Goode Mtn. and Cascade Pass

One-way Boy Scout hike from
  Prince Creek to Cascade River 50 miles
Allow at least 6 days
Elevation gain 5900 feet,
  loss 2600 feet
Park Service backcountry permit required

A classic and historic cross-Cascades route from the Columbia River to Puget Sound. The trip can begin from either side of the range, but for a well-ordered progression of soup, salad, main course, and finally dessert (rather than the reverse) the approach from the east is recommended. The journey can be a quick-and-easy 9 miles or, by starting at Prince Creek, a Boy Scout "50-mile hike."

Voyage Lake Chelan, elevation 1098 feet. (See Hike 76 for boat schedule.)

Begin the 50-mile hike at Prince Creek (Hike 76), then walk the quiet road from the Stehekin boat landing to Cottonwood Camp, 2800 feet, 23 miles from Stehekin and the end of automobile traffic. Hikers who don't need a merit badge may ride the shuttlebus this far (Hike 78). Note that this is the last permitted camp between here and the Cascade River road-end; the haul must be done in one hard day, leaving precious little time and energy for explorations.

At Cottonwood Camp the way emerges from woods into avalanche greenery and goes along the valley bottom, with views of ridges above, to the grassy-and-bouldery avalanche fan at the crossing of Basin Creek, 3100 feet, a long mile from Cottonwood. In another ¾ mile, at 3600 feet, is the junction with the route to Horseshoe Basin (Hike 81).

Excellent trail climbs an enormous talus to Doubtful Creek, 4100 feet, ¾ mile from the Horseshoe Basin junction. The ford can be difficult and extremely dangerous in high water, and falls above and below forbid any easy detour. Now the trail rises into a hot slope of slide alder, ascending in 12 gentle switchbacks to the crest of the wooded

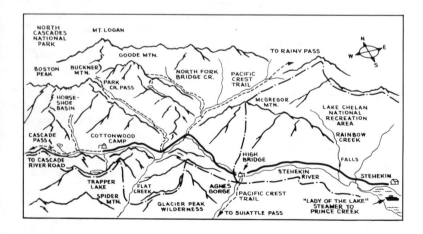

Stehekin valley and McGregor Mountain from Cascade Pass trail

ridge above Pelton Basin and views.

A short mile more leads to 5400-foot Cascade Pass and broader views. A supertrail descends 3¾ miles to the end of the Cascade River road, 3600 feet (Hike 30).

83 Foggy Dew Creek

Round trip to Sunrise Lake 13 miles
Hiking time 7½ hours
High point 7200 feet
Elevation gain 3700 feet
Best mid-July to October
Backpack
USGS Hungry Mtn. and Martin Peak

The name has magic for those who love the folk song, and the scene has more. Maybe the stiff climb of 3700 feet doesn't usually stir the poetry in a hiker's soul, but the loud waters of Foggy Dew Creek do, and the lake in a horseshoe cirque amid meadows, cliffs, and park-like larch and alpine firs. Try it in late September when the larch has turned to gold. However, since hunters are here then, maybe you'd prefer the midsummer solitude, caused in no small measure by the fishless condition of the shallow lake. A party could spend many days happily here, exploring the sidetrails on both sides of the divide, and, as well, the Chelan Summit Trail (Hike 77), to which this trail leads.

A note is appropriate here concerning driving to trailheads in the Methow-Twisp area. If you're coming from the Seattle area or south, Winthrop is the approximate swing point: for hikes starting up the Methow valley from there, the North Cascade Highway up the Skagit and over the mountains generally is the fastest approach from Seattle; for hikes starting down the Methow, including those in the Twisp valley, the old and honorable approach via Chelan and the Columbia River generally is fastest.

From Pateros on the Columbia River, drive the North Cascades Highway 17 miles toward Twisp. Just before crossing the Methow River, for the seventh time, turn left on a narrow county road 1 mile to a Forest Service sign. Here turn left on road No. 3109. (From Twisp drive 15 miles toward Pateros. Just before crossing the Methow River, for the third time, turn right on a narrow county road. In 1.5 miles turn right at the above-mentioned Forest Service sign.) Whichever way you reach it, from this sign drive South Fork Gold Creek road No. 3109 for 5 miles and turn left on road No. 3110. At 9.1 miles are the road-end and trailhead, elevation 3490 feet.

Foggy Dew trail No. 417 starts in selectively-logged (all the big pines) forest, climbs steadily, and at 2½ miles passes Foggy Dew Waterfall, something to sing about. At 3½ miles the valley and trail turn sharply right. At 4 miles cross a small tributary and at 5 miles come to a junction with the Martin Peak trail and the end of the motorcyclists.

At 5½ miles, 6700 feet, steepness lessens and the path ascends moderately in ever-expanding meadows. At 6 miles is a junction with a way trail to Sunrise Lake.

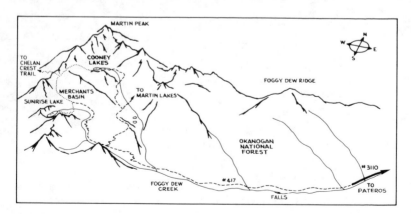

Sunrise Lake

From here the Foggy Dew trail to the Chelan Summit is seldom traveled and virtually vanishes in the meadow; a USGS map is essential to further navigation.

The well-used Sunrise Lake trail climbs ½ mile to the shores at 7200 feet, 6½ miles from the road. Campsites are lovely, explorations abound, and every prospect pleases. The lovely water may be contaminated by horses, though, so consider boiling or chemically treating before use.

84 Eagle Lakes Trail

Round trip to Lower Eagle Lake
  10 miles
Hiking time 5 hours
High point 6490 feet
Elevation gain 2200 feet in,
  200 feet out
Best mid-June through September
Backpack
USGS Martin Peak

Round trip to pass 13 miles
Hiking time 8 hours
High point 7590 feet
Elevation gain 2900 feet

Pretty Eagle Lakes under beetling crags. A 7590-foot pass overlooking Boiling Lake. A bushel of byways to other lakes and meadows. Easy-roaming routes to summits over 8000 feet, often-nameless points that are higher than many great and famous peaks elsewhere in the North Cascades. Views over forests and sagebrush to ranches in the Methow Valley, over vast deeps of the Lake Chelan trench to ice giants of the main range.

The first 4½ miles of the trail have been rebuilt smooth and wide. If you feel like running, the corners are nicely banked. But don't suppose the fancy design is for the benefit of racing hikers or galloping horses. The motorcyclists spoke up and the hikers didn't, and the hikers' former trail was turned into a motorcycle path. As typically happens when wheels churn dry Eastern Washington soils, by summer's end the trail is inches deep in a choking, powdery dust. To avoid dust and noise and the danger of being run over, it is recommended you do this trip in late June or early July when snowpatches still stop wheels but not feet.

Drive road No. 3109 (Hike 83) to the junction with road No. 3110 and stay on 3109 for 1.6 more miles to a Y. Take the left 6 miles to the road-end and the start of Eagle Lake trail No. 431, elevation 4700 feet.

After a nearly-level first mile traversing under cliffs, ascent begins and continues steadily. At ½ mile pass the Crater Lake trail, climbing 1700 feet in 3½ miles to two small lakes. At 2¼ miles pass the Martin Lake trail, going by several lakes and in 9 miles joining the Foggy Dew trail. At 2¾ miles is a tiny spring and a possible camp. At 4½ miles, 6900 feet, is a Y. The left drops 200 feet, at 5 miles from the road reaching Lower Eagle Lake, 6490 feet, with plentiful campsites. The right, the main trail, continues up, passing a short, unmarked way trail to 7110-foot Upper Eagle Lake and at 7½ miles reaching 7590-foot Horsehead Pass.

The trail descends 1 mile to Boiling Lake, a name that has led unknowing hikers to

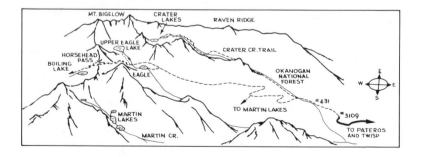

Eagle Lakes trail

imagine it must be a hot puddle in a sunbaked desert. Not at all — it's a cool pool in green meadows, with pleasant camps in the trees. The "boiling" is a common phenomenon in mountain lakes, bubbles of air rising from bottom mud. The trail continues down a bit more to join the Chelan Summit Trail (Hike 77).

Scatter Lake

TWISP RIVER

85 Scatter Lake

Round trip 9 miles
Hiking time 7½ hours
High point 7047 feet
Elevation gain 3900 feet
Best mid-July through October
Backpack
USGS Gilbert

If you want a definition for "grueling," try this, and don't be fooled by the mere 4½ miles of hiking because they gain 3900 feet, unmercifully hot in the midday summer sun. Why do it, then? You'll know when you get there. From the cirque walls scooped in the side of 8321-foot Abernathy Peak the sterile brown talus, streaked with mineralized yellow and red, slopes to the shore of a stunning blue gem ringed by larches, their delicate green a striking contrast to harsh colors of the rock.

Drive the North Cascades Highway (Hike 83) to Twisp and follow the Twisp River road, signed "Gilbert," 22 miles (pavement ends 14 miles). Just before crossing Scatter Creek go off right on a sideroad — actually the old river road. In 200 feet this road crosses Scatter Creek and forks. Go right 500 feet, passing a corral, to the start of Scatter Creek trail No. 427 (sign may be missing). Elevation, 3147 feet.

The route begins on a cat track dating from selective logging (all the big pines were selected). In ¼ mile the way becomes regular footpath (motorcycles banned). The first mile makes long, gentle switchbacks above the Twisp valley. The second mile traverses and switchbacks high above Scatter Creek. At 2½ miles the creek is close enough to get water. Be sure to do so.

At this point whoever built the trail apparently got tired of switchbacks; from now on when the hill is steep so is the path. At 3½ miles cross the Scatter Lake fork of Scatter Creek and follow the right side of the stream (USGS map is wrong). At 4 miles is a delightful camp in sound of a waterfall. The trail climbs above the falls, levels out, passes a tiny tarn, and reaches the shore of Scatter Lake, 7047 feet. It was worth it. Numerous pleasant camps but little wood.

The highest point of the cirque wall is Abernathy. The summit is to the left of the point with a red cap.

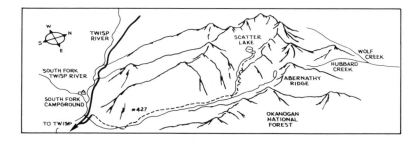

86 **Louis
Lake**

Round trip 10½ miles
Hiking time 5½ hours
High point 5351 feet
Elevation gain 2200 feet
Best mid-July through October
One day or backpack
USGS Gilbert

Beneath one of the most rugged stretches of Sawtooth Ridge is Louis Lake, large for this part of the Cascades, lying under terrific cliffs of 7742-foot Rennie Peak on the left and a nameless 8142-foot peak on the right. So narrow is the gash of a valley that even in midsummer the sun only touches the floor several hours a day.

Drive the Twisp River road (Hike 85) 22½ miles and just beyond South Creek Campground find the start of South Creek trail No. 401, elevation 3200 feet.

When motorcycles became popular the managers of this National Forest began spending tons of money reconstructing perfectly adequate hikers' trails into motorcycle highways. This is one of the racetracks, smoothly graded and easy on the anatomy of sit-down adventurers. Due to the trail's continuing into the North Cascades National Park, interagency agreement led to its being closed to machines in 1977. Unfortunately, there was a lack of comments from hikers and a clamor from motorcyclists and the trail was reopened in 1978.

The trail ascends gently in sound of South Creek cascading down a narrow canyon. At 2 miles, 3800 feet, is a junction. The main motorcycle trail continues up South Creek another 5½ miles to the National Park and a junction with Rainbow Creek trail. Go left on Louis Lake trail No. 428, dropping a bit to camps and a bridge over South Creek. The path, rough by previous comparison but plenty good for feet, switchbacks 500 feet up the hillside overlooking South Creek. South Creek Butte can be recognized by its red crest. Far upvalley the motorcycle highway is plainly visible slashing through the terrain, as highways are wont to do.

At about 3½ miles the path enters Louis Creek valley; a hiker has the dark suspicion he's entering a trap, a cul de sac with no escape through precipices. The trail contours high above Louis Creek with many ups and a few downs. At 4 miles, where the way parallels the stream, an opening appears in the otherwise unbroken expanse of high walls and the route proceeds through it to the lake and camps, 5351 feet.

The setting is spectacular. On the far shore is a small, tree-covered island. The lake surface is largely choked with enormous masses of driftwood from gigantic winter avalanches.

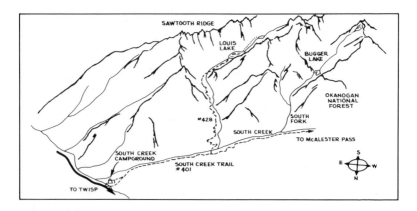

Louis Lake

A second lake, tiny, is 1 mile away and 500 feet higher, which sounds like an easy amble, but it ain't, the access mostly over broad bad fields of big boulders. If determined to get there anyhow, find a trail of sorts that goes from the camp around a thicket of slide alder, then parallels the shore.

TWISP RIVER

87 Twisp Pass—
Stiletto Vista

Round trip to Twisp Pass 8 miles
Hiking time 6-8 hours
High point 6064 feet
Elevation gain 2300 feet
Best late June through October
One day or backpack
USGS Gilbert and McAlester Mtn.
Park Service backcountry permit required
  for camping at Dagger Lake

Climb from Eastern Washington forest to Cascade Crest gardens, glacier-smoothed boulders, dramatic rock peaks, and views down into Bridge Creek and across to Goode and Logan. Then wander onward amid a glory of larch-dotted grass and flowers to an old lookout site with horizons so rich one wonders how the fire-spotter could ever have noticed smoke. For a special treat, do the walk in autumn when the air is cool and the alpine country is blazing with color.

Drive the Twisp River road (Hike 85) 25½ miles to the end. A short bit before the road-end is a parking area and the trailhead, elevation 3700 feet.

The trail begins by ascending moderately through woods, with occasional upvalley glimpses of pyramid-shaped Twisp Mountain. At 1½ miles are a junction with the North Fork Twisp River trail, a camp, and the last dependable water for a long, hot way. Ascend fairly steeply on soft-cushioned tread to 2½ miles; stop for a rest on ice-polished buttresses and views down to valley-bottom forest and up to the ragged ridge of Hock Mountain, above the glaciated basin of the South Fork headwaters. The trail emerges from trees to traverse a rocky sidehill, the rough tread sometimes blasted from cliffs. At about 3½ miles the route enters heather and flowers, coming in a short ½ mile to a small stream and pleasant campsites. A final ¼ mile climbs to Twisp Pass, 6064 feet, 4 miles, on the border of the North Cascades National Park.

For wider views, ascend meadows north and look down to Dagger Lake and Bridge Creek and across to Logan, Goode, Black, Frisco, and much more.

The trail drops steeply a mile to Dagger Lake and 4 more miles to Bridge Creek and a junction with the Pacific Crest Trail.

Don't go away without rambling the crest south from the pass about ¼ mile to the foot of Twisp Mountain and a magical surprise — a hidden little lake surrounded by grass and blossoms and alpine forest, a mountain home.

The open slopes north of the pass demand extended exploration. And here is another surprise. Hikers heading in the logical direction toward Stiletto Peak will stumble onto sketchy tread of an ancient trail. Follow the route up and down highlands, by sparkling creeks, to a green shelf under cliffs of 7660-foot Stiletto Peak, a fairy place of meandering streams and groves of wispy larch. Then comes a field of

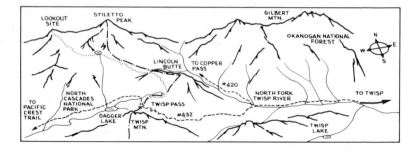

Dagger Lake from Twisp Pass

photogenic boulders, a rocky ridge, and the 7223 foot site of the old cabin. Look north over Copper Creek to Liberty Bell and Early Winter Spires, northwest to Tower, Cutthroat, Whistler, Arriva, and Black, southwest to McGregor, Glacier, and Bonanza, and south to Hock and Twisp — and these are merely a few of the peaks seen, not to mention the splendid valley. Stiletto Vista, former lookout site, is only 2 miles from Twisp Pass, an easy afternoon's roundtrip.

88 Wolf Creek

Round trip to basecamp 23 miles
Allow 2-5 days
High point 6000 feet
Elevation gain 2600 feet
Best June through October
USGS Midnight Mountain and Gilbert

A long walk up a long valley to meadows, old mines, wanders under tall walls of Abernathy Ridge, and glorious views from the crest of the ridge. Hikers have tended to neglect the area, put off by cows, horses, and motorcycles. However, none of these have as much fun as backpackers, who sweat a bit but then are free for the particular joy of this trip, the high-country roaming, that is forever impossible for folks who do their exploring sitting down.

From Winthrop drive the North Cascades Highway (see Hike 83 for discussion of how to get to Winthrop) east, the highway's downvalley direction, and at the town edge cross the Methow River. Immediately over the bridge, where the highway turns left to Twisp, go straight ahead, upvalley, 4 miles to pavement end and a Y. Go left on road No. 351 (unsigned in 1978). At 4.9 miles from Winthrop keep left, and at 5.0 miles left again on a road signed "Wolf Creek Ranch." At 5.6 miles the road is gated at a large parking area, the start of Wolf Creek trail No. 527 (unsigned in 1978). Elevation, 2400 feet.

The first 2 miles are high above Wolf Creek in partly-private pastures containing llamas, of all things; be sure to close all stock gates. Then, near the creek, the way enters forest and proceeds with easy ups and downs, crossing North Fork Wolf Creek and passing a junction with North Fork trail No. 528 (unsigned in 1978). At 4½ miles, just beyond a corral, an unsigned trail goes left to a very old patrol cabin and riverside camps that are very nice if not muddied by crowds of cows.

Around 5 miles the path changes from kindly to stern, with frequent steep ups and occasional gentle downs. At 8½ miles pass Abernathy trail No. 527 and at 9¼ miles Hubbard Creek trail No. 527B. Now the way steepens more, gaining 1200 feet in 1½ miles. At 10 miles begins a series of meadows and at 11 miles, 5800 feet, are Gardner Meadows and a good look to Abernathy Ridge. Forest is reentered and at 11½ miles, 6000 feet, is a great basecamp for explorations if not occupied by cows. The trail continues another ½ mile up Wolf Creek and ends.

The major attraction is up toward Abernathy Peak. Between the 11-mile marker and the suggested basecamp look for a long-abandoned mine trail partly hidden in brush;

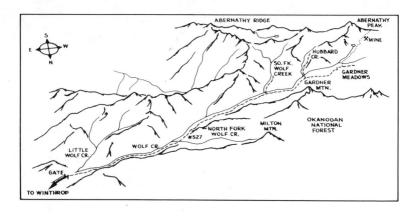

Abernathy Peak from Gardner Meadows

if you don't find it, just follow the stream up to Abernathy Lake. The trail goes by the little lake to the mine at 7400 feet, a place for marveling at the scenery and marveling at all the rusting equipment hauled laboriously up here. Don't enter the mine — it's dangerous. For more wanderings continue to the top of the ridge.

MIDDLE METHOW RIVER

89 Setting Sun Mountain

Round trip 6 miles
Hiking time 6 hours
High point 7253 feet
Elevation gain 2500 feet in,
  300 feet out
Best June to mid-October
One day
USGS Mazama

A long-abandoned lookout site on the south edge of the Pasayten Wilderness gives tremendous panoramas north into the Wilderness and west over the Methow Valley to great, craggy peaks of just plain wilderness in the Gardner-Silver Star area.

The Forest Service has abandoned the trail that until 25 years ago led easily to the top of the mountain from the Methow Valley. Reopening the route shouldn't take too much work, since the tread is still there; until that's done, though — and the Forest Service has no such plans at present — the start is hard to find and the tread is hard to follow, blocked by many fallen logs. Should hikers nevertheless want to give a try, from the Lost River landing strip drive the unmarked Yellow Jacket Creek road (sometimes impassable) that in recent years has shortened the trail by climbing to 4200 feet, and search for the unmarked trailhead. Several spots offer camping.

For the simplest way (1978) to climb the mountain, drive the North Cascades Highway to the Mazama junction (see Hike 83), turn off ½ mile to Mazama, and there turn east (right) 2 miles. Turn left onto road No. 375 and at 2.7 miles left again on road No. 3729. In 7 miles keep left at an unsigned junction, at 10.5 miles left again at another such, and at 11.8 miles right at still another. At 14 miles reach a pass; park just beyond a cattleguard. Elevation, 5000 feet.

You maybe were expecting a trail? There is none. But the route is easy and obvious, though advised only for clear weather with no danger of getting lost in clouds. Ascend straight up the slope on the north (right) side of the road, the hillside quite steep but with very few obstacles. Gradually the hill narrows to a ridge, but whatever you call it, it's steep, the angle not easing until near the top of a 7125-foot false summit. The true summit is ¾ mile to the northwest; follow the connecting ridge, losing 300 feet, then climbing to the 7253-foot top. Near the end walk remnants of old trail.

An abandoned telephone line goes from Setting Sun east along the ridge-crest Wilderness boundary, possibly connecting to a telephone line on an old trail up

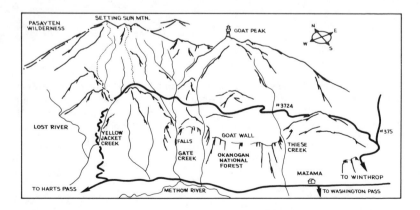

Silver Star Mountain from Setting Sun Mountain

Roundup Creek. Once there must have been a trail along the whole ridge, but investigations for this book didn't go into that.

On the way up, pay strict attention to the return route. Don't blaze trees or drape plastic ribbons — those methods no longer are acceptable. Just look over your shoulder frequently and memorize landmarks.

There's no water on the route so carry plenty; there can be lots of sun and sweat.

EARLY WINTERS CREEK

90 Cutthroat Pass

Round trip to Cutthroat Pass from
    Cutthroat Creek road-end 12 miles
Hiking time 6-8 hours
High point 6800 feet
Elevation gain 2300 feet
Best July to mid-October
One day or backpack
USGS Washington Pass

One-way trip from Rainy Pass to
    Cutthroat road-end 10½ miles
Hiking time 6-7 hours
High point 6800 feet
Elevation gain 1900 feet

A high ridge with impressive views, one of the most scenic sections of the Pacific Crest Trail. If transportation can be arranged, one can start at Rainy Pass and end at Cutthroat Creek, saving 400 feet of elevation gain. However, because a short side-

Cutthroat Peak

trip to sparkling Cutthroat Lake makes a refreshing rest stop, the trail is described starting from Cutthroat Creek.

Drive the North Cascades Highway east from the Skagit Valley over Rainy and Washington Passes, or west from the Methow Valley 14 miles from Winthrop to Early Winters and 11 miles more to Cutthroat Creek. Beyond the bridge turn right on the Cutthroat Creek road 1 mile to the road-end and trailhead, elevation 4500 feet.

The trail quickly crosses Cutthroat Creek and begins a gentle 1¾-mile ascent amid sparse rainshadow forest to a junction with the Cutthroat Lake trail. The 4935-foot lake (no camping) is ¼ mile away, well worth it. Fill canteens here — the upper regions are dry.

The next 2½ miles climb through big trees and little trees to meadows and a campsite (no water in late summer). A final short 2 miles lead upward to 6800-foot Cutthroat Pass, about 6 miles from the road-end.

It is absolutely essential to stroll to the knoll south of the pass for a better look at the country. Cutthroat Peak, 7865 feet, stands high and close. Eastward are the barren south slopes of Silver Star. Mighty Liberty Bell sticks its head above a nearby ridge. Far southwest over Porcupine Creek is glacier-clad Dome Peak.

If time and energy permit, make a sidetrip 1 mile north on the Pacific Crest Trail to a knoll above Granite Pass and striking views down to Swamp Creek headwaters and across to 8444-foot Tower Mountain, 8366-foot Golden Horn, and Azurite, Black, and countless more peaks in the distance. This portion of the Crest Trail may be blocked by snow until mid-August; if so, drop below the tread and cross the snow where it isn't dangerously steep.

From Cutthroat Pass the Crest Trail descends Porcupine Creek a pleasant 5 miles to Rainy Pass, the first 2 miles in meadows and the rest of the way in cool forest with numerous creeks. The trail ends a few hundred feet west of the summit of 4840-foot Rainy Pass.

The best camping is on flat spots near the head of Porcupine Creek, but none are close to water. At 3½ miles from Rainy Pass, ½ mile off the trail to the west, is a well-watered meadow camp.

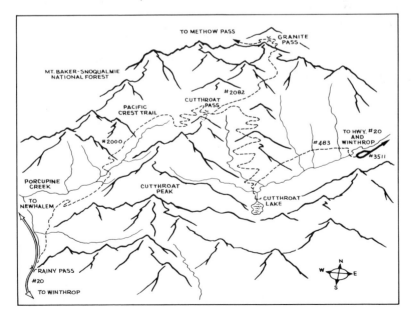

Corteo Peak from Maple Pass

EARLY WINTERS CREEK

91 Maple Pass

Round trip to pass 8 miles
Hiking time 4½ hours
High point 6600 feet
Elevation gain 1800 feet
Best mid-July to mid-October
One day
USGS Mt. Arriva, McGregor Mtn.,
and Rainy Pass

Lakes, little flower fields, small meadows, and big views sum up this delightful hike. The Forest Service built the trail to the pass, intending it to be a segment of the Pacific Crest Trail, only to discover what should have been obvious before, that the impact on fragile meadows would be disastrous. One wishes the trail never had been built, and certainly hopes it never will be completed; there are enough problems with it as things stand now.

Drive the North Cascades Highway west from the Skagit Valley or east from the Methow Valley (see Hike 83) to Rainy Pass and park at the south-side rest area. Find the trail signed "Lake Ann-Maple Pass." Elevation, 4855 feet.

As is typical of the Pacific Crest Freeway, the trail was blasted wide enough for a cavalry charge. However, unless this does become part of the Crest Trail, horses will continue to be banned, as they now are, and that's a mercy for the meadows. Elevation is gained at the easy grade typical of the freeway. At 1½ miles, 5400 feet, is a spur to Lake Ann, destination of most hikers. The ½-mile path goes along the outlet valley, nearly level, by two shallow lakelets, around marshes, to the shore. No camping at the lake but possibly at sites ¼ mile downstream.

The main trail ascends across a large rockslide, by 2 miles getting well above Lake Ann. At 3 miles is 6200-foot Heather Pass; from a switchback, look west to Black Peak, Lewis Peak and the cirque of Wing Lake, out of sight under the peak. The trail contours above cliffs 1000 feet above Lake Ann to Maple Pass at 4 miles, 6800 feet, and there abruptly ends.

Boot-beaten tracks go left and right. The path west leads to a 6870-foot high point with close views of Corteo and Black Peaks. The path east leads to a shoulder of Frisco Mountain and views down Maple Creek and out toward icy-white Dome Peak, Spire Point, Mt. Resplendent, and Glacier Peak.

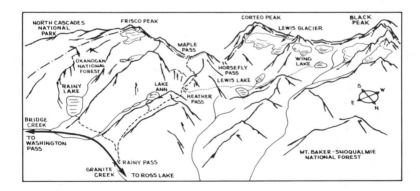

92 Robinson Pass

Round trip to Robinson Pass 18 miles
Hiking time 11 hours
High point 6200 feet
Elevation gain 2700 feet
Best late May through October
Backpack
USGS Slate Peak, Robinson Mtn.,
    Pasayten Peak, Mt. Lago, and Mazama

The geography here is not of the big glacier-monster crag sort characteristic of the North Cascades National Park, but spectacular it is — high, massive, shaggy ridges, naked and cliffy, reminding of Montana, and enormous U-shaped glacial-trough valleys, and awesome swaths of climax avalanches sweeping down from crests thousands of feet to bottoms and up the other sides. Also, lovely streams rush through parkland forests. And among the greatest appeals, trips in what the local folk call the "**wilderness** Wilderness" are like taking a ride in a time machine back to the 1930s. Solitude! Though Robinson Creek is a main thoroughfare into the heart of the Pasayten Wilderness, and a favorite with horsepeople, most come in the fall hunting season. Summer is lonesome even on the main trail, and on byways one can roam a hundred miles and maybe never see another soul.

Drive the North Cascades Highway (Hike 83) 1½ miles east of Early Winters Campground and turn left, cross the Methow River and go .4 mile to the hamlet of Mazama and turn left again, upvalley. At 7 miles pavement ends. At 9 miles cross Robinson Creek and turn right into a small campground, parking area, and trailhead, elevation 2500 feet.

The trail follows the creek ¼ mile, then switchbacks a couple hundred feet above the water. At 1½ miles enter the Pasayten Wilderness and shortly cross a bridge over Robinson Creek. Partly in rocky-brushy opens, partly in forest of big Ponderosa pines, then smaller firs, the way climbs steadily, moderately, just short of 3 miles crossing a steel bridge over Beauty Creek, which waterfalls down from Beauty Mountain, at 4 miles recrossing Robinson Creek on a bridge. The avalanche country has been entered, wide aisles cut in the forest, huge jackstraws piled up; from here on the way is a constant garden.

At 6 miles are a log crossing of Robinson Creek, now much smaller, and Porcupine Camp, in the woods and unappealing except in a storm. To here, avalanche meadows have broken the forest. From now on strips of forest break the ridge-to-creek meadows. A nice camp is located in the first broad meadow above Porcupine, and an

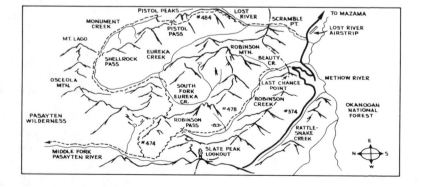

Robinson Pass and Slate Peak

even better in the second, at 6½ miles, 4900 feet, by the creek in a grove of large spruce trees.

But that may be the last water for camping, the creek dwindling fast and the trail anyhow leaving it to sidehill through the flower fields, rock gardens alternating with avalanche gardens, up to Robinson Pass at 9 miles, 6200 feet, a great broad gap through which the continental glacier flowed, which long-ago forest fires have cleared of big timber, where now the wildflowers blaze. In early summer water can be found for camping.

The pass is a trip in itself, but also is the takeoff for longer journeys. To begin, the open slopes above the pass invite easy roaming — to the left, up to big views from Peak 6935 and onward to Slate Pass, just 2 miles from Robinson Pass, and another mile to Slate Peak, or the other way on the long, lonesome heights of Gold Ridge; to the right, up to Peak 7720, and maybe along the ridge a mile to Devils Peak, or — climbers only — 2 miles more to 8726-foot Robinson Mountain, the neighborhood giant.

If trail-walking is preferred, descend Middle Fork Pasayten River, through gaspers of avalanches from Gold Ridge, the most impressive series of swaths in the Cascades; 15 miles from the pass is Soda Creek, and in another 8 miles, Canada. The classic long loop of the region is down the Middle Fork 6½ miles; up by Freds Lake to a 7100-foot pass, down by Lake Doris and around the headwaters of Eureka Creek, under Osceola, Carru, and Lago, three peaks between 8585 and 8745 feet, and up to Shellrock Pass, 7500 feet, 8 miles from the Middle Fork trail; 8½ miles down forests of Monument Creek and up by Lake in the Woods to Pistol Pass, 7100 feet; and 10¾ infamous miles down down and down, hot and thirsty, to the Lost River and out to the Methow road, reached at a point 2 miles from Robinson Creek; total loop, 43 miles, mucho elevation gain and loss, allow a week.

UPPER METHOW RIVER

93 Grasshopper Pass

Round trip 11 miles
Hiking time 6 hours
High point 7000 feet
Elevation gain 1000 feet in,
  1000 feet out
Best July through October
One day or backpack
USGS Slate Peak

Wide-open, big-sky meadow ridges with grand views of giant peaks and forested valleys. The entire hike is above timberline, contouring hillsides, traversing gardens, and sometimes following the exact Cascade Crest.

Drive the North Cascades Highway and turn off to Mazama (Hikes 83, 92), continue 20 miles upvalley to 6198-foot Harts Pass. From the pass turn left on the Meadow Campground road 2 miles, keeping right at a fork, to the road-end and trailhead, elevation 6400 feet.

The Pacific Crest Trail immediately leaves the trees, going along an open slope below diggings of the Brown Bear Mine and above a pretty meadow. The first mile is a gentle ascent to the 6600-foot east shoulder of a 7400-foot peak. The way swings around the south slopes of this peak to a saddle, 7000 feet, overlooking Ninetynine Basin at the head of Slate Creek, then contours 7386-foot Tatie Peak to another saddle, 6900 feet, and a magnificent picture of Mt. Ballard.

A moderate descent, with a stretch of switchbacks, leads around a 7500-foot peak. In a bouldery basin at 4 miles, 6600 feet, is the only dependable water on the trip, a cold little creek flowing from mossy rocks through a flower-and-heather meadow ringed by groves of larch. Splendid camps.

The trail climbs gradually a final mile to the broad swale of 6800-foot Grasshopper Pass. (Fine camps in early summer when snowmelt water is available.) But don't stop here — go ¼ mile more and a few feet higher on the ridge to a knob just before the trail

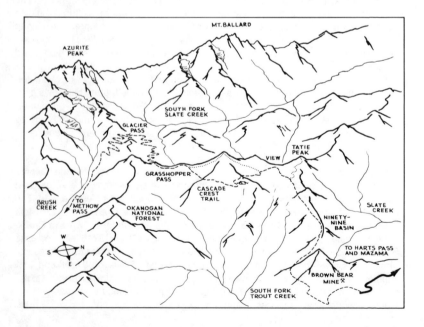

Azurite Peak and Grasshopper Pass

starts down and down to Glacier Pass. The views are dramatic across Slate Creek forests to 8440-foot Azurite Peak and 8301-foot Mt. Ballard. Eastward are meadows and trees of Trout Creek, flowing to the Methow.

Each of the peaks contoured by the trail invites a sidetrip of easy but steep scrambling to the summit, and the wanderings are endless amid larches and pines and spruces, flowers blossoming from scree and buttress, and the rocks — colorful shales, slates, conglomerates, and sandstones and an occasional igneous intrusion.

Experienced cross-country hikers don't really need the trail, but can scramble up and down the crest from road-end to Grasshopper Pass, climbing all three peaks. This route is not recommended for backpacking, but actually is the easiest way in early summer, when steep snow blocks the trail in several cold corners.

Round trip to Windy Pass 7 miles
Hiking time 5 hours
High point 7000 feet
Elevation gain 500 feet in,
**   1000 feet out**
Best early July through October
One day or backpack
USGS Slate Peak and Pasayten Peak

94 Windy Pass

In all the hundreds of miles of the Pacific Crest Trail in Washington, this ranks among the easiest and most scenic segments. The hike starts in meadows and stays high the entire way, contouring gardens thousands of feet above the trees of Slate Creek, magnificent views at every step.

Drive to Harts Pass (Hike 93) and turn right on the Slate Peak road about 1½ miles to the first switchback and a small parking area at the trailhead, elevation 6800 feet.

If the trip is being done in early July, don't be discouraged if the road beyond Harts Pass is blocked by snow and the trail beginning is blinding-white; snow lingers here later than on any other portion of the hike, and mostly-clear trail can be expected after a frosty start.

The Pacific Crest Trail gently climbs a meadow shelf the first ½ mile, contours steep slopes of Slate Peak, and drops into lovely little Benson Basin, with a creek and nice camps a few hundred feet below the tread. The way swings up and out to a spur ridge, contours to Buffalo Pass and another spur, and then descends above the gorgeous greenery of Barron Basin to 6257-foot Windy Pass and delightful camps in flowers and larch trees.

Sad to say, the wreckers have been here. Barron Basin is one of the most magnificent easy-to-reach glorylands in the Cascades, but much of it is private property and the miners have raised havoc, gouging delicate meadows with bulldozers, dumping garbage at will. This hike is bound to convert any casual walker into a fierce enemy of the ultra-permissive federal mining laws, which make it difficult if not impossible for the Forest Service to protect the land from professional swindlers-destroyers.

Sidetrips from the pass will make a person want the basin to be reclaimed for the public domain and placed within the Pasayten Wilderness, the boundary of which follows the divide, excluding the miner-mangled slopes to the west. Wander meadows north to the panoramas from 7290-foot Tamarack Peak, or walk the Crest

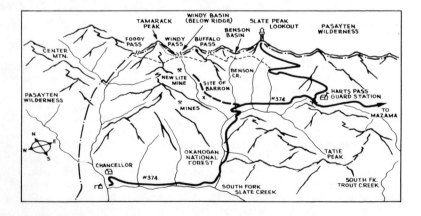

Trail a short mile into Windy Basin, offering the best — and most heavily-used — camps.

Views on the way? They start with Gardner Mountain, the Needles, Silver Star, Golden Horn, Tower Mountain, and especially the near bulks of Ballard and Azurite. Westerly, Jack and Crater dominate, but part of Baker can also be seen, and many more peaks. Easterly is the Pasayten country, high and remote.

Before or after the hike, take a sidetrip to the fire lookout on the 7440-foot summit of Slate Peak, the highest point in Washington State accessible to automobiles.

Crest Trail in Benson Basin. Mt. Ballard in distance

95 Three Fools Trail

One-way trip from Castle Pass to
 Ross Lake 27 miles
Allow 3-5 days
High point 7000 feet
Elevation gain about 10,000 feet
Best mid-July through September
USGS Slate Peak, Pasayten Peak, Shull
 Mtn., Castle Peak, Skagit Peak,
 and Hozomeen Mtn.

One-way trip from Harts Pass to Ross Lake
 54 miles
Allow 7-9 days

One-way trip from near Allison Pass
 (Canada) to Ross Lake 38 miles
Allow 5-7 days
Forest Service wilderness permit required

A classic highland wander from the Cascade Crest to Ross Lake, going up and down a lonesome trail through some of the wildest valleys, ridges, and meadows in the range. A one-way trip is recommended, starting at Harts Pass (or near Allison Pass in Canada) and ending at the lake. Special transportation arrangements are required: a drop-off at Harts Pass (or near Allison Pass); a pickup by boat from Ross Lake Resort (Hike 22) — though a party can, if desired, exit via the East Bank Trail.

Hike the Pacific Crest Trail (Hikes 94 and 101) 27 miles from Harts Pass (or 11 miles from near Allison Pass) to Castle Pass, elevation 5451 feet. Turn west on the Three Fools Trail (officially, Castle Pass trail No. 749), descending several hundred feet in ½ mile to a junction with the abandoned trail down Three Fools Creek. Turn right, climbing steeply in forest, then meadows. At 3 miles, 6000 feet, enter a little basin with a welcome creeklet — the first dependable water since before Castle Pass, and the last for several more miles. Sketchy tread ascends from the basin, swings around a spur, descends meadows to a saddle, and climbs the crest to a 6534-foot knob that ranks among the most magnificent viewpoints of the region: look north across the headwaters of Castle Creek to Castle Peak, Frosty Mountain in Canada, and Mt. Winthrop; look south across forests of Three Fools Creek to peaks along and west of the Cascade Crest; look in every direction and look for hours and never see all there is to be seen. The way drops from the knob and climbs ridgetop heather and parklands to 6 miles, 6400 feet, and a grandly scenic camp — but the only water, if any, is from snowmelt.

The trail angles down across a broad, steep flower garden, then switchbacks in

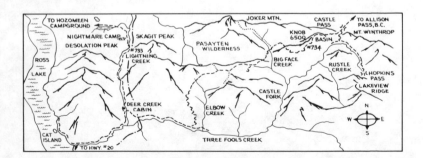

Woody Pass Peak from slopes of Three Fools Peak

what used to be forest until an avalanche roared down, wiping out a stretch of tread, to Big Face Creek, beneath the impressive wall of Joker Mountain. (At 6½ miles is a tumbling creek; below the trail here is a campsite on a tiny, wooded shelf.) At 8 miles, 5200 feet, the path reaches the valley bottom. For a mandatory sidetrip, fight through a bit of brush and climb the open basin to a high saddle with views out to Hozomeen and the Chilliwacks and below to a snowy cirque lake draining to Freezeout Creek.

The trail goes gently downstream in trees to a crossing of Big Face Creek at 8¾ miles, 4840 feet. Stay alert — tread proceeds straight ahead to a tangle of avalanched logs, but the trail actually turns right in a gravel wash to the ford. A possible camp here.

A long climb begins up forest to avalanche greenery; when tread vanishes in the grass go directly uphill, watching for cut logs. The ascent continues in trees, opens to meadows, and at 11½ miles, 6350 feet, tops out in the wide green pass, with broad views, between Big Face and Elbow Creeks. A sidetrail drops ¼ mile to a camp site and meandering stream in the glorious park of Elbow Basin. The main trail — tread missing for long stretches — contours and climbs north around the basin to a grassy swale (and a scenic camp, if snowmelt is available) near the ridge crest at 13 miles. Be sure to walk to the 6687-foot plateau summit of the ridge and views: east to the Cascade Crest; south to Jack Mountain; west to the Pickets, Chilliwacks, Desolation, and especially the nearby towers of Hozomeen; north into Canada.

The trail descends near and along the crest, with a look down to the tempting cirque of Freezeout Lake (accessible via a steep scramble), passing through a spectacular silver forest. A stern drop commences — down and down hot and dry burn meadows and young trees. The mouth grows parched, the knees loose and floppy. At 18 miles, 2350 feet, the trail at last touches Three Fools Creek and a possible camp; stop for an orgy of drinking and foot-soaking, and an understanding of why this trip is not recommended to begin at Ross Lake.

Hopes of an easy downhill water-grade hike are quickly dashed by a 1000-foot climb. The trail then goes down, goes up, and down and up, and finally on a forest bench to Lightning Creek at 23 miles, 1920 feet. Just before the crossing is a junction with the trail north to Nightmare Camp and Hozomeen (Hike 20). Just beyond the ford is Deer Lick Cabin (locked) and a campsite.

Again the trail climbs 1000 feet and goes down and up, high on the side of the Lightning Creek gorge, coming at last to a superb overlook of Ross Lake, a thousand feet below. The conclusion is a switchbacking descent to the lakeshore and Lightning Creek Camp, 1600 feet, 27 miles from Castle Pass.

Three Fools Peak from Lakeview Ridge, on the way to Three Fools Trail

Upper Goat Lake, near Crest Trail

Big Craggy Peak from Burch Mountain trail

96 Billy Goat Pass—
Burch Mountain

Round trip 10 miles
Hiking time 5 hours
High point 7782 feet
Elevation gain 3082 feet
Best late June through October
One day
USGS Billy Goat Mtn.
Forest Service wilderness permit required
for camping

Hike to the edge of the Pasayten Wilderness, climb toward an old lookout site, and see miles and miles of broad valleys and open ridges. Carry plenty of water and start early before the sun gets hot. This is big-scale country, often with long stretches between points of scenic interest. For hikers, therefore, early summer is the best season, when flowers and snowfields add variety.

Drive north from Winthrop on the paved Chewack River road. In 7½ miles cross the river and proceed up the west side of the valley. At 9 miles turn left on the Eightmile Creek road and follow it another 15 miles (The first 5 miles are paved. The last mile is steep and rough) to the road-end at a corral and old mine buildings, elevation 4800 feet.

The way is quite steep, climbing 1800 feet in 2½ miles through an open forest to Billy Goat Pass, 6600 feet, on the border of Pasayten Wilderness.

Hike a few hundred feet over the pass and find the Burch Mountain trail angling upward on the east (right-hand) side. This well constructed trail was once used by horses to supply a lookout on top of Burch Mountain, but it is now unmarked and doesn't show on any map. At first the tread is lost in meadows, but as the hillside steepens, the trail becomes distinct and, except for an occasional tree growing in the path, following it is no problem. The ascent is abrupt, quickly emerging to views southeast to Isabella Ridge and beyond to a horizon of 8000-foot peaks, the most dramatic being Big Craggy. Gaining some 600 feet in ¾ mile, the trail nearly reaches the ridge top then contours around a high rocky knoll to a broad saddle at 7200 feet. From there it switchbacks up to the 7782-foot summit of Burch Mountain 5 miles from the road-end. The lookout cabin has been gone for many years, but the views are still there.

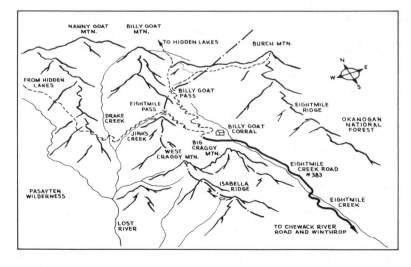

CHEWACK RIVER

97 Tiffany Mountain

Round trip from Freezeout Pass to the summit 6 miles
Hiking time 4 hours
High point 8242 feet
Elevation gain 1700 feet
Best July through September
One day
USGS Tiffany Mtn.

One-way trip via Tiffany Lake 8 miles
Hiking time 5 hours

A superb ridge walk to an 8242-foot summit with views west to distant peaks of the North Cascades, north into the Pasayten Wilderness, and east to farmlands of the Okanogan. The hike can be done as a round trip or — by use of two cars or a non-hiking assistant to move the car — as a one-way trip to either of two alternate trailheads.

Drive north from Winthrop on the paved Chewack River road. At 7½ miles, just before the paved road crosses the Chewack River, turn right on road No. 370. In less than 2 miles turn right again, still on road No. 370, which now follows Boulder Creek. In another 7 miles the road leaves Boulder Creek and goes up along Middle Bernhardt Creek. Continue 3 miles to Freezeout Pass and the trailhead, elevation 6500 feet.

(To place a car at the first of the alternate trailheads, drive 4 more miles to Tiffany Lake trail, 6240 feet. For the second, drive beyond the lake trail 5 miles on road No. 370 to a junction, turn right 1 mile on road No. 391 to Lone Frank Pass, and go another 6 miles to the trailhead, 4990 feet, signed "Tiffany Lake trail." If you reach Salmon Meadow, you've driven about 1 mile too far.)

From Freezeout Pass the trail climbs steadily 1½ miles through trees, then 1 mile above timberline, and begins a contour around the east side of the peak. Be sure to

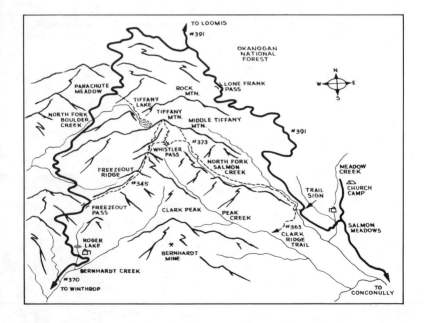

Tiffany Mountain from Tiffany Meadows

make the ½-mile (each way) sidetrip up grassy slopes to the unlimited views from the top of Tiffany Mountain, once the site of a fire lookout.

For the one-way trips, return to the trail and continue onward, descending through Whistler Pass to a 6800-foot junction, 3½ miles from Freezeout Pass, with the Tiffany Lake trail. Either go 4 miles to the road via 6480-foot Tiffany Lake or follow the open ridge above the North Fork Salmon Creek 2½ miles before dropping into trees and down to the road.

98 Horseshoe Basin (Pasayten)

Round trip to Sunny Pass 9 miles
Hiking time 6 hours
High point 7200 feet
Elevation gain 1200 feet
Best late June until mid-October
One day or backpack
USGS Horseshoe Basin
**Forest Service wilderness permit required
    for camping**

At the northeast extremity of the Cascades is a tundra country so unlike the main range a visitor wonders if he hasn't somehow missed a turn and ended up in the Arctic. Meadows for miles and miles, rolling from broad basins to rounded summits of peaks above 8000 feet, with views south over forests to Tiffany Mountain, east to Chopaka Mountain and the Okanogan Highlands, north far into Canada, and west across the Pasayten Wilderness to glaciered, dream-hazy giants of the Cascade Crest.

Drive west from Tonasket to Loomis and turn north. In 1.5 miles turn left at signs for Toats Coulee, cross the valley of Sinlahekin Creek, and start a long, steep climb up Toats Coulee on road No. 390. At 11 miles from Loomis is North Fork Campground and in another 5 miles a junction with narrow old road No. 390A signed "Iron Gate." Turn right and drive 7 rough and steep miles to the road-end and trailhead, elevation 6000 feet, at the new Iron Gate Camp (no water) on the boundary of the Pasayten Wilderness.

The first ½ mile is downhill along the abandoned road to the old Iron Gate Camp (no water). The trail from here begins in small lodgepole pine (most of this region was burned off by a series of huge fires in the 1920s) on the old road to Tungsten Mine, which operated as recently as the early 1950s. The grade is nearly flat ½ mile to cool waters of a branch of Clutch Creek, and then starts a moderate steady ascent. At 3¼ miles the route opens out into patches of grass and flowers. After a brief steep bit, at 4 miles the way abruptly opens from trees to the flowery, stream-bubbling nook of Sunny Basin and splendid Sunny Camp, 6900 feet.

The trail climbs ½ mile to 7200-foot Sunny Pass — be prepared to gasp and rave. All around spreads the enormous meadowland of Horseshoe Basin, demanding days of exploration. From the pass the Tungsten road drops left and the "pure" trail goes right, contouring gentle slopes of Horseshoe Mountain to grand basecamps in and near the wide flat of Horseshoe Pass, 7100 feet, 5¾ miles, and then contouring more glory to tiny Louden Lake, 6¾ miles (this lake dries up in late summer), and then on and on as described in Hike 99.

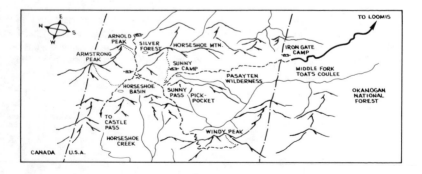

Horseshoe Basin

The roamings are unlimited. All the summits are easy flower walks — 7620-foot Pick Peak, 8000-foot Horseshoe Mountain, and 8076-foot Arnold Peak. The ridge north from 8106-foot Armstrong Peak has the added interest of monuments to mark the United States-Canada boundary. A more ambitious sidetrip is south from Sunny Pass 6 miles on the down-and-up trail to 8334-foot Windy Peak, highest in the area, and once the site of a fire lookout. Don't omit a short walk east through Horseshoe Pass to the immense silver forest at the head of Long Draw.

SINLAHEKIN CREEK

99 Boundary Trail

One-way trip (main route) from Iron Gate
    via Castle Pass to Harts Pass 94 miles
Allow 10 days or more
Best July through September
USGS Horseshoe Basin, Bauerman
    Ridge, Remmel Mtn., Ashnola Pass,
    Ashnola Mtn., Tatoosh Buttes,
    Frosty Creek, and Castle Peak
Forest Service wilderness permit required

As the golden eagle flies, it's 40 miles from the east edge of the Pasayten Wilderness to the Cascade Crest; as the backpacker walks it's twice that far, with some distance still remaining to reach civilization. Though the Pasayten country lacks the glaciers of more famous mountains west, and with few exceptions the peaks are rounded, unimpressive to a climber, there is a magnificent vastness of high ridges, snowfields, flower gardens, parklands, cold lakes, green forests, loud rivers. The weather is better and summer arrives earlier than in windward ranges. The trails are high much of the distance, often above 7000 feet, but are mostly snowfree in early July, an ideal time for the trip.

Length of the route precludes a detailed description in these pages. In any event the journey is for experienced wilderness travelers who have the routefinding skills needed to plan and find their own way. The notes below merely aim to stimulate the imagination.

Begin from the Iron Gate road-end (Hike 98) and walk to Horseshoe Basin and Louden Lake (6¾ miles). With ups and downs, always in highlands, the trail goes along Bauerman Ridge to Scheelite Pass (13¾ miles), the old buildings and garbage of Tungsten Mine (17¾ miles), and over Cathedral Pass to Cathedral Lakes (21¾ miles). The route this far makes a superb 4-7 day round trip from Iron Gate.

Continue west to Spanish Camp (26 miles) and the first descent to low elevation, at the Ashnola River (31½ miles). Climb high again, passing Sheep Mountain (34½ miles), Quartz Mountain (38 miles), and Bunker Hill (43¼ miles), then dropping to low forests of the Pasayten River (50½ miles).

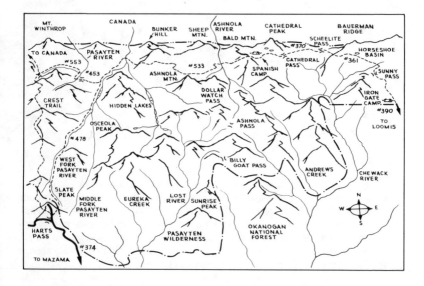

Boundary Trail through Horseshoe Basin

Follow the Pasayten River upstream to the Harrison Creek trail, cross a high ridge to Chuchuwanteen Creek (60 miles), and ascend Frosty Creek past Frosty Lake to Frosty Pass (66 miles) and on to Castle Pass (66¾ miles). From here take the Pacific Crest Trail 27 miles south (Hike 101) to Harts Pass, ending a trip of some 94 miles.

(For a shorter alternate, hike up the Pasayten River to Three Forks and ascend the West Fork Pasayten to Harts Pass. Trails branch west from this valley route to reach the Cascade Crest at Woody Pass and Holman Pass.)

However, for the true and complete Boundary Trail, go west from Castle Pass on the Three Fools Trail (Hike 95), hike south to Ross Dam and cross Ross Lake to the Little Beaver, and traverse the North Cascades National Park via Whatcom and Hannegan Passes (Hike 10), concluding the epic journey at the Ruth Creek road.

100 Chopaka Mountain

Round trip to Chopaka Mountain 4 miles
Hiking time 4 hours
High point 7882 feet
Elevation gain 1700 feet
Best mid-May through June,
  before cows arrive
One day
USGS Loomis and Horseshoe Basin

Stand on the absolute easternmost peak of the North Cascades. Look down a startling 6700-foot scarp to green pastures and orchards around Palmer Lake and meanders of the Similkameen River. Look east to the Okanogan Highlands, north into Canada and the beginnings of other ranges, and south over rolling forests of Toats Coulee Creek to Tiffany Mountain. And also look west across the Pasayten Wilderness to haze-dimmed, snowy summits of the Chelan Crest and Washington Pass. Aside from the geographical distinction of "farthest east," the special feature of the hike is the opportunity to wander alpine meadows as early as the middle of May, when windward ranges are so deep in snow that the coming of flowers seems an impossible dream.

Drive west from Tonasket to Loomis and turn north. In 1.5 miles turn left at signs for "Chopaka Lake-Toats Coulee," cross the valley of Sinlahekin Creek, ignore a road that goes right and uphill to Chopaka Lake, and start a long, steep climb up Toats Coulee on road No. 390. At 10 miles from Loomis, turn right 8 miles on the Ninemile Creek road (at this and all subsequent junctions follow "Chopaka Mountain" signs) to Cold Spring Campground, 6000 feet. The road generally is snowfree by Memorial Day; before then the way may be blocked by lingering snowfields, but if so this merely adds a mile or two to the hike. Carry water — Cold Spring has been contaminated by cattle. (The pleasant campground is fenced to keep cows **out,** but the cattlemen who "own" Chopaka use the fences to keep cows **in,** illegally employing the camp as a holding pen.)

Drive ¼ mile above Cold Spring to the road-end parking lot, elevation 6200 feet, with views west to Horseshoe Basin country. Hike a jeep track through spindly trees ½ mile. At 6600 feet, where the ruts start a sidehill contour northeast, find the first logical meadow opening and leave the track, climbing an obvious way toward the heights. The ascent winds amid clumps of alpine trees on open ground that would be flower-glorious were it not devastated by cattle. However, a slope of frost-wedged boulders stops the hooves and marks the upper end of mud-wallows and cow pies; the meadows now become genuine, clean, and natural. Emerge onto a broad plateau

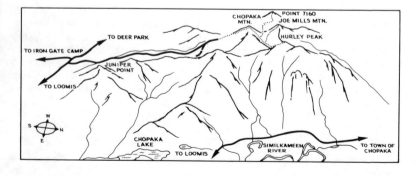

Rain shower approaching Chopaka Mountain

and amble a few more feet to the 7882-foot summit.

If another couple of hours are available, even better views can be had from Hurley Peak, a mile away. Drop north down a superb heather-and-flower meadow to a 7300-foot saddle and climb a gentle ridge to the 7820-foot top.

101 Pacific Crest Trail

**One-way trip from Allison Pass
  to Stevens Pass about 185 miles
Hiking time 20-25 days
Elevation gain about 30,000 feet
Best mid-July through September
Forest Service wilderness permit and
  Park Service backcountry permit
  required**

For rugged mountain scenery, the portion of the Pacific Crest National Scenic Trail between the Canadian border and Stevens Pass is the most spectacular long walking route in the nation. Undependable weather, late-melting snow, and many ups and downs make it also one of the most difficult and strenuous.

Few hikers have time to complete the trip in one season; most spread their efforts over a period of years, doing the trail in short sections. Those taking the whole trip at once generally prefer to start from the north, since pickup transportation at journey's end is easier to arrange at the south terminus. Though higher, the northern part of the trail lies in the rainshadow of great peaks to the west and thus gets less snow than the

Crest Trail on side of Slate Peak. Silver Star Mountain in distance

southern part; the north country and south country therefore open to travel simultaneously.

Note: If you ask U.S. Customs, U.S. Immigration, National Park Service, U.S. Forest Service, there is no practical legal way to backpack over the border. Hikers of both nations therefore find it better not to ask.

Drive the Trans-Canada Highway to E.C. Manning Provincial Park and find the trailhead on an unmarked side-road ½ mile east of the hotel-motel complex at Allison Pass. Hike 7½ miles up Castle Creek to the international boundary at Monument 78. Look east and west from the monument along the corridor cleared by boundary survey crews; in recent years the new growth has been cut or sprayed. Ascend Route Creek to Castle Pass, from which point south to Harts Pass the trail is almost continuously in meadowland, touching Hopkins Pass, climbing to Lakeview Ridge, crossing Woody Pass into Conie Basin and Rock Pass into Goat Lakes Basin, dropping to Holman Pass, swinging around Jim Mountain to Jim Pass, Foggy Pass, and Oregon Basin, crossing a shoulder of Tamarack Peak into Windy Basin, and from

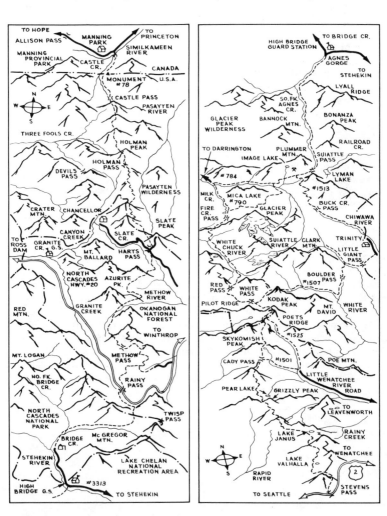

there continuing to Harts Pass as described in Hike 94. **Distance from Allison Pass to Harts Pass, 40 miles; elevation gain, about 8000 feet; hiking time, 4 days.**

From Harts Pass the next road junction is at Rainy Pass. The trail contours around Tatie Peak to Grasshopper Pass (Hike 93), drops to Glacier Pass, drops more into the West Fork Methow River, climbs over Methow Pass, and contours high around Tower Mountain to Granite Pass and on to Cutthroat Pass and down to Rainy Pass (Hike 90). **Distance from Harts Pass to Rainy Pass, 31 miles; elevation gain, about 4400 feet; hiking time, 4 days.**

The next segment is all downhill along Bridge Creek to the Stehekin River road. Walk east to the Rainy Lake-Bridge Creek Trail and descend forest to the road at Bridge Creek Campground (Hike 79). Hike 5 miles down the Stehekin River road to High Bridge Campground. **Distance from Rainy Pass to High Bridge, 16 miles; hiking time, 2 days.**

The next stage is the longest, with a difficult choice between the alternatives of going east or west of Glacier Peak. From High Bridge climb the Agnes valley to Suiattle Pass (Hike 78). Continue to Glacier Peak Mines (Hike 39) on the slopes of Plummer Mountain and choose either the west-of-Glacier or east-of-Glacier alternate.

East-of-Glacier alternate: Drop to Miners Creek, climb Middle Ridge, and continue to Buck Creek Pass (Hike 71). Descend Buck Creek to the old mining town of Trinity, walk the road to the Little Giant trail, cross Little Giant Pass (Hike 69) into the Napeequa valley, cross Boulder Pass (Hike 68) to the White River, and return via the White River trail to the Cascade Crest at Lower White Pass. **Distance from High Bridge to Lower White Pass, 79 miles; elevation gain, about 15,000 feet; hiking time 7 days.** The journey can be broken at either the Chiwawa River road or White River road.

West-of-Glacier alternate: Drop to the Suiattle River, climb the Vista Creek trail over ridges and down into Milk Creek (Hike 37), cross Fire Creek Pass to the White Chuck River (Hike 42), ascend the White Chuck to Red Pass (Hike 43), and continue via White Pass to Lower White Pass (Hike 65). **Distance from High Bridge to Lower White Pass, 66 miles; elevation gain, about 12,000 feet; hiking time, 6 days.** The journey can be broken by trail exits to the Suiattle River road, White Chuck River road, or North Fork Sauk River road.

The remainder of the way to Stevens Pass is comparatively level, wandering along the Cascade Crest with ups and downs, frequently alternating from east side to west side, mostly through open meadows of flowers or heather. From Lower White Pass (Hike 66) the trail stays high, dipping into forest only at Indian Pass and again at Cady Pass. From Cady Pass the route contours hillsides, traversing a mixture of forest and meadows past Pear Lake (Hike 58), climbing within a few hundred feet of Grizzly Peak, and proceeding onward to Janus Lake (Hike 60), Union Gap, Lake Valhalla (Hike 59), and finally Stevens Pass. **Distance from Lower White Pass to Stevens Pass, 32 miles; elevation gain, 5000 feet; hiking time, 4 days.**

For details of mileages and campsites, see the Forest Service map and log of the Pacific Crest Trail, available free from any Forest Service office, or one of the guidebooks to route.

Crest Trail on side of Indian Head Peak

STILL MORE HIKES IN THE NORTH CASCADES

This book covers the 100 miles from slopes of Mount Baker to the scarp of Chopaka Mountain and the 90-odd miles from Stevens Pass to Canada. A companion volume, **102 Hikes in the Alpine Lakes, South Cascades, and Olympics,** reaches south. Another, **103 Hikes in Southwestern British Columbia,** follows the North Cascades over the border to their end. Shorter walks than those herein are described in **Trips and Trails 1: Family Camps, Short Hikes, and View Roads Around the North Cascades.** The interface of Puget Sound lowlands and front ridges of the Cascades is treated in **Footsore 2 and 3: Walks and Hikes Around Puget Sound.** Approaches to and routes up peaks are the subject of **Cascade Alpine Guide**, a series of several volumes.

The 101 hikes have been selected to be representative of all the varied provinces of the North Cascades. However, it's a big country with hundreds of comparable trips. The books noted above describe many. Following is a sampling — some covered by the books, some not — that can be particularly recommended. The lack of detailed recipes may be compensated for by greater solitude.

Nooksack River

Twin Sisters Mountain

Church Mountain: Stiff climb to dramatic viewpoint

Silesia Creek from Canada: Reached from logging roads — lovely forest walk. Also accessible from Twin Lakes.

Bastile Ridge: Spectacular view of Coleman Glacier. Bridge gone (see Hike 2)

Middle Fork Nooksack to Park Butte: Glacier vistas and Mt. Baker views with sidetrip to Meadow Point

Keep Kool Trail to Yellow Aster Meadows: Steep trail to beautiful gardens also reached by Hike 4

Chilliwack River from Canada: Excellent forest walk from Chilliwack Lake

Green Creek Trail to Elbow Lake

Canyon Ridge: The loneliest trail in the vicinity, with many meadows and views

Price Lake: Climbers' path to rock-milky lake under Price Glacier

Easy Ridge: Abandoned trail to lookout site above Chilliwack River

Baker River

South Fork Nooksack to Bell Pass: Trail over 3964-foot pass. An interesting route to Park Butte

Elbow Lakes: 1½ miles on trail No. 679 and then cross-country to Lake Wiseman and Twin Sisters Mountain

Dock Butte: See **Trips and Trails.**

Boulder Ridge: Forest trail climbing to edge of Boulder Glacier

Swift Creek: Trail starts in meadows at Austin Pass and ends in forest near Baker Lake.

Anderson Lakes, Watson Lakes, and Anderson Butte: See **Trips and Trails.**

Shadow of Sentinels Nature Trail: ½-mile walk. See **Trips and Trails.**

Blue Lake: ¾-mile walk. See **Trips and Trails.**

Slide Lake: Easy 1-mile hike from road No. 347. See the massive rockslide that dammed the lake.

Shuksan Lake: 3-hour scramble on poor trail from road No. 3817 to lake in a deep cirque. Terrific views from trail

Skagit River-Ross Lake

Sauk Mountain: See **Trips and Trails.**

Pyramid Lake: A faint trail in forest to lake under Pyramid Peak

Diablo Lake trail: From Diablo Dam above cliffs to Ross Lake

Ruby Creek: Magnificent river walk near North Cascades Highway

Ruby Mountain: Abandoned trail, long climb, but spectacular views for the experienced hiker

Perry Creek: Sidetrip on virtually vanished trail from Little Beaver into a hanging valley

Silver Creek: Unmaintained valley trail on the west side of Ross Lake

Panther Creek and Fourth of July Pass: 10-mile forest hike to view Snowfield and Eldorado Peaks

Pierce Mountain Way: Alternate route up Sourdough Mountain

McKay Ridge

McAllister Creek: Dead-end trail from Thunder Creek

Jack Mountain: Little-used trail starting from Ruby Pasture and going 6 miles to end amid meadows and views and camps. From here climbers continue to summit of Jack.

Cascade River

Marble Creek: See **Trips and Trails.**

Kindy Creek: Little-used trail providing access to Kindy Creek and Sonny Boy Lakes

North Fork Stillaguamish River

Boulder River: See **Trips and Trails, Footsore 3.**

Whitehorse Glacier via Lone Tree Pass: 2 miles of very steep trail to viewpoint, then 2 miles of straight-up blazed route to pass, then a climbers' route to the ice.

Mt. Higgins: Hike or drive Seapost Road from a mile west of Hazel to reach trailhead in 3 miles. Trail climbs past Myrtle Lake to abandoned lookout site.

Suiattle River

Suiattle Mountain: From road No. 3304, 1 mile of unmaintained trail to Lake Tupso and White Creek road

Tenas Creek to Boulder Lake: Long trail hike to wooded lake, also reached by bushwhack from Tenas Creek road

Huckleberry Mountain: Old lookout site. The way is steep, the views big. Good hiking in May to snowline

Buck Creek: See **Trips and Trails.**

Sulphur Creek: See **Trips and Trails.**

Sulphur Mountain: Very steep trail to lookout site with commanding view of Suiattle River and Glacier Peak.

Canyon Lake and Totem Pass: A flower-covered ridge 5 miles from Image Lake

Suiattle River to Suiattle Glacier: Magnificent forests. Trail is lost beyond Chocolate Creek. From there on the route is for the experienced only.

Bedal Basin: Steep miner's trail to a small meadow beneath Sloan Peak

White Chuck River

Glacier Ridge: Shortcut to Pumice Cirque on a steep trail, partially maintained by a Boy Scout troop, past an old lookout site

Crystal Lake: 1½ miles to a lake in a deep valley

North Fork Sauk River

Cougar Lakes trail: Noted for its many waterfalls

Bald Eagle Trail: Little-used route with fine forests and meadows and great views

South Fork Stillaguamish River

Mt. Pilchuck: Popular hike to wide-view lookout (**Footsore 3**)

Big Four Glacier: See **Trips and Trails.**

Heather Lake: Very popular 2-mile hike to alpine lake (**Footsore 3**)

Lake 22: Very popular 2½-mile hike to alpine lake (**Footsore 3**)

Pinnacle Lake: 1½ miles of poor trail to beautiful lake with views (**Footsore 3**)

Meadow Mountain: Tiny meadows on wooded ridge from Tupso Lake

Mallardy Ridge trail: 14 miles of unmaintained trail on wooded ridge

Silver Gulch trail: 1½ miles on old miners' path to open ridges

Marble Gulch: Plans are to rebuild this old miners' trail.

Sunrise Mine trail No. 707 to Headlee Pass: Very difficult trail from road No. 3012

Martin Creek trail: Steep jeep trail to forested valley

South Fork Sauk River

76 Gulch: A route, no maintained trail, to old mines

Skykomish River

Mt. Stickney: A route on logging roads and through bushes to high views (**Footsore 2**)

Sultan Basin: Short trail climbing beside waterfalls to Little and Big Greider Lakes (**Footsore 2**)

Mineral City-Silver Creek: Rich in mining history. The walk follows old logging roads.

Howard Creek: No trail, a bushwhacking climbers' route to Spire Mountain

Troublesome Creek: Dead-end trail through the woods. See **Trips and Trails.**

West Cady Ridge: Miles of open ridge-walking — no water

North Fork Skykomish River: A long, forested, river-bottom approach to Crest Trail. Hike the trail now, before a logging road wipes it out.

Scorpion Mountain: An airy road leads to an airy ridge walk to a lookout site.

Meadow Creek to Fortune Ponds, Peaches and Pear Lakes, Quartz Creek: Steep, long trail through virgin forest to Curry Gap

Little Wenatchee River

Poe Mountain: Steep, easy trail to lookout site with big views

Cockeye Creek trail: Over Poet Ridge to Panther Creek. Easy access to Poe Mountain from road No. 2817C

White River

Panther Creek: Long valley approach gives access to Ibex Creek canyon and Cougar Creek-Cockeye Creek.

White River: 14-mile valley approach to Crest Trail, noted for beautiful forest

Indian Creek: 13-mile valley approach to Crest Trail

Twin Lakes: Easy hike to popular mountain lakes

Mt. David: A long 8 miles to a high lookout site

Chiwawa River

Schaefer Lake: 5-mile climb to high country of beautiful Chiwawa Ridge. Difficult river crossing

Leroy Creek: Steep trail to meadows and camps in a basin on the side of Mt. Maude, with access over the ridge to Ice Lakes

Red Mountain: Old mining road, then trail, goes 7 miles from Buck Creek trail to high on Red Mountain. From trail-end a short, easy route leads over Red Mountain Pass and down to Spider Glacier

Chiwawa Basin: The basin trail leaves the Red Mountain trail at basin entrance and winds through broad meadows, rejoining Red Mountain trail up high.

Phelps Ridge: A trail going from Red Mountain trail over the ridge, and down to Phelps Creek trail at a point just above Leroy Creek

Massie Lake: 6-mile trail from Chiwawa Basin up to Massie Lake and then up the ridge under Pass No Pass to join the Buck Creek trail

Basalt Ridge: Long, dry climb, partly steep and brushy, to magnificent scenery

Estes Butte: Steep and rocky trail to old lookout site. Few, if any, views

Carne Mountain: High meadows along the Entiat Mountains — possible sidetrip to Ice Lakes

High Pass trail: 3 miles of glorious ridge-walking from Buck Creek Pass

Entiat River

Pyramid Creek to Pyramid Peak: 16-mile trail along Chelan Mountains

Lake Chelan-Stehekin River

Domke Mountain: Sidetrail from Domke Lake trail climbs to old lookout site and views up Lake Chelan and Railroad Creek

Holden Lake: 4-mile sidetrip from Railroad Creek to a lake in a hanging valley. Views of Mary Green Glacier on Bonanza Peak

Flat Creek: Dead-end, 3.3-mile trail into a scenic valley under the LeConte Glacier, giving access to a tough cross-country trip to the Ptarmigan Traverse

Rainbow Lake: Popular trail to alpine lake

Devore Creek-Company Creek loop: A long hike through beautiful alpine meadows

Junction Mountain: Dead-end trail with views of Agnes and Stehekin valleys

Prince Creek, Canoe Creek, Fish Creek: Long, steep access trails from Lake Chelan to the Chelan Summit

Boulder Creek: To War Creek Pass and Chelan Summit

Rainbow-McAlester loop: Long trail over a high pass

McGregor Mountain: Long climb to long views from Lake Chelan to Glacier Peak

Twisp River

Copper Pass: Meadows reached via the 4½-mile North Fork Twisp River trail No. 420 — unmaintained

Hoodoo Pass: Easiest way into the heart of the Chelan Summit

Fish Creek Pass: Long, easy hike up Buttermilk Creek to Chelan Summit

War Creek: A much easier trail to War Creek Pass than the grueling approach from Stehekin

Reynolds Creek: Joins the Boulder Creek trail

North Creek: Steep, dry trail to a tiny mountain lake or down Cedar Creek to Early Winters

Oval Creek: To small, wooded mountain lakes under the Chelan Crest

Martin Creek: Trail to Chelan Summit

Crater Creek trail to Crater Lake: High alpine lake under the Sawtooth Range

Crater Creek trail to Martin Lakes: Beautiful alpine meadows and lakes

Early Winters Creek

Silver Star: Hunters' camp reached by blazed trail up Cedar Creek

Lake Ann-Rainy Lake: Easy hikes from Rainy Pass (see **Trips and Trails**)

Methow River

Goat Peak: Short hike to a lookout (see **Trips and Trails**)

Granite Creek

Panther Creek: Forest hike to 4th of July Pass

East Creek-Mebee Pass: Steep climb on old Indian-miners' route

Mill Creek-Azurite Pass: Stiff climb beginning on an old mining road

Canyon Creek: Forest walk on old narrow-gauge mining road to ghost town of Chancellor

INDEX